More Praise for
Creating the Innovation Culture

"Frances Horibe illustrates her very astute understanding of the forces at play inside organizations. By challenging our zealous devotion to vision, quality, teams and alignment, she points out how our best intentions conspire to stomp out the very innovation that we are all dependent upon. She offers pragmatic solutions for how to continue to hear dissent, how to keep it in the open, get it out of the underground, and prepare the ground for innovation. This is a must-read for leaders serious about creating the conditions for innovation."

> —*Rod Brandvold, Vice President, Organizational Development, Cognos Inc.*

"Frances Horibe has made a compelling case for leaders to encourage diversity of ideas and to embrace 'dissenters' for their organizations to be innovative and successful."

> —*Sol Kasimer, Chief Executive Officer, YMCA*

"We are on the edge of awareness that organizations have to learn how to really think, not just 'manage knowledge.' This book builds this awareness in plain, simple, and hard-hitting language."

> —*Dr. Min Basadur, Michael G. DeGroote School of Business, McMaster University*

creating the
INNOVATION CULTURE

Also by Frances Horibe

Managing Knowledge Workers
*New Skills and Attitudes to Unlock the
Intellectual Capital in Your Organization*

(ISBN: 0-471-64318-1, John Wiley & Sons, Canada Ltd.)

creating the
INNOVATION CULTURE

Leveraging Visionaries, Dissenters and Other Useful Troublemakers in Your Organization

FRANCES HORIBE

JOHN WILEY & SONS

Toronto • New York • Chichester • Weinheim • Brisbane • Singapore

John Wiley & Sons Canada Limited
22 Worcester Road
Etobicoke, Ontario
M9W 1L1

National Library of Canada Cataloguing in Publication Data

Horibe, Frances Dale Emy
    Creating the innovation culture : leveraging visionaries, dissenters and other useful troublemakers in your organization

Includes index.
ISBN 0-471-64628-8

1. Personel management. 2. Employee motivation.
3. Corporate culture. I. Title.

HF5549.H67 2001   658.3 044   C2001-901495-3

Production Credits
Cover design: Interrobang Graphic Design Inc.
Printer: Tri-Graphic Printing

Printed in Canada
10 9 8 7 6 5 4 3 2 1

TABLE OF CONTENTS

ॐ

ACKNOWLEDGEMENTS

Many people helped me take this project from idea to book. My thanks first to Roland Dumas, whose life role as dissenter, visionary, and thinker-out-of-the-box first gave me the idea. Then, David Carlson and Cliff Cullen—both practical men with deep insights—helped me to work through the first stumbling around. Susan Robinson, Louise Ross, and Sharon VanderKaay took these ideas even further, proving—as I have always known—that they are that most rare of all commodities—successful innovators.

Once an idea had formed into main themes, many others' reflections and expertise helped me to shape the content further. They are Dr. Min Basadur, Rod Brandvold, Rod Brazier, Alan Breakspear, Derek Burney, David Brown, Jonathan Caloff, Michel Cardinal, Maureen Donlevy, Mont Doyle, Roland Dumas, Joe Flynn, Sol Kasimer, Mike Norman, Rob Notman, Geoffrey O'Brien, Christiane Ouimet, Steve Quesnelle, Geoff Smith, Gisele Samson-Verreault, Chuck Seeley, and Marc Spooner.

Finally, four people, Lew Auerbach, Roxanne Cameron, Barb Mac-Callum, and Janet Mairs undertook the onerous and somewhat thankless task of reviewing and commenting on the entire book, applying their experience to what I had written and helping to focus the material still further. They have a unique capacity to ponder an individual idea or even phrase while holding the wholeness of the intent of the book and of the idea. Their comments have been invaluable in both the large and the small.

Throughout, my editor, Karen Milner, and my agent, Daphne Hart, have guided me ably and continued to listen to my ramblings with sympathy while tempering them with reality.

To all of these people, many thanks. Any errors of omission or commission are mine, but I know that any depth and range you find in this book is due primarily to their generous assistance.

The Need for Innovation

*Radical, category-breaking innovation is what
is needed today. Some companies can do it
consistently but most can't. Why not?*

The Need for Innovation

Time was, all a company needed to do was improve. If it did it continuously (and that was hard enough), it could expect to be successful. Those days are long gone. The information explosion, the global economy—all the things you'd have to have been in a coma to have missed—have conspired to change the rules. In fact, *Harvard Business Review* concludes that "pursuing incremental improvement while rivals reinvent the industry is like fiddling while Rome burns"[1] and *Business Week* believes that "what's likely to kill you in the new economy is not somebody doing something better, it's somebody doing something different."[2] Geoff Smith, VP of Business Development for Mitel, a manufacturer of telephone switching equipment, provides the perfect example. "Our competitors are not Lucent or Nortel," he maintains. "Our competitors are companies like Cisco that see voice communication as just another data application that they can give away. They're giving away our whole business."

---

[1] Gary Hamel, "Strategy as Revolution," *Harvard Business Review* (July/August 1996).
[2] Michael Bloomberg, "Winning at the Intersection of Fear and Opportunity," *BusinessWeek* (January 11, 1999).

So what is the new imperative? The Society of Management Accountants calls "*innovation*...fundamental to the quest for profitable, sustainable growth."[3] Peter Drucker, probably the most insightful management guru ever, deems it *the* one business competence needed for the future. *Fortune* magazine's advice to companies who want to be named to its Most Admired List? Innovate, innovate, innovate. Innovation currently accounts for more than half of all growth. And it is enormously profitable. A study done on the rate of return for 17 successful innovations showed a mean return of 56% compared with an average ROI of 16%.

Companies are catching on to this sea change. In an Ernst & Young study, European and North American companies called innovation the most important criterion for success in the future. Even technology firms who presumably are leading this charge consider "making innovation happen" the industry's single biggest problem.

Jack Welch, CEO of GE and seen as the world's greatest living manager, obsesses about his company's ability to "break the glass"—that is, continue to innovate. He worries whether it has "the right gene pool—do people who join big companies want to break the glass? We've got to break this company to do this—there's no discussion, we've just got to break it."[4]

So organizations need to innovate to survive and they know it. But before we explore this issue further, let's ask an important question.

What is Innovation Anyhow?

The commonly held view is that innovation is creativity—new ideas, knowledge creation. That's why companies spend mega-bucks for courses where people play with brightly colored blocks to get their creative juices going. But it isn't just that. It goes beyond idea generation to putting those ideas into action. Steve Wynn, CEO of Mirage Resorts—one of *Fortune*'s most admired corporations—points out that "the challenge is getting the steady stream of good ideas out of the labs and creativity campfires, through marketing and manufacturing and all the way to the customer." In other words, while you need to keep the pump primed with lots of great ideas, it will be for naught if they don't see the light of day. Management expert Rosabeth Moss Kanter has long maintained that "a good new idea means little—except risk—

---

[3] The Society of Management Accountants of Canada, *Collaborative Innovation and the Knowledge Economy*, (Management Accounting Issues paper 17).
[4] Thomas A. Stewart, "See Jack. See Jack Run," *Fortune* (September 27, 1999), pp. 124–36.

without...excellence in execution."[5] So, if you have a lot of off-the-wall thoughts, you're creative. If you can turn them into something of value, you're innovative.

In addition, in today's fast-moving, category-breaking business environment, building a better mousetrap may be effective, but it's not innovation. Innovation is using supersonic waves to beam the mice back to their native habitat; it's developing a whole new way to get rid of them. It is *not* about marginal improvement on a marginal product.

Accordingly, *Fortune* magazine maintains that only non-linear— that is non-obvious, non-incremental—innovation will produce long-term wealth creation. Radical innovation, the kind *inconsistent* with your present strategy, is no longer an option but an imperative. Geoff Yang, a Silicon Valley venture capitalist with one of best track records in the business (300% annual return on investment), agrees. "To come up with concepts for new products, CEOs have to encourage break-through thinking."[6]

So, to be innovative, the idea has to be creative and implemented. To be competitive, it has to be a great leap forward. Otherwise, close but no cigar.

What Kind of Innovation Is Required?

We know that innovation has to be creative, implementable, and radical. But on what? Products and services are the obvious place but there are many other areas where we need to rethink our old habits. Guy Kawasaki, former marketing guru for Apple and author of *Rules for Revolution*, says that habits will kill business in the new economy. I've listed some of them below:

• *Our product is less terrible than yours.* Realistically, in the old econ-omy and before the Internet, if consumers didn't know they could get your products 20% cheaper on the other side of town, you automatically made 20% more profit. What they didn't know fell directly to your bottom line. And if you were even mar-ginally better than your home-town competitor, you were in gravy. Today, everyone can reach far and wide to get products that aren't just less bad but actually work better.

---

[5] Rosabeth Moss Kanter, "Follow-up and Follow-through," *Harvard Business Review* (March/ April 1990), p. 8.
[6] Lori Ioannou, "Make Your Company an Idea Factory," *Fortune* (June 12, 2000), pp. F264N–F264R.

- *Budget is paramount.* If it's not in the budget, it doesn't exist, no matter how worthwhile. And budgets, the last time I looked, are not instruments of risk. By putting them above innovation, companies avoid those high-risk, high-payoff opportunities that are the essence of innovation.
- *Outsourcing saves money.* In the short-term, it does but it kills you in the longer term. In outsourcing the work, you also outsource your talent, your core competencies, and your capacity to innovate.
- *The best product wins.* I wish, I wish, I wish that were true. Then we'd all be working on Apples and playing our (rapidly disappearing) videotapes in Beta format. First to market seems to be the way to win. This means software with lots of bugs that will be fixed, later, honest. It is forcing us to rethink the value and the profitability of quality.

These habits are no longer useful and in fact will get us into trouble. We need to come up with new ways to address new challenges. We need to innovate our way out of old habits.

Some Organizations Are Great at Innovation

Some organizations have a marvelous history of innovation; not just the breakthrough that put them on the map, but a continuing stream. 3-M produces 30% of its revenue from products that didn't exist four years ago. Enron is a pipeline operator that has reinvented itself into a new economy trading powerhouse. In an e-business world still trying to figure out how to make things work, EnronOnline, its business-to-business site, traded $100 billion in its first year of operation. Its EVP, Steve Kean, knows "innovation is at the heart of sustaining a company's competitive advantage."[7]

Companies that innovate successfully understand the need to be radical. Hewlett-Packard makes both laser and ink jet printers, products that naturally compete. However, rather than try to avoid the competition, H-P encouraged the two divisions to cannibalize each other's markets. The result? It is the leader in *both* laser and ink jet printers.

Similarly, Jack Welch's success is at least partially attributable to his radical innovation. When he became CEO of GE in 1980, he figuratively blew up what was at the time the most successful company in

---

[7] Nicholas Stein, "The World's Most Admired Companies," *Fortune* (October 2, 2000), p. 183.

the United States. He demanded every GE business be first or second in
its field. With that strategy, GE today is consistently one of the most
admired companies in the world (i.e., most profitable, given this is *Fortune* magazine doing the admiring). But Welch has now realized that
the innovation imperative requires a new mindset. GE no longer wants
its member companies to be first in their field. To be more open to
innovation everywhere, it expects them to be players—not even necessarily the dominant one—in many markets.

Some companies can innovate successfully and are rewarded hand-
somely for it. But it is a fragile thing. Compare *Fortune*'s picks for most
innovative companies in 1999 and 2000. In 1999, it was Home Depot,
Intel, and Fortune Brands in that order. A year later, it was Enron,
Nokia, and Home Depot. Only Home Depot stayed within the top
three and it dropped from first to third. Needless to say, none of these
companies stopped innovating but it is clear that staying on top of the
innovation game is as hard as getting there in the first place.

Some Are Crummy

So some organizations seem to have the magic bullet. But most don't
and they know it. The American Management Association conducted
a survey of 500 chief executives. These executives, like the companies
in the Ernst & Young study cited earlier, named innovation as the top
answer to "what must one do to survive in the 21st century?" But only
6% thought they were doing the great job necessary for today's economy. There have been many failures.

Xerox's Palo Alto Research Center (PARC) is famous for innovations that Xerox did *not* exploit—like fax machines, laser printers, and
graphical user interface (GUI). The problem continues to exist. PARC's
strategy-integration manager Mark Bernstein reports that a number of
projects with money-making potential are orphaned, even though
industry analysts have urged Xerox to focus on PARC's new technologies to pull itself out of its present slump. But they are also skeptical
Xerox will do so, saying that a "central irony of Xerox's predicament is
that it may ultimately be undone by its inability to adapt to the com-
puter-driven, networked world its own lab helped to create."[8]

Procter & Gamble has a similar problem. It has a long history and is
credited with revolutionizing business with its use of brand marketing.
But its last major breakthrough was Pampers in 1961. The company
went from innovation to merely improving—Tide has had over 60 "new

[8] Jeremy Kahn, "The Paper Jam from Hell," *Fortune* (November 13, 2000), pp. 141–46.

and improveds." The company has fallen seriously behind its competitors. It had become known as "the land of the Proctoids—a place that squelches entrepreneurs, creative types, freethinkers—where 'troublemakers don't belong.'" In 1999, the new CEO, Durk Jager, promised to act aggressively to fix this problem. He said, "The core business is innovation. If we innovate well, we will ultimately win. If we innovate poorly, we won't win."[9] Seventeen months later, he was out of a job, the industry consensus being that he had pushed change too fast for the Proctoids.

Other companies struggle with innovation. Motorola resisted going from analog to digital and lost its commanding lead in cellular phones. McDonald's stuck to its successful formula too long, resulting in creative inertia and a string of innovation flops like McPizza, McLean Burger, and the "adult" Arch Deluxe. Levi Strauss stopped innovating and destroyed its brand name to such an extent that its estimated market value has gone from $14 billion to $8 billion while The Gap has gone from $7 billion to $40 billion in the same time period.

Pretty depressing. Much as organizations want innovation, they're not great at it. In fact, a study of 46 leading-edge companies in the United States, Canada, Europe, and the Middle East found that companies unintentionally kill it. They hire creative people and then prevent them from using their skills. The *Financial Post* calls this inability to innovate "the single most dangerous gap in business today."[10]

So here we are, knowing that innovation is the next competitive edge and also that generating and sustaining it has daunted many a talented and determined manager. Why? Well, that's what this book is about. Not only why companies can't sustain innovation but also what they can do to change.

About This Book

The first section of this book, Chapters 2 to 4, helps us understand how we got into this pickle and how the encouragement of dissent can play a central role in fostering a more innovative culture.

There are four main things managers need to do to encourage dissent and therefore innovation in their organizations. The first is to avoid inadvertently suppressing open dissent that naturally occurs. This topic will be covered in Chapters 5 and 6.

---

[9] Katrina Brooker, "Can Procter & Gamble Change Its Culture, Protect Its Market Share and Find the Next Tide?" *Fortune* (April 26, 1999), p. 150.
[10] *Financial Post*, "The Creativity Deficit is Described as the Single Most Dangerous Gap in Business Today," (October 25, 2000), p. c9.

Chapters 7 to 9 help managers work with people who have taken on the role of a dissenter. That is, they typically dissent no matter what. While they can be pains in the neck, they can also be very helpful in creating an innovative culture. These chapters will help managers identify them, coach them, and act as their political handlers in getting their ideas accepted in the company.

Much as dealing with open dissent is a challenge, it is even more difficult if it goes underground. Chapter 10 will help you identify if your dissent has gone underground and Chapters 11 and 12 help you to bring it to the surface again.

A culture that sustains innovation needs to incorporate ways to encourage continuing dissent. Chapter 13 will cover how to kickstart the move to an innovation culture, Chapter 14 deals with processes and mechanisms that support innovation, and Chapter 15 shows individual managers how they can help the culture change.

Chapter 16 deals with dissenters who are destructive and must be let go. The final chapter provides some thoughts on where to go from here in the evolving role of manager as promoter of innovation.

Summary

Even though having a great idea is, in and of itself, an accomplishment, the true test for any organization is getting it to market. The more we rely on innovation for success, the more we understand how tough that road is. The next chapter will explore how we have set up organizations that are inadvertently unfriendly to innovation.

Main Points

- Innovation is the key to long-term, sustained growth.
- It must be radical not incremental innovation.
- Some companies can do it but the majority can't.

References for This Chapter

Brooker, Katrina, "Plugging the Leaks at P&G," *Fortune* (February 21, 2000), pp. 44–48.

Colvin, Geoffrey, "America's Most Admired Companies," *Fortune* (February 21, 2000), p. 110.

Colvin, Geoffrey, "The Ultimate Manager," *Fortune* (November 22, 1999), pp. 185–187.

Hamel, Gary, "Driving Grassroots Growth," *Fortune* (September 4, 2000), p. 186.

Hamel, Gary, "Reinvent Your Company," *Fortune* (June 12, 2000), pp. 99–118.

Kahn, Jeremy, "The World's Most Admired Companies," *Fortune* (October 11, 1999), pp. 267–70.

Kawasaki, Guy, *Rules for Revolutionaries* (New York: HarperCollins Publishers, Inc., 1999), as quoted in *Fortune* (May 24, 1999), p. 296(d).

Kupfer, Andrew, "Xerox Jam is too Much for Thoman," *Fortune* (May 29, 2000), pp. 42–4.

Munk, Nina, "How Levi's Trashed a Great American Brand," *Fortune* (April 12, 1999).

Rose, Ian, "Valuing Intellectual Capital: Summary Report," IBR Consulting Services Limited (August 1997), p. 24.

Roth, David, "From Poster Boy to Whipping Boy: Burying Motorola," *Fortune* (July 6, 1998), p. 28.

Sellers, Patricia, "Big, Hairy, Audacious Goals Don't Work—Just Ask P&G," *Fortune* (April 3, 2000), pp. 39–41.

Sellers, Patricia, "Reinventing the Arch: McDonald's Starts Over," *Fortune* (June 22, 1998), p. 34.

Stein, Nicholas, "The World's Most Admired Companies," *Fortune* (October 2, 2000), p. 183.

Stewart, Thomas A., "3-M Fights Back," *Fortune* (February 5, 1996), p. 99.

The Society of Management Accountants of Canada, *Collaborative Innovation and the Knowledge Economy* (Management Accounting Issues paper 17) p. 40.

Valery, Nicholas, "A Survey of Innovation in Industry," *The Economist* (February 20, 1999), p. 7.

The Efficiency-Innovation Dichotomy

While on the road to efficiency, we have inadvertently created organizations that are inhospitable to innovation.

Innovation: Fantasy and Fact

If this were a better world, innovation would happen like this: A bright-eyed, respectful, and tidy young employee would bounce into your office with a category-breaking idea. You would immediately see its value. You would heap praise on Tidy, who would accept it with becoming bashfulness and never need any other recognition. You take Tidy's great idea up the line where you are hailed as a genius for seeing its potential. Amid acclaim and intimations of promotion, money is thrown at it and everyone drops everything to help you get the idea to market. You hit the market in record time, make mega-bucks, and *Fortune* is asking for an interview.

Well, if you work in a company where that happens, write to me. I want to work there too.

Instead, innovation is more likely to happen like this: Even if the first part of the scenario holds—Tidy bounces in, you get how big the idea is immediately—your next step is to take it up the line. Your own boss is a bit of a stick in the mud. She shakes her head. "I dunno. Can't see it working, can you? I mean, it's not sticking to our knitting, is it?"

You convince her to let you take it to the next level. You do a stunning presentation but a VP raises objections. "How can you be sure of the ROI projections? Haven't you inflated the market potential? This prototype is awfully hard to use. I don't think customers will go for it." You answer as best you can but feel the room going in his direction. You know his objections aren't for the good of the company. If you're successful, it will take business away from his area. His real objection is that it won't be good for *him*.

The VP convinces everyone they should look before they leap. You are asked to gather more consumer data. "But," you protest, "with category-breaking ideas, consumer data aren't any good. Because it's new, customers have to try it before they decide if they like it!"

"So you want us to buy a pig in a poke?" demands your nemesis.

"No, of course not, but..." The tide has turned against you and you have to agree to collect data you know won't tell you anything.

You launch the market study. While the focus groups are running, you get wind that the nemesis VP is quietly campaigning to tank your idea. He has even got to your boss. She comes in. "Do you really think this will work?" she asks, wringing her hands. "After all, it's so new. Will the customer understand how to use it?"

You answer as you have a million times before. "If we do our marketing well, I'm sure they will. It's not that complicated. It's just new."

"But Nemesis says we'll confuse the marketplace. Then everybody will suffer." Your boss leans forward and lowers her voice. "Confidentially, Nemesis has told me most of the other VPs are negative. He's pretty sure that when you go back, there won't be much support around the table. And if that's the case..." she shrugs. "You know our fearless leader. He won't go out on a limb."

"Just like you," you think to yourself. But you just repeat, "I'm sure the data will convince the committee."

Meanwhile, back at the ranch, Tidy is getting restive. "Why don't they get off their butts and approve it?" he demands. "And I want stock options for this." Threats about taking his marbles and going home are unspoken but in the air.

Knowing that the data will not give you the knockout punch you need, you start campaigning with the other VPs. You buttonhole every one you can and talk up the great and exciting potential. You let them paint the picture of the new idea as a way to take Nemesis down a peg or two. Most of the VPs are noncommittal but interested.

On the day of the pitch, you downplay the data, which are all you predicted—i.e., not helpful—and instead, give an impassioned plea for the idea as the wave of the future. You show the committee how they can be market leaders. Over the objections of Nemesis and with the tepid support of your own boss, the funding is approved and you breathe a sigh of relief.

You race back to Tidy with the great news. He looks down and shuffles his feet. "Gee, that's great, boss, but...." He looks up. "I just accepted an offer from e-Product. I was going to give my notice today."

"You can't take your idea with you!" you explode. "It belongs to the company!"

Tidy shrugs. "I know. But I've had a couple of others—completely different. E-Product has already lined up the funding."

You go back to your office and close the door. You know as well as Tidy that the basic prototype isn't enough. He's the only one who really understands how it works and how to take it to a viable product. Even if you could get a replacement tomorrow, just getting the person up to speed will take months. And you promised to hit the market by spring!

A knock at the door. Nemesis sticks his head in. "Congrats on the funding," he said, his shark teeth spread into a grin. "Didn't think you'd pull it off." He walks in and puts out a hand. You shake it gingerly.

"No hard feelings, of course," he says.

"Of course," you reply weakly. "After all, I'm going to need your help to market."

Nemesis nods. "We'll do everything we can to make this a success. After all, what's good for the company is good for us, no?"

You straighten. "I really appreciate that, Nemesis. Why don't we meet next week to get the ball rolling?"

Without a blink, Nemesis shakes his head. "Next week...no can do. I'm in Stockholm."

"Can Linda sub for you?"

"No, no...Linda's fully committed. Couldn't let her go."

"What about Ralph?"

Again, the shaking of the head. "I don't think Ralph has the big picture you'd need...no, not Ralph."

"Well, when would you be available?"

Nemesis shrugs. "I dunno—what with that acquisition fallout. I'm pretty booked right now." He straightens. "But call Vicky and see where she can fit you in. I'm sure we can do it for such an important project." With that, he waves and is gone.

You put your head in your hands. You know the drill. You'll call Vicky and, wonder of wonders, Nemesis is completely booked for months and months. And nobody can commit Nemesis's resources except him. You know he's just begun to fight.

The Drive for Efficiency

The old guard protecting its turf against a new idea is a challenge for any innovation. However, in addition to office politics, there is something else—even more embedded in the way we do things—that makes creating and sustaining innovation difficult. It is our drive for efficiency.

Ever since Frederick Taylor held a stopwatch over some hapless factory worker, a large part of our work has been focused on efficiency. Because efficiency turns into profit, we constantly ask ourselves, *How do we get more done in a shorter time?* Today, that drive is captured in our obsession with speed. First to market is the winner. We need speed to compete in this restless global economy. It's the early bird on steroids with faxes and e-mails, FedEx, and downloading to help.

Because we've worked at it, we're pretty good at it. We have discovered that Taylor's time and motion studies might have been all right for the simpler manufacturing work of the last century, but today we need more sophisticated ways. And we have hit on three very effective ones. The first is vision. Rather than ordering everyone to go in the same direction, policing to make sure they do, and punishing those who don't, we engage staff in a common vision because, over the longer haul, it is a much more efficient and effective way to reach our goals. We also have leaders who are, by and large, pretty talented in getting us to the finish line. Finally, we use teams because, although it may take more time up front to build a team, they are marvelously efficient in the longer term to get things done. So visionary companies, good leaders, and well-functioning teams all help us be as efficient as possible. And every one of them contributes to a climate that is relatively unfriendly to innovation. How can that be?

Innovation and Visionary Companies

Visionary companies are ones we all want to work in. They have a strong sense of where they're going; everyone is committed to that goal. Often the leader is held in high esteem, and his or her pronouncements have the ability to move the organization quickly in new directions. Loyalty is a strong feature, and the sense of everyone pulling together keeps people eager to come to work and contribute. Recognizing how fundamentally efficient this kind of culture is, companies have made many efforts to create it.

But, for all its positive characteristics, it has downsides. A company strongly committed to a goal will suppress, push out, or just not recruit those who think a different one is better. Research shows that like-minded people talking only among themselves (as would happen in a company with a unity of purpose) reinforces their intolerance for different ideas. Conference Board studies have concluded that organizations have difficulty developing a new perspective because they are blind to their own assumptions. C.J. Nemeth, in a *California Management Review* article, goes even further by saying that "there is evidence that the atmosphere most likely to induce creativity [innovation] is one diametrically opposed to the 'cult-like' corporate culture."[1]

This has a ring of truth, don't you think? Ever been in a company where high quality is valued? What do you think of a person who does less than his best? If you're a really fine human being, you might just shrug and think, "To each his own," but if you're like the rest of us, you're more likely to have dark thoughts about his parentage and personal habits. You might avoid working with him because he won't put in the extra hours and you'll be stuck with everything. In a culture that reinforces high quality, there is very little sympathy for someone who just gets by. And yet, isn't it possible that sometimes this guy is right? Is it always necessary to do things perfectly? Aren't there times when good enough is good enough, especially in our first-to-market era? But an organization committed only to the best and one that silences those who think differently will have little ability to recognize, much less act on, that trend.

Discouraging different views might be effective as long as the current goal is viable. But once that goal is achieved or, worse, has become irrelevant while you're still working toward it, a culture that suppresses dissident views will have no one around to point that out.

"Wait a minute!" you may be scoffing. "There are lots of companies that are both innovative and have strong, committed cultures. Like the ones profiled in the last chapter." True. But Nemeth believes that these companies are successful because the *leader* is the innovator. If that's the case, having a committed and loyal company to implement the idea is a distinct advantage.

But there is a downside: The leader had better be right. Because, right or wrong, her idea will be implemented. There are many examples of committed people enthusiastically embracing a disastrous innovation. In one of China's Great Leaps Forward during the reign of Mao Tse-tung, the populace was asked to kill sparrows as they were considered a menace. It undertook the task so vigorously that sparrows were almost driven to extinction there. The results? The people busy

---

[1] Charlan Jeanne Nemeth, "Managing Innovation: When Less Is More," *California Management Review* (Vol. 40, No. 1, Fall 1997), p. 64.

killing sparrows didn't plant crops. What crops were planted were destroyed by insects that were usually eaten by sparrows. There was widespread crop failure and famine.

Thus, single-minded implementation of a bad idea can have tragic consequences. But even in the business world, stupid ideas beautifully executed cost us precious time and money. Remember Scott Paper's disposable dresses, Crystal Pepsi, or Nullo internal deodorant (yes, you really were supposed to ingest it to remain odor-free). And what about Ford Pintos or the Earring Magic Ken doll—presumably the suitable companion to an alternative Barbie? Not to mention the Edsel. And yet, someone at some point thought these were great ideas and all made it to market.

The strength of visionary companies is their ability to implement. But their capacity to foster and sustain innovation throughout the organization is limited. It's kind of like life, isn't it? Visionary companies have traveled down one road—to commitment and singleness of purpose—with many positive results. But they have the weakness of their strengths. The very focus that makes it possible to deliver quickly and well also makes it harder to take a different direction when needed.

Am I Advocating Tossing Vision and Teams?

Not at all. Vision and teams have been and are positive forces in organizations. However, I am asking you to consider that, while not bad, they might not be unadulterated good either. We haven't spent much time questioning whether they have a dark side. Albert Hirschman, in his excellent book *Exit, Voice and Loyalty*, pointed out that danger. He noted that "happy slaves"—those who are committed to the way things are—can agree to participate in what they might otherwise see as morally unacceptable systems. How otherwise can we explain Nazi Germany, South Africa under apartheid, or the southern United States before the Civil War or even well into the 1950s? These were not entire nations of immoral and malevolent people, but rather those who did not question the status quo. So while commitment to the ways of an organization or of a society is generally a good thing, without those lone voices who speak against the comfortable, the acceptable, and the normal, great evil can be missed by otherwise responsible and caring people.

Innovation and Senior Management

You'd think senior managers would encourage innovation since they know its importance. But T.J. Watson, founder of IBM, is famous for stating categorically that not more than five computers were ever going to be needed in the world. In 1977, Ken Olsen, founder of Digital Equipment Corporation, declared that "there is no reason anyone would want a computer in their home."[2] Even innovative GE can slip. In 1994, one of its employees, Glen Meakem, proposed that suppliers compete for GE's orders in live, open, electronic auctions. GE couldn't see the point. Five years later, Meakem's company, FreeMarkets Inc., had a market cap in the billions by running live, open, electronic auctions. GE missed leading the business-to-business Internet revolution. So how is it that these talented managers and companies missed such big boats? Because they are often unsuited, both by training and inclination, to be its champions.

The manufacturing era may now be passing into history, but we still have a management system built on its premises. A manager was trained to plan, organize, direct, and control. Innovation? Something the engineers and researchers did. The regular people just followed their bosses' lead.

Even today, it's still important to plan, organize, direct, and control. In fact, it's an even bigger challenge for e-businesses than their old-economy counterparts. In the past, to make your business dreams come true, you usually needed some kind of manufacturing capacity. Once you were set up to make cars, it wasn't possible for your employees to make teacups. But CEOs of e-businesses know that "at [companies like] Yahoo, Intuit or eBay, where the primary capital equipment is brainpower, employees can start to pursue radically different strategies in an eye blink....Soon your assets are utterly uncoordinated, unless the e-CEO reinforces the strategic focus relentlessly."[3] Even today, a normal manager's business is not about continually shifting focus or strategy. It is largely about implementing an already agreed upon one.

In addition, a manager has to know what to expect so she can tell when things are going wrong. But paradigms that help you decide whether things are on track can also prevent you from seeing things that don't fit. To illustrate the point, let's talk sunspots. Even without telescopes, Chinese astronomers reported their existence *centuries* before Europeans. Were the Chinese smarter or did they have better

---

[2] Mark Borden, "Thinking about Tomorrow," *Fortune* (November 22, 1999), p. 170.
[3] Geoffrey Colvin, "How to be a Great E-CEO," *Fortune* (May 24, 1999), p. 107.

eyesight? Unlikely. The major difference was that Chinese astronomy did not preclude the possibility of change in the cosmos whereas the prevailing belief in Europe was that the heavens were immutable. Chinese astronomers could see sunspots because their paradigm allowed it while European astronomers could not because theirs precluded it.

Innovation, by definition, is not about normal business. It is always about doing things a different way. But normal business is what managers are good at. Their ability to run a business efficiently may contribute to their inability to see innovative possibilities. A paradigm, be it astronomical or manufacturing, is helpful in making sense of the world, but it can also make it harder to see what doesn't fit.

You Can't Tell Where an Innovation is Going

The long-term consequences of any successful innovation cannot be foreseen. Peter Drucker says, "Innovation always has the power to change everything. The unexpected always happens."[4] Danny Hillis, a Disney fellow and technology thinker, agrees that "those of us close to technology have been certain of the uncertainty for a long time."[5]

History gives us many examples of the unpredictable consequences of innovation. The invention of the printing press led to mass literacy. For the first time in human history, it was possible to access knowledge directly, without the involvement and interpretations of a third party. People could decide for themselves what they thought about the world. This ability to question the established order led to the Protestant Reformation, which was based on an individual's right to make his own way to God. And if you could decide your relationship to God, how much more logical to also determine your relationship with the state. And that led to democratic movements. So, the printing press, invented originally simply to avoid the onerous task of copying out by hand, led to democracy that still shapes our world.

Other ways that innovations have changed our lives in unexpected ways:
- In the early part of the 20th century, the spread of the car caused the need for horses to disappear so quickly that the conversion from hay to other crops prompted an agricultural revolution.

---

[4] Brent Schlender, "Peter Drucker Takes the Long View," *Fortune* (September 28, 1998), p. 170.
[5] Danny Hillis, "Why Do We Buy the Myth of Y2K?" *Newsweek* (May 31, 1999), p. 12.

• The introduction of radio blurred regional differences, wiped out vaudeville, and enabled the rise of national consumer brands.
• The invention of batteries helped to bring down totalitarianism—cell phones are used to communicate between rebels when the dictators control the telephone lines.
• The U.S. South grew into an economic force to be reckoned with when air conditioning became widespread.
And finally my favorite—a prediction about the course of innovation itself. In a lovely burst of confidence, Charles Duell, a former commissioner of the U.S. patent office, said in 1899 that "everything that can be invented, has been invented."[6] Guess his face is red wherever he is today.

Innovation and Teams

Teams have often been touted as the engine of innovation in organizations. On the theory that many heads are better than one, they're often formed to tackle some vexing problem or suggest a new way to do things.

However, my observation has been that teams rarely make startling decisions or come up with significant leaps forward. They don't make worse decisions nor have worse ideas than their managers; they just don't have better ones. I was part of a group that was supposed to come up with an innovative way to restructure a company. Everyone worked long and hard, but in the end, the "new" organization looked suspiciously like the one in place. This group wasn't any less innovative or insightful than the average, but things like turf and fear of change and protecting sacred cows got in our way.

Research shows that groups tend to be less creative than individuals alone. People are very swayed by others' opinions. The public "yes" of some can override a person's private "no." This can be a downward spiral. Even though I'd prefer to say "no," I feel pressured to say "yes." My public "yes" encourages still others to disregard their own feelings and agree also. Groups are inclined to adopt the strategy the majority favors to the exclusion of other possibilities. Thus, they are relatively unable to detect original solutions.

Groups will tolerate a range of opinions but only if they stay within the boundaries of the accepted philosophy. That is, as long as you believe in quality, your opinions are welcome. If you don't, your views

---

[6] Borden, op. cit., p. 170.

will be censured. In democracies, the danger of allowing only certain opinions is well recognized and special pains have been taken to address the problem. Freedom of speech guarantees me the right to my opinion even if others vehemently disagree, even if my world view is repugnant. But while we have this right as citizens, it is not so clear this tolerance extends to our work life. In organizations, freedom of speech is a rarer commodity. Thus, while groups are excellent vehicles to generate commitment and get things done, they are not necessarily stellar at coming up with the best ideas. They can impose a kind of group-think—a Proctoid culture—that discourages innovation.

So we have been marvelously successful in creating efficient business practices that get us to our goals in the shortest time possible. But as *Fortune* columnist Stewart Aslop points out, "Much of the technology underlying our efficient economy was developed under conditions that did not demand an immediate return on investment." The microprocessor was developed at AT&T Labs. Local area networking, GUI, laser printers, and graphical word processes came out of Xerox's Palo Alto Research Center, the mouse out of Stanford Research International, the Internet protocol from the Defense Advanced Research Projects Agency, and the main protocol for the World Wide Web from a British programmer at a Swiss research lab. "Everyone's so busy being efficient and profitable," Alsop says, "that I wonder where we'll get those stupid, outlandish ideas that will drive growth beyond the Internet."[7] I wonder too.

Order and Innovation

In the 1400s, the Chinese had all the technology needed for an industrial revolution—iron and steel, gunpowder, the compass, the rudder, the printing press, drills for natural gas. But they did not exploit them for that aim. They had already created an enormously successful empire based on a Confucian view of the world in which order and hierarchy were paramount. It was a self-contained and self-satisfied world that was reluctant to trade with the West (desperate to get China's porcelain and silks) because everything it needed or thought it would need could be found within its borders.

So despite the existence of these inventions early on within its society, China continued along its stable path until the West used the rudder and compass to sail into the country's water and gunpowder, iron, and steel to conquer it.

---

[7] Stewart Aslop, "What's a New Economy without Research?" *Fortune* (May 15, 2000), p. 92.

Ways around This Dilemma

At some intuitive level, organizations have recognized the problem of creating and sustaining innovation internally and have tried several ways to address it. They have isolated their innovators in skunk works—units effectively walled off from the rest of the company, exempt from normal rules, and given the task of designing some desired innovation. There have been some legendary successes, such as Apple's Macintosh. But the evidence is building that the way the Mac came into existence was an anomaly rather than a beacon. Researcher Eric Trist studied large organizations such as General Foods and found that skunk works and other pilot projects almost never influence the rest of the organization.

In fact, a *Harvard Business Review* article concluded that "new-venture divisions, skunk works, and the musings of research fellows are no more likely to engender an industry revolution than is an annual planning process."[8] Going even further, *Fortune* columnist Michael Schrage believes that "skunk works are…a signal of management that has given up on innovation.…Top management effectively acknowledges that their corporation is incapable of internal organic innovation."[9] So skunk works may not be the answer to our innovation prayer.

Clayton Christiansen, in a very influential book called *The Innovator's Dilemma*, proposes another tack. He notes that success often hogties innovation—that is, companies with a leading technology usually do a good job improving what they have but rarely develop a new one to displace the old. Too many vested interests (money, time, talent, assets, mind-set) are tied to the existing product line. His solution is to set up innovations as separate companies outside the main one.

Along similar lines, *The Economist* has noted the trend for large companies to buy up smaller ones entirely for their innovative product or service. Thus, innovation is happening less and less within established organizations.

This may be part of the New Business Model—that innovation happens in start-ups that then make mega-bucks selling the idea to a company with a distribution channel. And in the big picture, at the level of market and economy, that's fine since innovation happens no matter what.

However, this trend is the death knell for today's integrated corporations. If innovation is fundamental to profitable, sustainable growth and it occurs outside established organizations, we face multiple problems down the road. For one, if the ability to identify and develop new

---

[8] Gary, Hamel, "Strategy as Revolution," *Harvard Business Review* (July/August 1996), p. 80.
[9] Michael Schrage, "What's That Bad Odor at Innovation Skunkworks?" *Fortune* (December 20, 1999), p. 338.

ideas resides largely outside the organization, we will gradually lose the capacity inside even to recognize the potential of an innovation. Even if the innovation is recognized as valuable and therefore bought, an anti-innovation culture will tend to reshape and mold the innovation to what already works. A non-innovative culture will make it difficult to fully exploit an innovation brought in from the outside.

Finally, if organizations become largely distribution networks (and even that might be questioned, given the Web), how interesting is the work going to be and how easy will it be to hold onto knowledge workers? Post offices are not usually considered to be challenging places to work.

Interestingly enough, Lester Thurow, professor of management and economics at MIT and former dean of the Sloan School of Management, doesn't believe that start-ups are the engines of innovation. Rather, he thinks that "new ideas don't come from small companies but from big companies who refused to use them."[10] So big companies may be sitting on gold mines that, if they could exploit them, would lessen their reliance on outside innovation considerably.

No matter how you slice it, it seems that organizations that do not foster their innovative capacity will be tomorrow's losers in the new economy. It's a high price to pay for efficiency today.

Summary

Some days you just can't win. Here you have been doing all kinds of things to be as effective as possible, and some—while efficient—are actually relatively ineffective if we're talking innovation. C.J. Nemeth of the Institute of Management, Innovation and Technology believes that "creativity and innovation may require a culture different from and opposed to that which encourages cohesion and loyalty."[11] I'm not sure I agree that a total change is necessary and I'm not suggesting you make a wholesale trade of efficiency for innovation. Companies need both. But it is the yin and yang of organizational life. If you're too efficient, you stifle innovation. If you're not efficient enough, you go out of business. I'm not arguing that you abandon one for the other, but we have pursued productivity for many decades. While it has provided us with tremendous benefits, the pendulum may have swung too far.

What we need is a culture of innovation that will generate new ideas and make it easy for them to be adopted and brought to market.

---

[10] Lester Thurow, "Knowledge as the New Organizational and Societal Wealth in the 21st century," Address to Canadian Centre for Management Development, November 7, 2000.
[11] Nemeth, op. cit., p. 59.

We want a culture where innovation occurs *because* of the culture and not *in spite* of it. Organizations have become more efficient; they now need to become more innovative. Chapter 3 will talk about that.

Main Points

- A visionary organization can actually prevent innovation from flourishing.
- Efficient managers can do the same.
- Work groups or teams also stifle innovation by a kind of "groupthink."
- Skunk works and buying your innovation may not work.

References for This Chapter

Chen, Christine and Tim Carvell, "Hall of Shame," *Fortune* (November 22, 1999), p. 140.

Christensen, Clayton M., *The Innovator's Dilemma: When New Technologies Cause Great Firms to Fail* (New York: Harper Business, 2000).

Dixon, Nancy M. *Report to the Conference Board of Canada on Organizational Learning* (January 1993), p. 14.

Fox, Justin, "How New is the Internet, Really?" *Fortune* (November 22, 1999), p. 176.

Hirschman, Albert O., *Exit, Voice and Loyalty: Responses to Decline in Firms, Organizations and States* (Cambridge, Massachusetts: Harvard University Press, 1970).

Kleiner, Art, *The Age of Heretics: Heroes, Outlaws and Forerunners of Corporate Change* (New York: Currency-Doubleday, 1996), p. 67.

Nemeth, Charlan Jeanne, "Managing Innovation: When Less Is More," *California Management Review* (Vol. 40, No. 1, Fall 1997), p. 62.

Samuelson, Robert J., "The Internet and Gutenberg," *Newsweek* (January 24, 2000), p. 45.

Stewart, Thomas A., Alex Taylor III, Peter Petre, and Brent Schlender, "The Businessman of the Century," *Fortune* (November 22, 1999), pp. 109–28.

Stewart, Thomas A., "How Teradyne Solved the Innovator's Dilemma," *Fortune* (January 10, 2000), pp. 188–90.

Stipp, David, "The Theory of Fads," *Fortune* (October 14, 1996), p. 52.

Tully, Shawn, "The B2B Tool That Really Is Changing the World," *Fortune* (March 20, 2000), pp. 132–45.

Valery, Nicholas, "A Survey of Innovation in Industry," *The Economist* (February 20, 1999), pp. 4–28.

CHAPTER 3

॥∞॥

The Need for Dissent

Organizations fail to innovate because they do not recognize that, by its nature, innovation is disruptive to settled patterns. This disruption takes the form of dissent— of people wanting to go in a different direction from the generally accepted. Rather than suppress these dissenting voices, organizations need to encourage their expression. This chapter will cover why the encouragement of dissent is critical to the innovative process.

Resisting Innovation

To succeed in today's world, we need to drive single-mindedly toward the prize while keeping an eye out for the next big win; we need a way to be both efficient *and* innovative, even though they are kind of opposites. Organizations have trouble doing that, not just because of their efficiency drive, but also because they resist the new. AT&T couldn't see the future in cellular phones. GE spent three years trying to prove that transistors wouldn't work because the vacuum tube (the precursor of the transistor) was its most profitable line. These companies are neither incompetent nor shortsighted but they had trouble understanding the basic principle of innovation—that organizations get smarter by constantly challenging their operating norms. And who is most wedded to those operating norms? According to London School of Business professor Gary Hamel, they are those with the "least diversity of experience, largest investment in the past [and] greatest reverence for industrial dogma."[1] That is, executives. The very people who should be pushing hardest for innovation are, as we discussed in the previous chapter, by training and temperament, not all that likely to know it when they see it. What companies need are people who are willing to speak truth to power.

Speak Truth to Power

Companies need people who will not give up on an idea. In fact, *The Economist* points out that often breakthrough innovation succeeds from "the sheer bloody-mindedness of individual engineers who refuse to abandon a pet idea."[2] Let's talk about two companies—3-M and GE—that seem to know how to get people to speak truth to power.

Thinsulate is an ultra-thin but warm product made by 3-M. It's probably lining your winter gloves. It has been an outstanding success but 3-M's CEO tells audiences that he tried five times to prevent it from going into production. Think about the kind of company where this could happen. First, it has to be a place where you can keep coming back to your bosses and saying, "You're wrong." In most organizations, you have only one chance to pitch an idea. If you're not successful, the idea is dead. Not only that, but if you try to revive it, you get "What part of 'no' didn't you understand?" But 3-M has created an environment where it is acceptable to persist. Not only that, but think about the culture that must exist if the CEO *himself* tells the story about his inability to stop a project. Here, it seems, is a CEO who accepts he is not the final decision-maker and that, moreover, he could be wrong and needs people around telling him that. Again, not standard equipment in most companies. It is a completely different view of hierarchy and the role of senior managers.

GE has a similar capacity. *Fortune* columnist Thomas Stewart attributes GE's success in part to a willingness to tell the boss he's all wet. They have a process called WorkOut. Employees can call a meeting without managers to discuss a problem at any time. Once they've concluded what needs to be done, the responsible manager must respond to their recommendations on the spot. The process, now honed over a good number of years, has taught people to speak their minds and even subvert traditional executive authority. It is so much part of their culture that every GE business has appointed a maverick—an e-commerce fanatic—who reports to the business's CEO and is empowered to break every GE rule except the company's values.

---

[1] Hamel, Gary, "Strategy as Revolution," *Harvard Business Review* (July/August,1996), p. 74.
[2] Valery, Nicholas, "A Survey of Innovation in Industry," *The Economist* (February 20, 1999), p. 14.

Ronald Heifetz, one of the world's leading authorities on leadership and director of the Leadership Education Project at Harvard, believes that a willingness to speak up and speak out is the root of innovation. "Companies tend to be allergic to conflict...but conflict is the primary engine of creativity and innovation. People don't learn by staring into a mirror; people learn by encountering difference. So hand in hand with the courage to face reality comes the courage to surface and orchestrate conflicts."[3] Cultures well positioned to innovate teach their people to challenge the assumption that the best employee is the one who goes along.

Honoring Those Who Speak Truth to Power

It's all very well to cite "a willingness to tell the boss he's all wet" as the answer to our innovation problem but it's another when you actually try to make it happen. Deposed CEO Durk Jager of Procter & Gamble knew that "to innovate, you have to go away from the norm. You have to be rebellious or non-conventional,"[4] but he wasn't notably successful in getting it. So even if your intent is to create a culture that will allow people to speak up, where do you start?

In every organization, there are people who want to tell you when you're wrong. They are the troublemakers, the visionaries, the dissenters. One of the most important ways to start your organization down the innovation road is to honor those who naturally want to speak truth to power, even if they feel infuriating to deal with. Sony, Microsoft, Nortel, and Hewlett-Packard have all found that honoring their troublemakers has paid off.

As you may know (as you certainly know if you have a teenage boy in your household) Playstations 1 and 2 are hugely popular. How Playstation started shows us the importance of listening to the people who cause grief. Ken Kutaragi, a Sony employee, was playing with his daughter's Nintendo (Sony's bitter rival, by the way) one day in the mid-1980s. He realized that the product would be much better with a Sony digital audio chip. He started secret negotiations with Nintendo. Naturally, at one point, he had to disclose what he was doing. His bosses were predictably furious. But he had one farsighted champion in the then-president (now CEO and chairman) Norio Ogha, who protected him from their wrath and mandated going ahead with the project.

---

[3] Taylor, William C., "The Leader of the Future," *Fast Company* (June 1999), p.132.
[4] Brooker, Katrina, "Can Procter & Gamble Change Its Culture, Protect Its Market Share, and Find the Next Tide?" *Fortune* (April 26, 1999), p. 149.

Eventually, the relationship with Nintendo fell through but Kutaragi was able to convince Sony to develop its own video games device despite the general view that it was not the high-end, sophisticated tool Sony liked to sponsor.

Microsoft has a similar history. On the one hand, it has been called "a single, formidably organized army, designed to fulfill a unified mission."[5] On the other, it is considered a badge of honor if you can shout Bill Gates down. Though I'm a bit doubtful whether who can yell the loudest is a really good predictor of innovation, Microsoft president Steve Ballmer says that "it's important to avoid that gentle civility that keeps you from getting to the heart of an issue quickly. He [Gates] likes it when a junior employee challenges him, and you know he respects you when he starts shouting back."[6]

Nortel Networks had a big success at a crucial stage in its development thanks to a stubborn rule-breaker. Nortel started out as the research arm of a phone company and has grown to a telecommunications giant that threatens the hegemony of Lucent and Cisco. When the company was first getting into fiber optic cabling, it decided to farm out a crucial part of the development to a Japanese firm. Dr. Rudolph Kriegler, a scientist with Nortel, was adamantly opposed, so much that he and a general manager got into a screaming match about it. Kriegler was reprimanded and ordered to toe the party line. Instead, he secretly started a team working on the component that had been contracted out. At the critical moment, the Japanese were not able to deliver, as Kriegler had predicted. Nortel's reputation and chance to move into this new field were in jeopardy. Kriegler saved the day by having an already-working device. Nortel recognized his contribution by appointing him a Nortel Fellow, an honor given to only three others in the company's history.

In the past, Hewlett-Packard also has honored those who speak truth to power. David Packard once gave a medal for "extraordinary contempt and defiance beyond the normal call of engineering duty" to a maverick named Chuck House. House ignored Packard's orders to quit work on the development of a new display technology that later turned out to be a financial success. Recently, HP has recognized that it needs new thinking to lead to new products, new services, and new ways of doing business. To do this, it's trying to revive its tradition of embracing mavericks.

---

[5] Levy, Steven, "Joel Klein, Entrepreneur," *Newsweek* (May 8, 2000), p. 36.
[6] Dess, Gregory G., "Leadership in the 21st Century," *Organizational Dynamics* (Winter 2000), p. 30.

Research of leading-edge organizations in the United States, Canada, Europe, and the Middle East has found that although "innovators may seem like 'troublemakers,' [they] are an organization's greatest resource."[7] Organizations are beginning to understand that the first step to building a culture that can create and sustain innovation is to listen to those who will not toe the party line.

Heretic, Troublemaker, What?

The title of this book talks about "visionaries, dissenters, and other useful troublemakers." I've also called them people who speak truth to power, heretics, and mavericks. So can we settle on one term to cover this phenomenon?

This quality of persisting in pushing a new idea or pointing out when things aren't going right doesn't generally have a positive tag in organizational life. Well, perhaps "visionary," although the term reminds me of an old joke. "Today, they won't hire me without a vision. Fifteen years ago, they would have locked me up if I had one." I don't think "visionary" is the best term for this phenomenon. You can have a vision of where the company should go but unless you push for it, nothing will happen. Having a great thought off in a corner, while visionary, doesn't help innovation, even though it is an important element of it.

"Troublemaker" is another possibility, and people I'm describing are seen as such by those in power. But troublemakers are not necessarily innovative. They can be just, well, troublemakers. I'll talk more about how to sort out the useful troublemakers from others in a later chapter but generally, I think we need to lose the idea that people who push new ideas are trouble. "Revolutionary" is a possibility but it's way too scary for most managers. And moreover, inaccurate. The great value of these people is that they *don't* want to destroy the institution. They are making a fuss because they want to make things better. They are into fixing, not overthrowing. "Heretic?" Well, possibly, although it has burning-at-the-stake connotations that aren't as prevalent in today's organizations as those of the past.

I think the word to best capture what I mean comes from the worlds of politics and religion: "dissenter." A dissenter has always been willing to speak truth to power. There have been religious

---

[7] Rose, Ian, *Valuing Intellectual Capital: A Summary Report* (IBR Consulting Services Ltd., 1997).

dissenters, such as the Pilgrim Fathers, and political ones, such as anti-war protesters, who have been around almost as long as the institutions against which they dissent. Dissent has an honorable tradition. In many spheres of our history, dissent has led to great things. Whatever your opinion of unions in today's environment, we owe a debt to those men and women who died in the twenties and thirties so that we can take for granted our right to work in physically safe conditions or so our children are not forced to work rather than learn. In some spheres, we have even institutionalized dissent. It's common for Supreme Court and lower level judges to publish a view that dissents from the majority decision. In the British parliamentary tradition, the party not in power is called the Loyal Opposition. These are integral parts of the fabric that makes democracy strong.

Dissenters have been responsible for many important advances in our society and so, even in a management context, I think it is the right label for the kind of people I want to talk about.

How Honoring Dissenters Helps Innovation

Honoring dissenters helps innovation in two ways. First, the group or corporate culture doesn't typically overly influence dissenters. This makes them hard to get along with[8] but research indicates that these types of people are also more likely to be innovative. If you are oblivious to or can resist the culture's attempts to keep you in line, you are more likely to see new possibilities. Dissenters help alleviate the danger of a culture so unified behind a goal that it can't see when it's time to change.

Second, research shows that groups think better with a dissenter in their presence. They tend to come up with more original ideas if a dissenter challenges their views. However—and this is important—the dissenter has to continue to be heard. There are many ways we cut off people who are a pain. We can actively discourage them from speaking. Even more subtle and dangerous is a mental blowing off. "There he goes again," we sigh internally and shut down our listening. A dissenter helps a group generate better ideas only if he continues to be ' taken seriously.

---

[8] A note: Just because someone is a dissenter in relation to his bosses does not mean he is with respect to his family or his colleagues. Sometimes, a dissenter may exercise that quality only with reference to authority.

Interestingly enough, the dissenter doesn't have to be right to foster more independent thought and less groupthink. In fact, he could be completely wrong, but the act of reacting to his prodding seems to be enough to generate better ideas. Research shows that even a single dissenter can break the sway of majority thinking.

That's how dissenters help organizations be more innovative. They may have the great idea themselves and be annoyingly persistent in their support of it. Or they may force others to challenge their own assumptions and ways of doing things. Either way, they are a valuable commodity. They have the ability not to be caught in and shaped by the culture. They are the little boy who could say that the Emperor had no clothes.

People Can't See What's Different

Psychologists Bruner and Postman did a fascinating experiment that illustrates how difficult it is to see what is different from what we expect. They asked experimental subjects to identify playing cards given a short exposure to them. Most cards were normal but some were anomalies. For example, there might be a black four of hearts.

Even on the shortest exposure times, subjects were able to identify the normal cards. In addition and without hesitancy, they transformed the anomalies into what they expected. Thus, the black four of hearts would be called either a four of spades or hearts.

When the time of exposure lengthened, subjects began to hesitate. They couldn't name the anomalous card but they knew something was different. As the exposures grew, most participants were able to say, "That's a black four of hearts" but even at 40 times the normal exposure, more than 10% of anomalous cards could not be identified even though this awareness of the anomaly caused the test subjects considerable distress.

So novelty emerges with difficulty. It's hard even to see innovation, much less use it profitably. We need people who are naturally inclined to look where no one else does.

Managing Conflict and Managing Dissent

There may be some asking, "Isn't dissent just another word for conflict? Isn't this an old sheep trucked out in new fleece?" I don't think so. To me, conflict is a general term that covers anything from personality clashes to fundamental disagreements about the direction of the organization. Managers don't typically differentiate between the two; they try to get rid of both. They do this, to some extent, because we lack a vocabulary to distinguish between healthy and unhealthy conflict.

Unhealthy conflict can derive from interpersonal issues that prevent people from coming up with the best solutions. I dislike you, not because you have a better way to do things, but because you treat my ideas with contempt. Managing conflict is about, "I don't like you, you don't like me, but we have to work together." It's very worthwhile and necessary for organizations to minimize this friction. But managing dissent is about listening to voices that convey valuable information on values, strategy, and tactics, even if negatively expressed. It is about finding that fine balance between encouraging an open expression of dissent and allowing anarchy to reign. Organizations need both to be single-minded in pursuit of their goals and open to the lone voice saying, "You're going in the wrong direction."

It's understandable why conflict and dissent are confused since dissent can sometimes be disguised as a personality conflict. If you don't agree with what someone is saying and he keeps saying it, it can be annoying and then rude and then downright insulting. Also, focusing on the other's personality problems shifts the blame to him and absolves you of the need to do anything—like admitting that something's wrong either in the organization or in you.

The skills used to manage conflict will be useful in managing dissent, but they have fundamentally different objectives. You manage conflict to minimize it and you manage dissent to highlight it and use it productively.

When Dissent Is Useful

There are any number of ways dissent can help an organization to be more effective and innovative.

Killing a Wrong/Out-of-Date Idea

One company was being bought by another. Brave New World, the buyer, had decided that Marketshare had a product complementary to its own. The plan was to buy Marketshare, cross-sell to each other's customers and thus increase both products' profitability. Brave New World waved a dazzling amount of money in front of Marketshare's owners and the race to merge was on.

However, several people in Marketshare kept saying that Brave New World's products were not complementary but competitive. Brave New World's strategic objective of growth through cross-selling was doomed to failure. They were going after the same finite customer base. However, these people were labeled as difficult, turfy, and short-sighted. They were silenced.

The farther everyone got into the merger preparations—as client lists and strategies from the two companies were shared—it became clear even to the architects of the deal that the dissenters were right. But by that time, the merger had already been announced with great fanfare to both Boards of Directors. Bonuses and credibility were riding on its successful completion. Because the dissenters had already been silenced, there was no one to raise the issues again and the deal went through, even though everyone knew it would not be good for either side.

This conspiracy of silence occurs more often than one might hope. For example, it has been well-documented that decision-makers during the Kennedy administration's ill-fated invasion of Cuba were uneasy about its advisability. But a visionary leader and a strong sense of assumed consensus made people stay silent. With disastrous consequences.

Dissent may prevent you from going down a path that will ultimately prove fruitless. It points out the problems either with the idea or its implementation. Managers are often uncomfortable with dissent because it looks like it slows things down. But speed to market is not just about running as fast as you can—you have to be traveling in the right direction. There's no point in getting there first if nobody wanted to get there at all.

Making course corrections or even throwing out a strategy needs to be done in a matter of months or even days. To have this capacity, you need people willing to speak up when they believe the organization is taking a wrong turn, *even or perhaps especially if it is the received wisdom.*

Getting at Tacit Knowledge

Managing an organization's knowledge is becoming more and more important. Knowledge is usually divided into two kinds—tacit and explicit. Explicit knowledge is documented in procedures, the policy manual, reports on best practices—anything that has been recorded for public consumption. Tacit knowledge is what's carried in people's heads. It can be knowledge that either never makes it into a public document (how to manage the boss when he's in a snit) or that makes meaning of the explicit. The budgeting process is documented, how to maneuver through it is tacit. Experts estimate that the tacit part represents roughly 80% of knowledge.

When a new venture is undertaken, it's not unusual for some team members to shake their heads and say, "It'll never work." Managers, impatient to get onto an exciting new challenge, are often tempted to brush off this reaction as resistance or sour grapes. But sometimes "It'll never work" hides a wealth of tacit knowledge of what has been tried before, what didn't work, what did, and how this new venture can be undertaken. If the dissenter is silenced, none of this critical knowledge will ever come to light.

Getting at the Real Issue

In a very similar way to tacit knowledge, dissent can help get at the real issue. Apparently, Jimmy Carter disliked the posturing, arguing, and haggling that were part of his Cabinet meetings. However, such dissent can cue us to the real issues. For example, a proposal is opposed by a dissenter who says it will have disastrous consequences. No one else feels the fallout will be as dramatic but the dissenter will not be moved off his mark. Finally, when things don't go his way, he shakes his head and says, "I don't know what my people will think...this is the third time we've lost." Bingo. The real issue. He's worried about his credibility with his staff and at least part of his objection was due to that.

While one might argue that this dissenter shouldn't be concerned about his reputation, the reality is that he is and no amount of arguing about the benign consequences of the decision is going to sway him since that's not what's sticking in his craw. Dissent can help us identify the real issue and allow us to deal with it and not the façade.

Breaking out of a Bad Pattern

Organizations, like people and societies, can get into bad patterns. And these patterns have an equilibrium that is difficult to upset. Think about the computer keyboard. The placement of the letters and numbers on it was decided when manual typewriters were first invented. If the keyboard is arranged alphabetically, many commonly used letters occur together (e.g., "bed"). The typewriter keys would tangle if the typist typed faster than the time it took for a key to strike the page and return to its slot before another was struck. To avoid this problem, the present-day QWERTY keyboard was developed, separating commonly used keys from each other. Great innovation, very useful at the time, and completely useless now. In fact, the QWERTY keyboard makes it *more* difficult to learn to use a keyboard. But we are stuck in a bad pattern that would take an enormous amount of effort to change.

Organizations have the same problem. I know a company with a long history that was struggling. Although it was agreed that the problems were temporary and the market would eventually correct itself, in the short term, the company was facing disaster. An influential executive was positive the answer was layoffs. He was articulate and compelling about the need to use them. Anything less lacked courage and business acumen. The slash and burn option began to emerge as synonymous with visionary and bold.

However, another executive was troubled by this view and asked HR to trace how the company had handled adverse conditions in the past. They went back to records of the Depression and found that, during that whole period, the company had not laid off a single worker. They had reduced salaries, cut hours of work, and lowered benefits but no one had lost their job.

When this was presented, several managers who had been silent until then spoke. The Depression story reminded them of who they were as a company, that they had a long tradition of working with their employees in adversity. By connecting with their own history and tradition, they were able to break out of the pattern of assuming layoffs were the only option.

However, they would not have been able to do so unless a dissenter had pointed out that they were in a bad pattern. Sometimes agreement, and not dissent, is the major problem in an organization.

Won't All This Dissent Run Amok?

As you read through this, the hairs on the back of your managerial neck may have started to rise. Even if you agree that dissent can make a valuable contribution to innovation, you may have a legitimate fear that it will run amok, causing chaos and, even more importantly, paralyzing the organization. In addition, you might have to tolerate constant badgering from dissenters, complaining about situations you can't do anything about.

Good points. Certainly, how much dissent you allow depends on your business. Military organizations and churches might be less inclined to tolerate it while fields such as journalism or academia have a well-established tradition of people who don't fly in formation. But the examples cited above show it is possible to have an organization that both encourages dissent and accomplishes its goals. Rather than opening the gates to anarchy, dissent is actually an economical way to produce innovation.

Having said that, however, it's not easy. It will require managers to think about the unwritten rules they have about dissent. But the payoff can be significant. Making a place for people with great ideas even if they don't have the requisite political and interpersonal skills is an important contribution to future success. More of that in the next chapter.

Summary

A wise CEO once said, "I don't shoot messengers—therefore I have them." Organizations that don't allow dissent inadvertently discourage innovation. Dissent and innovation are opposites only in the same way exhaling and inhaling are. You must exhale to be able to inhale. You must have dissent to have innovation.

Main Points

- Speaking truth to power is an important component of an innovative culture.
- Managers may fear that dissent will create chaos but it is possible to welcome dissent while still moving forward.

References for This Chapter

Colvin, Geoffrey, "The Ultimate Manager," *Fortune* (November 22, 1999), pp. 185–87.

Hamel, Gary, "Driving Grassroots Growth," *Fortune* (September 4, 2000), p. 176.

Harvey, Jerry B., *The Abilene Paradox and Other Meditations on Management* (San Diego: University Associates, 1988).

Kuhn, Thomas S., *The Structure of Scientific Revolutions: Third Edition* (Chicago: University of Chicago Press, 1996).

MacDonald, Larry, *Nortel Networks: How Innovation and Vision Created a Network Giant* (Toronto: John Wiley and Sons, 2000).

Nee, Eric, "Hewlett-Packard's New E-vangelist," *Fortune* (January 10, 2000) pp. 166–67.

Stamps, David, "Is Knowledge Management a Fad?" *Training* (March 1999).

Stewart, Thomas A., "3-M Fights Back," *Fortune* (February 5, 1996), p. 98.

Stewart, Thomas A., "See Jack. See Jack Run," *Fortune* (September 27, 1999), pp. 124–36.

Stewart, Thomas, "Today's Companies Won't Make It and Gary Hamel Knows Why," *Fortune* (September 4, 2000), pp. 386–88.

Taylor, William C., "The Leader of the Future," *Fast Company* (June 1999), p. 134.

The Nature of Dissent in Organizations

Dissent does not always confine itself to the areas managers find acceptable. It's not possible to have a culture that encourages it only in areas sanctioned by management. Dissent has to flow free.

Introduction

When I was speaking once at a conference, someone told me a story he thought was a great one about managing knowledge workers. It was, but it was an even better story about managing dissent.

He was working at a brokerage firm that traded in Asia. Traders had to get up at the crack of dawn to check opening prices on the Tokyo exchange. Then they would come into work. Because of the long and demanding days, attrition and absenteeism were very high. A manager suggested to the Board of Directors that they install a "crash room"—nothing more than couches and music so traders could sack out for a few hours when fatigue got them. The Board pooh-poohed the suggestion. After all, *they* had made it through the ranks without mollycoddling. The traders could just tough it out.

But the manager went ahead and installed the room anyway. Sure enough, absenteeism dropped almost to nothing when traders knew they could just take a nap rather than skip a whole day's work. Attrition also dropped. When the Board saw the results, they realized the value of the idea and allowed other rooms to be set up. But they fired the manager. They fired him because he *disobeyed a direct order.*

In hindsight, the firing seems pretty stupid. First of all, the Board cut itself off from any other innovative ideas that manager might have. In addition and even more importantly, it sent a signal to the rest of the organization that, no matter the public pronouncements, innovation would be punished.

However, while I think it was a stupid and shortsighted decision, I also have a sneaking sympathy for the Board. How *do* you run an organization if everyone feels free to disregard your orders? How can you accomplish anything if nobody listens? While I don't think the company resolved those questions very effectively, it was using a tried and true management paradigm. We have a long tradition of assuming that only certain people are supposed to make decisions or think, and woe betide those who make different decisions or think differently. In fact, early 20th-century management guru Frederick Taylor stated emphatically that "all possible brain work should be removed from the shop."[1]

Suggestions from lower down the chain of command were seen as counterproductive, implied disapproval, and were a challenge to an executive's authority. Critical thinking was synonymous with criticism. Therefore and not surprisingly, managers developed a fairly sophisticated ability to ensure that any signs of thinking—such as disagreement, disapproval, and dissent—were suppressed. In fact, given the beliefs of the day, it would be surprising if they hadn't been.

Stages of Suppressing Dissent

Unfortunately, even though we know today that suppressing critical thinking is both erroneous and destructive, the management approaches that have grown up around that unquestioned assumption have been hard to break, as shown by our example. Although we know a free exchange of ideas is more effective, we don't always act as if that were the case. Many organizations still have a very well developed ability to suppress dissent. This legacy is so much part of the culture that it often isn't seen and certainly not remarked upon. But it is a powerful influence nevertheless. Organizations tend to suppress dissent in some pretty standard ways. I bet you will recognize the stages:

Stage 1: Arguing

At Stage 1, it is assumed the dissenter just doesn't know any better and is amenable to "rational" discussion. Some of the arguments you'll hear:
>   *"It'll never work."*
>   *"The boss will never go for it."*

---

[1] Thomas Petzinger, Jr., "A New Model for the Nature of Business: It's Alive!" *The Wall Street Journal* (February 26, 1999).

"It's not what we do around here."
"Things are okay as they are."

Stage 2: Listening But Not Hearing

If the dissenter persists in his wrong-headed view, things stay polite but subtle messages are sent.

"Yes, we've heard from you on that. Anybody else got some different ideas?"
"Thanks for your contribution."
"Maybe you should put that in writing so we all have a good idea of what you mean."

Stage 3: Laughing It Off

Before they hit this stage, most team players are astute enough to realize they need to tone down their advocacy. But those who don't get it begin to get teased about their persistence.

"This is a real hobbyhorse, isn't it? When are you going to get off and give somebody else a chance to ride?"
"If you're so smart, how come you ain't rich?"
"Can I give you a quarter to phone somebody who cares?"

You note that nowhere are people talking about the real issues—like how inconvenient, threatening, or difficult it will be to implement the dissenter's idea. Often, it's *because* the idea is inconvenient, threatening, or difficult that this whole process gets invoked to begin with. It is at this point that the focus moves from the dissenter's *ideas* to the dissenter himself. It stops being about whether the idea makes sense and starts being about the dissenter's personality flaws.

Stage 4: Ignoring

If ridicule doesn't work, the powers-that-be start to get a little ticked. Although they'd never say it, they're beginning to feel that if the dissenter had any sensitivity or even manners, he'd stop bothering them. They bring into play one of the most powerful weapons—silence. When the dissenter speaks, no one replies; the conversation continues as if he had never spoken. If he protests or persists, he gets:

"We've been over that ground before. I was looking for new ideas."
"I don't think we'll get to your item today. Maybe next time."

While in the previous stage people kept their expressions carefully neutral, now nonverbal cues are more evident. Rolling eyeballs and sighs are prominent.

Stage 5: Making Invisible

Still some people don't get it. They persist despite the increasingly unfriendly environment. The heat is turned up. Not only will the boss refuse to engage in further discussion but also funny things start to happen. Somehow, the dissenter's name gets left off distribution lists. Invitations to important meetings aren't forthcoming. Decisions are taken without his input. It's as if he has disappeared.

Stage 6: Forbidding

Some dissenters won't take their invisibility lying down. Then the big guns come out. If the dissenter continues to push his unpopular views, someone will finally drag him into a room and say:

"You are to focus on assigned projects, not just on the ones you want to do."
"Stop wasting other people's time by pushing your pet project."
"I forbid you to work on that idea."

Sanctions may or may not be threatened. If the dissenter has taken the issue this far, he may see his fight as a matter of principle. Backing down would be a comment on him, on his integrity. But equally, the boss has had it, and the idea the dissenter has will be implemented only over several dead bodies.

Stage 7: Getting Rid of the Dissenter

If the situation gets to this stage, war has been declared and both sides are focused not on what's good for the company but on winning. And, just given the way of the world, the power is on the side of the higher-ups. If the dissenter ignores the previous injunctions, any number of things can happen.

"I don't think your skills are up to this position. There's a job for a paper-pusher in Division M."
"You need to report through Bob now. He'll vet any of your ideas."
"Somebody has to be laid off. I regret it has to be you."
"We don't have a place for you in this organization."

Sound familiar? You might even have experienced at least the first stages of this model. If you've survived and even thrived, you know what dissenters are not as clear on—that you sometimes have to back down to fight another day. That makes good political sense. You can't influence an organization you don't belong to.

However, the problem for organizations and innovation is that, early on, the whole thing stops being about the idea and starts being about the dissenter as a difficult employee. Thus, the value of the idea gets buried in a contest of wills, and a potential innovation gets lost in the playing out of other issues. And while the loss of one innovation isn't all that horrifying, the idea that there is a well-developed system in place that regularly suppresses them is.

Why Do Dissenters Stay?

Why do dissenters stay in organizations? As you can see, much as they are annoying to us, it's no picnic for them either. They have to endure a modern kind of shunning that is irrelevant only to someone with absolutely no human feelings.

It's more comprehensible why people dissent for religious or political reasons. Until maybe the last hundred years, it wasn't easy and sometimes impossible to change either your country or your religion. Execution or imprisonment was not uncommon for trying. Since you couldn't switch, your only choices were to knuckle under or dissent.

However, that's not true in today's work world. Those who speak up are staying when it would be just as easy to leave. Some may feel captive to personal or professional bonds, or security or even stubbornness, but I also think there is an element of wanting the organization to be better. And that needs to be respected, no matter how annoying or inexpertly expressed.

Consent and Dissent

History is littered with attempts to suppress innovators. When Edward Jenner proposed a smallpox vaccine in 1797, the Royal Society of London ridiculed him for recommending something "so at variance with established knowledge and withal so incredible."[2] Hungarian physician Ignaz Semmelweis figured out that physicians' unwashed hands were causing fatal infections among new mothers at the University of Vienna in the 1850s. They fired him. Barry Marshall first reported his findings on the infectious cause of ulcers in 1983, but his peers ignored the discovery until 1990 when the *National Enquirer* got hold of the story and told the world. Makes you want to rethink your views on whether aliens really did abduct Michelle Pfeiffer, doesn't it?

---

[2] Geoffrey Cowley, "The Real 'Hot One,'" *Newsweek* (November 27, 2000), pp. 66–7.

Even Playstation inventor Ken Kutaragi talks about being exiled to an internal Sony wilderness as he struggled to get his idea adopted. Success was a lonely road. "I was the outsider," he reports. "I was homeless. People inside Sony hated us."[3] So the tools of ridicule, ignoring, etc. are common when we are faced with ideas that don't fit our world view.

Why does this happen? Why does this proclivity to suppress dissent, to suppress speaking truth to power, continue to be so well exercised in organizations, despite its deleterious effects?

One of the executives I interviewed for this book gave me a clue. "I'll tolerate dissent before the decision is taken. But after?" He shook his head. "After that, it's insubordination. I can't run an organization if I have to keep protecting my back."

When I initially heard that, I thought, "Yeah, makes sense. After all, you've got to deliver." Intuitively and most particularly in our information economy, managers understand that their effectiveness depends to a remarkable degree on the active consent of their employees. Without willing compliance, the cost of management can be too high. The taxman and the military know this. If the majority of taxpayers don't pay willingly and honestly, the cost of collecting taxes will outweigh the revenues. In fact (and this is a deep, dark secret I share with you), I used to work in the tax department and the rule of thumb was that it cost $1.05 to generate $1.00 in taxes if payment wasn't voluntary. Similarly, with conscription. It works only if the majority of citizens comply willingly. If even a minority does not, as happened during the Vietnam War, the cost both monetarily and socially of enforcing the policy is prohibitive.

You know that from your own experience. Have you ever had an employee who didn't do what you asked? Eventually, you end up spending so much time checking up on her that you can't do your own job. The employee becomes a liability because you cannot trust her. So, because managers understand how necessary active consent of their employees is, they are leery of anything that suggests it will not occur.

Not only that, but managers know that too much dissent—too many people with too many divergent ideas—is a recipe for chaos. An organization that cannot make up its mind is paralyzed. You may fear the situation Levi Strauss found itself in. Former CFO George James discovered that "unless you could convince everyone to agree with your idea, you didn't have the authority to make the decision."[4]

---

[3] Gary Hamel, "Driving Grassroots Growth," *Fortune* (September 4, 2000), p. 176.
[4] Nina Munk, "How Levi's Trashed a Great American Brand," *Fortune* (April 12, 1999).

Finally, even though most managers know that communicating with and convincing employees will pay off in the long run, they reasonably cannot spend all their time doing it. They may fear they'll have to if there is a dissenter in their midst.

But for all that, the more I think about it, the less I agree with the executive's statement.

For one thing, if free and open debate prior to a decision is helpful, why is it no longer acceptable after? Why useful before and insubordination after? Say you really have made the wrong decision. Don't you need people around you, like the Thinsulate guy, who will tell you that, no matter how far down the road you are?

"But," you might be objecting, "there are lots of times when a decision, even if it's not the best, can be made to work if everybody gets behind it." Clearly true. The old Betamax and VHS debate is an example. Betamax was the better technology for videotaping but the VHS system won out completely. Given that, you want everyone to put their all into making the decision work rather than being stuck at "but it was the wrong decision to begin with." Understandable, but I think that view raises other issues worthy of challenge.

When the manager says, "I can't run an organization if I have to keep protecting my back," he is making two assumptions. The first is that dissent is subversive and the other that the dissenter doesn't have the best interests of the company at heart. But are either true?

In the first case, if you disagree with a decision, will you really do everything you can to tank its success? Management theorist Gary Hamel of the London Business School doesn't think so: "What the defenders of orthodoxy see as subversiveness, the champions of new thinking see as enlightenment."[5] He points out that dissenters are subversive but their goal is not subversion. They may not toe the party line but it doesn't follow that they are therefore trying to destroy what has been built. New thinking is disruptive, and disruption is often seen as trying to subvert the goals of the organization.

As to the second reason, that you don't care about the company—well, when you think about it, that doesn't add up either. If you had nefarious designs and thought the company was going down a path of error and failure, wouldn't you do everything in your power to make sure that the company *adopted* that path rather than speak out against it? Or wouldn't it make most sense just to leave?[6] Why stick around to undergo the unpleasant consequences of disagreeing with the received wisdom?

---

[5] Marshall Loeb, "When to Rat on the Boss," *Fortune* (October 2, 1995), p. 183.
[6] I realize that leaving or not leaving a job has many more components than just dissent.

However, since dissent is synonymous with nefarious motives and sabotage in most managers' minds, they fear it. And because they fear it, they actively discourage any signs, so much so that they often impose an unstated but powerful expectation: Only 100% agreement is acceptable. You have to pretend to agree even if you don't. This can lead to the ridiculous situation in which everyone says they support an initiative when they don't and their boss knows they don't. Is that logical? That the boss *prefers* people to lie to him? There's only one way I can make sense of it: Managers suppress dissent because they see the situation as binary—that is, there are only two choices: 100% agreement or chaos. If you believe that there is no gray area and that your only choices are between having people lie to you and a descent into anarchy, then faking it probably is preferable.

But dissent isn't an on-off phenomenon. It is a continuum, from the kind that is useful to that which is divisive and destructive. It's not that subversion and sabotage don't occur. We know they do. But they are the extreme end of dissent. By being unaware that a continuum exists, managers can inadvertently shut off useful dissent and throw the baby out with the bath water.

A Season for Dissent?

Are there periods in the life cycle of an organization when dissent is more acceptable or at least less unacceptable? Rod Brandvold is Vice President of Organizational Development for Cognos, Inc., the world's largest and most successful business intelligence software company. He speculates that, in start-up phase, there may be more room for "misfits." Early on, before the organizational culture has jelled, a wider diversity of behavior may be tolerated as innovation ranges high, wide, and handsome. However, as the company gets more successful and grows, there is pressure to put aside the wild early days for the more mature, responsible, grown-up ways that instill confidence in stockholders and stock markets. And perhaps, somewhere along the line, the magic gets put aside too.

A Dissent Continuum

As I said, dissent runs on a continuum from that which helps innovation to that which is destructive. There are four stages and they tend to be sequential as illustrated in the figure below.

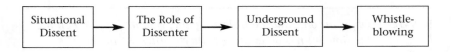

Situational Dissent

Situational dissent is the first and most easily tolerated type. It is usually driven by circumstance. An employee who is committed to the company's strategic direction may find herself at odds with it in a particular situation. If the issue can be resolved, the dissent is dissipated. This is how it might look.

> **Terry** *Hey Greg, I have a bone to pick with you!*
> **YOU** *Really?*
> **Terry** *You shouldn't let Merrimount Corp. access our client base.*
> **YOU** *Well, we are sister companies.*
> **Terry** *But we're also competitors. What's to prevent them from trying to knock us out of the 14-to-18-year-old market?*
> **YOU** *They're not big there now.*
> **Terry** *But they're making noises like they want to be.*
> **YOU** *Really?*

From the dissent point of view, it actually doesn't matter how you resolve this. You may try to prevent Merrimount's access or stand pat. What's important is that you listened to the dissenter. Not all that difficult, is it? You probably do it every day. Most managers deal with this level of dissent well.

The Role of Dissenter

Not all situations are resolved that easily though. You may not think Terry is very credible. Even if she is, you may not agree on what the future holds or be unable to listen to her. Once their boss has put the kibosh on their dissent, most employees would give up. But some take on the role of dissenter and persist, even after you've taken the decision.

> **Terry** *Greg, I really have a bad feeling about the Merrimount thing.*
> **YOU** *Lookit, Terry, it's a done deal. Let's move on.*
> **Terry** *But I tell you, they're ready to wipe us out in the 14-to-18s. I just know they are. Giving them our client base is opening our shirt for the knife.*

> **YOU**   *Oh, come on...that's a little dramatic, isn't it? I mean, nothing Merrimount has done suggests they're after our market share.*
> **Terry** *Not yet.*
> **YOU**   *Well, until they do, we've got to cooperate.*
> **Terry** *But by the time they take action, we'll be sunk. They have deep pockets. We can't outspend them.*
> **YOU**   *We may not need to.*
> **Terry** *I'm sure we will. I just know it.*

If you have dealt with dissenters, you know this conversation could go on a lot longer and get not much further. Because dissenters can't seem to take no for an answer, you may feel stuck in endless and fruitless discussions. If you cover the same ground again and again, the need to cut it off and get on with things is understandable.

But what if Terry is right? You want to avoid shutting her down completely while continuing to move forward. In following chapters, I'll show you how.

Underground Dissent

The previous kind of dissent is annoying and frustrating, but it is preferable to this next stage. Underground dissent, as the name implies, is disagreement that is not expressed openly. This is where sabotage and subversion kick in.

Dissent that has not been handled effectively in the previous stages doesn't go away. If employees believe that differing ideas are not welcome, dissent gets expressed in obscure ways.

> **YOU**   *Terry, I just got a call from Bill Paxton over at Merrimount. Apparently, they're having trouble accessing our database. They keep getting a "corrupted file" message.*
> **Terry** *Really? Gosh, I wonder what happened.*
> **YOU**   *Did you make the arrangements for access?*
> **Terry** *Of course. I guess the Merrimount guys just don't know what they're doing.*
> **YOU**   *Bill says he's been trying to get you for the last two days.*
> **Terry** *Well, I've returned all his calls. It's not my fault we haven't been able to connect.*
> **YOU**   *Could you call him and straighten this out?*
> **Terry** *Sure thing.*

Terry will call Bill back but my bet is she'll do it over the lunch hour or after the end of the day when she can leave yet another message to "prove" she is cooperating. Will the problem get fixed? Probably and eventually, but only if you check up on her and spend a whole lot more time on it than you should have to.

Given our reliance today on knowledge work that happens entirely in people's heads, this kind of dissent is especially dangerous. So, much as open dissent is a nuisance, underground is worse.

Whistle-blowing

An employee can go to the media, the police, or some regulatory body with internal information she believes is immoral or illegal. When this happens, even if it is useful to the public at large, it is almost always disastrous for the organization. Whistle-blowing is an extreme form of dissent clearly aimed at forcing the organization along a path it wasn't intending to take. I'm not going to provide a dialog for this situation since, once the employee blows the whistle, your legal and HR departments should be advising you on what is no longer strictly a management matter.

People being people, they don't always follow the continuum exactly as laid out. A dissenter in stage two might move to whistle-blowing without going underground first. Or she might leave the organization completely and never get past the dissenter role. However, typically speaking, people don't move from situational dissent directly to whistle-blowing. Nor do most people start out as underground dissenters. They are usually driven to it by (dare I say?) how effectively the manager handles open dissent.

So, in summary, dissent is on a continuum from situational to whistle-blowing. Generally speaking, people get pushed farther along the dissent continuum if the organization invokes one or more of the suppression tactics I've already covered. Some tactics are more likely with certain types of dissent and the figure on the next page illustrates that.

When dissent is situational, the sanctions are usually relatively mild. However, as things heat up, they get more important. It's interesting to note that most sanctions tend to be used at the second stage—the role of the dissenter. It's almost as if managers are putting their all into suppressing dissent exactly at the point they should be trying their hardest to keep it in the open.

So dissent is not a binary function but a continuum. It needs to be encouraged to help innovation flourish, but it's productive only if it

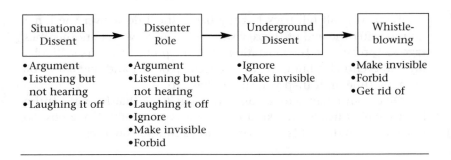

can be kept in the open. If you want dissent to spur innovation, you need to work very hard at keeping it at the first two stages. Once it goes underground or into whistle-blowing, its potential to provoke innovation is pretty much over and you have an entirely new set of problems. In fact, I'd bet if you're in either of the latter stages, you're not worrying about innovation; you're worrying about staying alive.

Dissent and Politics

Dissent is uncomfortable because it gets expressed as politics—another dirty word in organizational life. Company politics is always the thing we want to rise above and condemn others for engaging in. We tend to think life would be so much easier if it didn't exist.

But you know what? Office politics can be an instrument of innovation...because both politics and innovation are about people. It would be easy if innovators were typically shy retiring types.[7] If only they would propose their ideas in a timid voice, shake their heads, and say, "No, I didn't think it would work either." But they don't. Innovators and dissenters want to make things happen and more often than anyone is happy with, they argue, cajole, go behind your back, go above you, or do it anyway. They play politics and that, in and of itself, is disruptive. But politics are one of the ways new ideas and perspectives emerge in organizations.

However—and this is an important "however"—politics are helpful to dissent only if they are open and aboveboard. If they are underground and malicious, they are the destructive force we fear. I'll deal more with that in the chapters on underground dissent.

---

[7] It's important to remember our definition of innovation. Innovation is actually transforming an idea into something of value. An *inventor* may be a shy retiring type, but an innovator rarely is.

Good Dissent and Bad

After reading all this, you may be thinking, "Okay, maybe I buy allowing dissent to encourage innovation. Even if it's annoying. But I'm going to put up with it only where I want innovation."

It makes sense to want to distinguish between good dissent—that which will assist innovation—and bad dissent—that which will not. We want encourage the good and discourage the bad. I don't think anyone would disagree this is a worthwhile objective.

The question is, how? I've outlined one way. Keeping it aboveground will avoid a lot of its destructive and unproductive expressions. However, even if you do that, you might be tempted to limit the nuisance value further by restricting the topics open for dissent. Product development, sales and marketing, and customer service are all desirable targets for innovation and therefore worth tolerating a little dissent. What about financial and human resources practices? Hmmm—getting iffy. Are you really going to allow people to make a fuss about how the books are kept or how you hire people? But there might be some innovation possibilities there, too, so maybe you have to let it happen there also. Okay, but definitely not mission, vision, and values. They have to stay rock solid.

However, history provides us with some disturbing examples of how an immutable mission can cause damage. Let me tell you a story that might give you pause. It happened a while ago but I tell it because the elapsed time gives us enough perspective to see the long-term effects.

The Catholic Church, like any religion, is an interesting study for organizations because it is a pure form of mission and values. It doesn't have a product or service that needs mission and values to bring it to life. It *is* a mission and set of values that have some products and services to amplify and expand it.

The 1960s were a time of ferment in the world, and the Catholic Church was not exempt. A major debate centered on birth control, and in 1968, an encyclical ruled against artificial means to prevent conception. Given the Church's core belief in the sanctity of human life, it's easy to see how difficult and perhaps even impossible it was to conclude otherwise. However, the decision seems to have prompted several important consequences.

First, there was opposition to the decision within the Church[8] and many radical priests and nuns were either pushed out or left voluntarily. With weakened internal voices, the Church's capacity to hear societal concerns was damaged and this, arguably, led to an ossification of its structure.

---

[8] Although this was not the only issue on which dissent was active at this time.

Some who stayed also opposed the ruling. A friend who was planning to marry at the height of the controversy remembers an interview with her parish priest. He said to her, "I am going to ask a question, but I don't want you to answer it." He repeated the statement and then said, "Are you planning to use artificial birth control?" Obviously, he had been instructed to refuse to marry anyone who answered yes. To express his dissent, he asked the question but avoided hearing the answer. He followed the letter of his instructions but not the spirit. Thus, the Church's intent was not carried out even by some of those who chose to stay within it. The dissent had gone underground.

Finally, many parishioners continued to use birth control even after it was expressly forbidden. This is a dangerous point for any organization. By persisting in a policy that was actively flouted, the Church inadvertently sent the message that its instruction could be ignored. People learned they didn't need to listen. This contributed to the erosion of the parish priest's strong and well-accepted position of authority in the community. Without minimizing other causes, the Church's inability to tolerate dissent can be seen as a contributing factor to the fall in numbers of Catholics after the 1960s and in the Church's diluted ability to guide its members' daily lives.

An unanswerable but fascinating question is whether the Church would have altered its decision on birth control had it known the consequences for its influence. My guess is not; it was seen as fundamental to the fabric of the religion's belief system. But the Church's unwillingness or inability to adapt its values and beliefs resulted in a diminished willingness of its people to listen at all.

Let me stress that I am not addressing the rightness of the Church's decisions, but rather what seems to be an interesting phenomenon— that even in debates on issues as fundamental as values, institutions that protect themselves by pushing out or suppressing dissent may find, by that act, they weaken the institution itself.

I am coming around to the view that dissent is a unitary concept. It may not be possible to say, "Bring your brains to work but apply them only where we want." You can't support innovation in products but not strategy, or in operations but not values. You may have to encourage it (and therefore dissent) in all aspects of work life.

Nor do I think it's possible to parcel dissent into major and trivial issues. It would certainly be more efficient to expend energy only on those issues that matter. But you need to remember two things. First, the person raising the issue presumably doesn't think it's trivial. And who knows, she may be right. Second and even more important, if you suppress dissent on the small things, will people come back on the big stuff? The more likely train of thought will be: "Well, he really blew me off about the photocopier. I can just imagine what he'll do if I bring up the problem with the distribution chain."

I'm beginning to believe that dissent needs a kind of Prime Directive. If you remember, *Star Trek*'s Prime Directive forbade interference with another culture's development. They had found that, no matter how pure the motives, the consequences of intervention could not be predicted and were sometimes disastrous. Rather than try to predict which actions would be beneficial and which harmful, they opted for none.

So it is with dissent. Because it's difficult to know where or when dissent is appropriate, a Dissent Prime Directive might go something like this: All open dissent is acceptable and will not be suppressed.

Realistically, this can't be. There will be times when you need to concentrate people's attention on one issue or when you just don't have time to argue whether Styrofoam cups are the answer. But it's something to keep in mind. Innovation and therefore dissent cannot easily be focused and its encouragement may well need to be across the board.

Stupid Dissent

I can imagine you mumbling into your beer, "All very well to encourage dissent if we're talking about somebody with good ideas but what about Blaire?" We've all managed them. Good-hearted, hard-working, enthusiastic, great with people, and wouldn't know a good idea if it walked up and introduced itself. Unfortunately, the Blaires of the world always seem to take up a lot of airtime on their "great" ideas.

It's hard to tolerate this boundless, stupid enthusiasm. But you need to. Not for Blaire, but for the others in the group. If others see you stomping on her, they won't know you're going to do it only to her. They're more likely to assume you don't want new ideas. In addition, even off-the-wall ideas can spark innovation. It's annoying that all the off-the-wall stuff comes from one person, but there you are. If "ifs" and "ands" were pots and pans, there'd be no need for tinkers, as an old aunt of mine used to say. (I know, I didn't know what it meant either. It means—if you could have the stuff that follows "if" and "and" as easily as you buy pots, you'd not need a repairer of pots, a tinker. On second thought, that doesn't make sense either. I digress.)

If Blaire continually comes up with hare-brained ideas, you may need to sit her down and make sure she understands the strategic direction and how it applies in your area. May help, can't hurt, and yes, I would say you need to tolerate Blaire's "great ideas" with as much grace as possible.

Your Tasks in Supporting Dissent

Collectively, we have developed a very efficient and effective dissent suppression mechanism. To start to move your organization to one more open to innovation, you need to lower the price dissenters pay for dissent and increase the dissenter's ability to be effective without domesticating him.

You can begin that process with four things. First, you need to avoid suppressing dissent that occurs naturally. Second, you can learn how to handle dissent in such a way that people will continue to speak up but will not impede meeting your objectives. Third, you have to re-surface underground dissent. Finally, you need to put into place new structures, mechanisms, and procedures to move toward a more innovative culture.

The four things apply to all managers, no matter their level. Executives need to encourage dissent with their direct reports as does any junior manager. This is important for their own direct reports' innovation but also as a model for the rest of the organization of what is acceptable or even required behavior. But beyond that, executives have some special responsibilities to put the structures and mechanisms in place that will promote dissent and innovation.

If you follow these steps, you are well on your way to creating a culture that can sustain innovation. I'll cover how to do these things in upcoming chapters. Some of what I'll be saying will be the plainest common sense but other points will ask you to walk a tightrope, between that which is efficient and that which promotes innovation. Some advice might even be counterintuitive. But all of it underscores the point that if fostering innovation were easy, we would have done it long ago and I wouldn't need to write this book.

Summary

I know this sounds like chaos in the making. You probably have pictures of dissenters running wild through the corridors, creating mayhem as they go. But it doesn't have to be that way. I'm not advocating turning the asylum over to the inmates, but rather introducing ways to help innovation range more freely while still remembering that you have a business to run. The next chapter will help you avoid some things that suppress dissent.

Main Points

- In the old manufacturing economy, a sophisticated system of suppression of dissent was developed.
- This system still functions well and has seven stages.
- Dissent is on a continuum.
- Keeping dissent in the open keeps it productive.

CHAPTER 5

Ways You'd Never Suppress Dissent— Would You?

Managers are very effective at shutting down dissent.
Even when they're not trying to, their actions may be
interpreted that way and the net effect will be the same.
This chapter will outline how managers
shut down dissent and how to avoid doing so.

Introduction

This chapter and the next focus on your first task as a manager— avoiding the suppression of naturally occurring dissent. Usually, this dissent is situational, i.e., it occurs when an employee who supports the strategic direction tells you about a disconnect. If most dissent could be kept situational, you'd probably increase your level of innovation while remaining efficient. But while this is desirable, it's surprisingly difficult to do because, as I think these examples will show, it is easy to suppress.

Shooting messengers, sending mixed messages, playing politics, and intimidating are tactics that some—not many, but some—managers use with regularity in the workplace. Not good at the best of times, but they have the added problem of suppressing dissent. I know you don't engage in them. You're not That Kind of Person. But a surprising number of managers don't realize that the purest of motives can be interpreted by the recipients in exactly those ways. It doesn't take much for politically savvy employees to know when to shut up. And while it's efficient to have everybody do what they're told, it's not a source of innovation. So keep reading—this might apply to you after all.

For each behavior I discuss, I'll cover what it is, how it suppresses dissent, and how to avoid it. The situations are not obviously dissent related. This highlights how easy it is to miss their effect on dissent.

Shoot the Messenger

We think we've got it bad. In ancient Roman times, bearers of bad news were sometimes literally killed. You've got to think some of those emperors had low impulse control. Today, we don't actually shoot messengers but we do the non-Criminal Code equivalent and it's just as effective. Here's a typical situation.

Roger *Hi, boss, got a minute?*

YOU *Of course, Roger. My door is always open.*

Roger *I know you wanted the Telus report by today but it's just not possible.*

YOU *What! With Linda breathing down my neck as it is!*

Roger *I know, I know. Until a couple of hours ago, I thought we were okay. But we reran one of the analyses, just to be sure, and found incomplete data. Once we got everything in, the revenue projections looked weird.*

YOU *You're just telling me now!*

Roger *But I didn't know until now it was going to affect revenues.*

YOU *I don't care...you do this to me all the time...*

Roger *What!*

YOU *Well—like last week—with the Singapore thing.*

Roger *Wait a minute—that wasn't my fault! And this one isn't either—I told you—Amerinet gave us incomplete data. If Phyllis hadn't caught it, we'd be doing pie-in-the-sky projections...*

YOU *You should have thought of that before...*

Roger *Thought about what? I should have told the subsidiaries to send in complete data? Is that what you mean?*

YOU *You should have been checking and double-checking...*

Roger *I told you...it wasn't our fault...in fact, we're the heroes...if Phyllis....*

YOU *Yeah, yeah, you've told me that already...*

And so on. You just know this isn't going anywhere good. You're angry and that's understandable if your boss is expecting the report. However, it's not so clear at whom this anger should be directed. Is it really Roger's fault? Could he have done anything else to ensure the report got to you when promised? If, truthfully and reasonably (the "check and double-check" crack aside), he could not, you have shot the messenger.[1]

Of course, we don't think we're shooting messengers. We think we are having an honest discussion about why the problem cannot be fixed, why the solution has already been rejected, or why this is a recurring issue. And that is indeed happening. But shooting-the-messenger discussions also have an element of unwarranted blame. The "you do this to me all the time..." and "You should have thought of that before..." suggest you are casting around for someone to point the finger at without really trying to get to the bottom of the matter.

Shooting messengers has all kinds of unfortunate consequences. Eventually, nobody will tell you bad news and you'll wonder why you're continually blindsided. Part of the reason Coke's CEO, Doug Ivester, was forced out was because he was "blind to his own weaknesses and unwilling to take advice. He became increasingly isolated."[2] Ivester didn't make it easy for people to tell him what was wrong and eventually, nobody did.

In addition, if you shoot messengers—even on fairly trivial matters seemingly unrelated to innovation—it sends the signal that you're unable to tolerate hearing things you don't like. While understanding *why* something went wrong is the first step to fixing it, an organization that needs to find one person to blame creates employees who know it's better to keep their heads down and never try to make things better— innovative culture be damned.

So how do you avoid shooting the messenger? Let's pick it up when Roger tells you the bad news.

Roger   *I know you wanted the Telus report by today but it's just not possible.*

YOU   *What! With Linda breathing down my neck as it is!*

Roger   *I know, I know. Right until a couple of hours ago, I thought we were going to be okay. But we reran one of the analyses, just to be sure, and found incomplete data. Once we got everything in, the revenue projections looked weird.*

YOU   *Oh no! How could this have happened?*

Roger   *I dunno. Actually, we wouldn't have caught it except Phyllis thought Amerinet's numbers looked funny.*

---

[1] Of course, if he could have reasonably avoided this or it is part of a pattern as you were implying, that's a different story. That's a performance problem, and its resolution needs to be approached differently.

[2] Betsy Morris and Patricia Sellers, "What Really Happened at Coke," *Fortune* (January 10, 2000), pp. 114-16.

> **YOU** *So Amerinet gave you incomplete data?*
> **Roger** *And didn't tell us...If we hadn't spotted it, we would really have been in trouble.*
> **YOU** *Look, Roger—I'm in a fix. I can tell Linda about the Amerinet snafu but she still needs those numbers for the executive committee. I promised them by close of business today.*
> **Roger** *I know but we can't go with bad numbers...*
> **YOU** *I agree but...*

Not all that hard, was it? At the critical moment, you asked, "How could this have happened?" rather than giving rein to your frustration. It doesn't take all that much to avoid shooting. But it has an important benefit—you illustrate by your actions that you can tolerate hearing things different from what you want or expect and thereby create a climate that supports dissent and innovation.

There may not be a happy resolution to this situation. Not shooting the messenger doesn't solve the problem, but it does help you get at the real one instead of spiraling into a round of recrimination and finger-pointing.

One final thing. Roger's boss started the conversation with "My door is always open." My observation is that managers who say this think it means that the piece of wood separating them from the rest of the world isn't flush with the wall. But their employees know that although the door is open, the mind behind it is closed. I'd avoid saying this door-is-open thing at all. If you demonstrate that you really listen to people's concerns, the position of the lumber will be irrelevant.

Send Mixed Messages

It has a variety of names—walking the talk, putting your money where your mouth is, following through, being sincere. All basically the same thing—and often poorly done.

Making a grand pronouncement and then contradicting it by their actions is a besetting sin of managers. You know what I mean:

- *You're invaluable but we can't afford to keep your skills current.*
- *Treat customers well but take whatever abuse I heap on you.*
- *We're against workaholism, but we admire it* ("Can you believe that Warren? Pulled an all-nighter again! The guy's a man of steel."), *reward it* ("Well, who else for Employee of the Year...I mean, the

hours he puts in!"), *and promote it* ("Warren Appleby, Sales VP"). *Moreover and subtly, we make "no" unacceptable* ("I know she's good, but does she have the stamina, the dedication for this assignment?").

There are many good and important things that companies try to accomplish and they almost always start with a statement of intent whether it's a vision, mission, objective, or plan. But words need to be translated into actions. And where words and action meet is a dangerous intersection.

If words and actions contradict each other, employees do what every human being does. They believe the actions and discount the words. So even if managers are completely sincere, nobody believes them if their actions aren't consistent with their words. On the other hand, if they are consonant, they act as multipliers of each other, strengthening the message as well as the belief in it. It's possible to mix messages without even trying.

Carol   *Hi, Pat, I've got my travel forms. Can you sign off?*

YOU   *Sure. [Pause] Ah, isn't the airfare a little high? I know you're going during high season but I would have thought we could get a cheaper fare.*

Carol   *Well, yeah, I booked business class—I mean, it's a 15-hour flight and Mr. Yang is going to meet me at the airport to take me to Soo Enterprises.*

YOU   *Carol, you know the policy. Business class travel only for directors and above.*

Carol   *But that doesn't make sense. I need to be as rested as possible if I'm going into a meeting the moment I touch down.*

YOU   *I agree but that's the policy.*

Carol   *Well, so much for the CEO's thing about everyone's work being equally valued. There are obviously some people who are more valuable than others.*

YOU   *Come on—we can't have everybody traveling business class. Do you know what that would cost?*

Carol   *So why is it okay for you guys but not me?*

YOU   *It's a perk, Carol, you know that.*

Carol   *But you guys already get paid more anyhow. Why do you need perks?*

YOU   *Salary is based on skills. Perks are different.*

Carol   *Why different?*

> **YOU**   *Lookit—I've been with this company a lot longer than you. I haven't flitted from place to place, looking for the best deal. I've earned my perks.*
>
> **Carol**   *Earned them? How can you earn perks? Don't they just come with the job?*
>
> **YOU**   *You know what I mean—they're a payoff for loyalty, staying with the company.*
>
> **Carol**   *So I have to be here a million years just to fly business class? Even if I can't be at my best when I'm meeting one of our biggest clients?*
>
> **YOU**   *Carol, I can't do anything about it—it's company policy.*

Ah, perks. The organizational outward signs of inward grace. Every company has them. The office by the window, the special furniture, the parking spaces, business class travel. They are usually little things people can put years into achieving. While they may confer only limited extra comfort, they often confer a whole lot of status.

Carol is going away without feeling she got a good answer and it's hard not to sympathize with her. She has a point. Business class does allow the traveler to arrive more rested and if that's so for executives, why is it less true for their equally traveled, less exalted juniors? How can a company have perks based on rank and also maintain that everybody's work is equally valuable?

I'm not trying to resolve this issue here. The main point for us is that Carol pointed out a mixed message and you didn't address it. In fact, you kind of defended the whole thing—both the perks policy *and* mixed message coming from the company. I know you thought you were just talking perks, but by not addressing the mixed message, you implied support of it. You need to separate the content of the discussion (the advisability of perks) from the context (sending mixed messages is okay). If you don't, employees see a lack of honesty even if it is unintentional.

An even more troubling outcome of mixed messages is the promotion of a hear-no-evil, see-no-evil culture. Say you arrange an elaborate programmers' celebration after exhorting employees to save money. You justify it to yourself. "These guys are the engine of the company. The quarter's results are okay. My message to save was a long-term, way-of-life one, not a here-and-now one." You've convinced yourself it is unrelated to walking your talk.

If someone suggests you sent a mixed message, you say shortly: "Lookit, we have to treat them specially. If we don't, we'll be down the tubes." Thus, you shut down any discussion about what you're doing. You also make it clear to people that there are issues they're not allowed to point out. If it weren't so destructive, you'd have to admire the elegance of the whole thing.

Mixed messages create a climate in which an idea's acceptability is more important than its utility or uniqueness, a climate in which the only ideas raised are those that everyone already knows will be well received. And that is anathema to innovation. You're doomed to a life of always getting what you've always gotten.

I know you don't mean to send mixed messages but you need to fix them if you inadvertently do so. Mixed messages stay mixed no matter how they got that way. You'll keep dancing around this miscommunication unless you do something about it. Let's try the previous conversation again.

YOU	*Carol, you know the policy. Business class travel only for directors and above.*
Carol	*But Pat, that doesn't make sense. I need to be as rested as possible if I'm going into a meeting the moment I touch down.*
YOU	*You're right. It doesn't.*
Carol	*Not only that, but what about the CEO's thing about everyone being equally valued?*
YOU	*There does seem to be a disconnect, doesn't there?*
Carol	*Well, yeah. So can I upgrade?*
YOU	*Carol, if it were up to me, I'd say go for it. I think we could even swing it in the budget.*
Carol	*So what's the problem?*
YOU	*Well, the finance people are pretty sticky. They won't reimburse you for the upgrade if they don't agree. You don't want to be out that money.*
Carol	*Of course not! It's on company business!*
YOU	*I agree. So why don't I call finance and see if we can get an exemption?*
Carol	*Okay, but the rule is still stupid.*
YOU	*It's sort of a hangover from the old days, isn't it? I'll bring it up at the next management meeting and see if John will lobby finance to change it.*
Carol	*Those guys! I don't think so!*
YOU	*Maybe not, but I don't know what else I can do. I can't change the rules myself.*
Carol	*I know, Pat. You're right, I guess that's the way to go.*

Realistically, you can't change every rule that's prompting a mixed message. Reasonable employees don't expect miracles as long as their point of view has been heard and acknowledged. What is important both to them and for your credibility is that you don't try to defend the indefensible. Companies are constantly changing and striking out in new directions, so it's natural that not everything is in sync all the time. But even though you can't immediately resolve the issue, you can signal your willingness to listen when things are out of whack. It is an important way to encourage the expression of dissent and, ultimately, of innovation.

One final related point. A way to send mixed messages at the speed of light is by not following your own rules. You know them: Nobody is to have coffee at their computer except me because I'm just a bear without it first thing. Everybody has to clean up after themselves in the kitchen except when I'm just too busy with important things. Everybody has to turn their expense claims in by the end of the month and I'll do mine just as soon as I get around to it. Unlike the Queen, you are not above the law (and if you'll notice, it hasn't done her much good). To give that impression sends a mixed message par excellence.

Instead, be like Continental Airlines CEO Gordon Bethune. He shifted Continental's on-time arrivals record from one of the worst in the business to one of the best. During this period, Bethune boarded a flight quite close to departure time. He paused at the entrance and the gate agent said, "Excuse me, sir. You'll have to sit down. The plane has to leave." "That's Mr. Bethune!" said one of the flight attendants, horrified. To which the agent said, "That's very nice, but we gotta go. Tell him to sit down."[3] How many bosses do you know would have been mightily offended that one of their minions had ordered them around? By following his own rules, Bethune signaled that his messages applied to everyone, even himself. Following your own rules avoids mixing messages and, hence, the dampening of dissent and innovation.

By the by, this story is also a good example of the point I made earlier. Here the employee was following Bethune's strategic direction not dissenting against it. Dissent isn't necessary nor desirable all the time everywhere. It needs to live side by side with those things, such as vision, that make you efficient.

Never Apologize (Never Be Wrong)

Some people act as if they are infallible although, if you challenged them, they'd say, "No way…I make mistakes just like the next guy." But

---

[3] Gordon Bethune, *From Worst to First: Behind the Scenes of Continental's Remarkable Comeback—A Flight Plan for Success* (New York: John Wiley and Sons, 1998).

you'll notice that raising specific examples of that fallibility gets the cold shoulder and of course, they never, never apologize. "Sorry" is not a word that figures largely in the vocabulary of most managers but with these people, I'm quite convinced they've never actually heard of it.

Yet making mistakes is an important component of innovation. Moreover, signaling that it's okay to make mistakes is critical to creating a climate that values risk. Innovation isn't possible without risk. So how do you signal that making mistakes is okay? One of the best ways: *Apologize* after you've made one yourself.

Apologizing is different from just admitting a mistake. The latter simply notes your judgment was napping. The former says you made a mistake *and* you're sorry about the damage it caused. Of course, you could regret this privately in your office, with the door closed and the blinds down. And while that may be good for the soul and even for your future mastery, this private penance will do almost nothing for the here-and-now damage you've caused, however inadvertent.

This ostrich approach does more harm than you can imagine. At one point in my management career, I got a reputation for "fixing" troubled groups. One constant in every one of these situations was a backlog of resentment and unresolved injuries. One employee was still smarting from an injustice that had occurred seven years and three bosses ago! These hurts don't go away but go underground and turn dissent into sabotage.

Apologizing can be the fastest way to deflate the anger and endless arguments. It can move both parties quickly out of finger-pointing and into constructive discussion about how to fix the damage.

Equally important, apologizing creates a climate in which mistakes can be quickly acknowledged. Saying the unpopular thing or attacking a sacred cow becomes easier for your staff because you've demonstrated that, even if the dissent turns out not to be well-founded, it's possible to make the mistake, rectify the damage, and move forward without negative consequences.

Let's use a non-dissent example to underline that point. Say you've blown up in a meeting about Sam's quarterly results. You've had it with his excuses. However, on reflection, you realize the outburst did nothing to help Sam be more productive, and it also shut everyone else down at the meeting.

You need to apologize to Sam for the outburst. Groveling is not necessary (and managers are notoriously short on this skill anyway), but you could say:

	YOU	*Ah, Sam, just wanted to mention—I was sort of out of line yesterday. Sorry about that.*
Don't follow up with anything like:		*I was under a lot of pressure.* Yes, we know that. However, this is not about you, this is about the other person.
Also a no-no		*But you really did screw up on the quarter results.* This is not about apportioning blame. It's about admitting you didn't handle the problem successfully.
If Sam is a wonderful human being, he'll say:	**Sam**	*Thanks, Bill. I appreciate the effort it took to say that. No hard feelings.* Kiss and make up. (Okay, a hearty pat on each other's backs.)
If Sam is just a nice human being, he'll say something like:	**Sam**	*Don't mention it. I guess you were under a lot of pressure.*
You do *not* reply:	**YOU**	*Yeah, I was. It was a really bad day...I can't tell you the stuff coming down from headquarters...* Not only do we start talking about you but also leave the impression, however inadvertent, that on *really* bad days, it's okay to humiliate people. Nope.
Instead, try:	**YOU**	*Well, it's true, I am under a lot of pressure. But that's no reason to take it out on you...*
If Sam is just your normal guy, he'll say:	**Sam**	*Ah, gee, boss. That's okay. Forget it.* And you can move onto other things.
If you are a really fine human being, you could say:	**YOU**	*I appreciate that. I'll try to hold onto things better next time.* Not required, but a nice touch if you can manage it.

If Sam is sort of a stinker, he may say:	**Sam**	*Well, I thought you were getting bent out of shape for nothing. I mean, I can make it up the next quarter...* Take a deep breath and get that blood pressure under control.
Don't say:	**YOU**	*No way, José. You've been saying that for the last two quarters. Don't give me that bull. I'm sick and tired of...* You can fill in the rest. He got your goat, admit it. You're back in the same trap.
Instead say:	**YOU**	*No, I'm not apologizing for being ticked about this quarter's results. I still think it's a problem and I want you to pursue the lines we've discussed. What I'm talking about is how I said it.* You need to take this groveling only so far. You've done your duty and don't need to take it any further.

How you respond will in some part depend on Sam. If he is a regular human being, this should be a short non-event that puts things right. If he's a bit of a poop, he might try to use your openness to wiggle out of taking action on his own failings. You don't have to buy that if you remember to distinguish between the behavior (not meeting the quarter's targets) and your reaction to it. You can still disapprove of missing targets while deploring how you expressed that disapproval. Don't confuse the two. If you start talking about the unacceptable behavior while apologizing, it looks like you're blaming Sam for the way you reacted. You aren't and shouldn't. It's quite legitimate to talk about how to rectify Sam's poor performance but don't use it as a reason to justify yours.

Not all that hard, is it, once you get into it? It doesn't have to be a big thing. No hair shirts or whips.

If you get used to apologizing when necessary, it can become part of normal interactions. You can replace the tension of everyone pretending they don't know you screwed up with the ease of a quick apology accepted at face value that allows everyone to get on with things. If the objective is to keep dissent both alive and aboveground, apologizing for your occasional slips is an excellent way to signal your wish to keep the discussion open and flowing even if you don't always do it perfectly.

Don't Let Apologizing Be the Only Thing You Do

Apologizing is critical, but you also need to quit doing whatever you're apologizing for. I once had a boss who attacked every time she felt unsure or threatened. Later she would fall on her sword beautifully and I would be flattered by the sincerity of her regret. However, that was only the first couple of times. After she established the pattern of personal attack, abject apology, and personal attack, it was obvious she thought apology was enough. It's not. If you apologize, you implicitly admit you have some work to do personally. It's not that you can't ever get mad again, but it does mean your apologies on that issue need to decrease over time. Otherwise, it's just a clever way to avoid adjusting to a world where dissent is welcome.

Play Politics

I had been consulting with one organization long enough to know it was troubled—it had particular problems making decisions and getting people to implement them. One day, I met with my client and her CEO, Alex. After the meeting, my client said, "Alex doesn't like me." I was astounded. "Why do you say that?" I asked. She shrugged. "He didn't make eye contact with me through the entire meeting."

I was about to pooh-pooh the idea and dismiss her as paranoid when I realized she was probably right. In this culture and with this CEO, subtle cues like eye contact were the way messages about being in favor were communicated.

This is playing politics at its worst (or best, I guess, depending on your point of view). Playing politics is the art of manipulating without looking like you've manipulated—even though everyone knows you have. People who use intermediaries to send bad news are playing politics, as are those who express their displeasure by cutting the offender out of the information loop, assigning him to a bad job shift, or giving him a poor performance review. These actions may be justified, but the way they are done can signal that secretive behavior is the modus operandi. If you can't do business in an aboveboard manner, you're certainly not going to deal with dissent tolerantly. This attitude makes it very easy for dissent to go underground—in fact, requires it. It is a subtle but effective way to discourage innovation.

How do you avoid playing politics, even in an environment that supports or requires it? Realistically, you need to be careful. You could try to be straight with colleagues and even superiors, but they are doubtful choices off the top unless you already trust them. However, one group you should take a risk with is your own employees. You need their innovation and dissent, and their openness will pay off. Let's walk through how to do this.

You have decided to form a cross-functional task group to come up with a strategy for a recent rash of customer complaints. Art is your manager of Customer Relations. You've broached the idea with him and this is your second meeting.

	YOU	*So, what do you think?*
	Art	*Great idea. This team stuff is the way to go.*
All right, right away, I'm suspicious. Most people are reluctant to give up control. Ask some questions.	**YOU**	*Really? It won't cause you or your guys problems?*
	Art	*Nope, nope. Of course, my people will need to be on the team—no point in reinventing the wheel.*
Is he trying to control the group?	**YOU**	*True, but I don't want the team tied to past solutions—that's the point.*
	Art	*Oh, absolutely—I'll tell them that.*
	YOU	*How many of your people do you want in the group?*
	Art	*Just a few. Probably Gladys, because she's call center. And Andrew, for policy issues. Jackie would be good because….*
	YOU	*Whoa, whoa, that's too many! I mean, the point is to get other points of view.*
	Art	*Well, my guys have to be represented…*

It doesn't seem to me you're talking repre-sentation. Art seems unwilling to say what he thinks. You need to intervene.

YOU *You know, Art, I'm getting the feeling that maybe there's something else bothering you...*

Art *No, no, I think it's a great idea...*

YOU *Really? So how come I'm getting the idea that something is sticking in your craw?*

Art *Well, Sal, can't help you there.*

YOU *Come on, Art—nobody here but us chickens. What's the problem?*

You're in luck. Art trusts you enough to let his hair down.

Art *Well, now that you mention it—some of my guys are wondering whether this task force is a comment on their work. I'm all for it and I've told them that...but yeah, they're worried.*

Whether it's really Art or Art's guys who are worried is irrelevant. Address it anyway.

YOU *What are they worried about?*

Art *Now I don't believe this myself, I'm just passing on the message...*

YOU *Yeah, got it. What are they worried about?*

Art *Well, some of them think they should be allowed to solve the problem themselves—they're the experts in customer service, after all. What do a bunch of operations and marketing people know?*

YOU *So, this task group is horning in on their territory...*

Art *I wouldn't put it exactly that way, but kind of...*

YOU *So what do you think we can do about it?*

The problem Art raises is an important one. If the Customer Relations people feel slighted, any recommendations from the task group will gather dust. How you resolve the problem can vary. You may go ahead anyhow and ask Art to work with the staff to change their attitudes. You may decide that Art is right and change your approach.

Whatever you do, the important thing from the innovation standpoint is that you got him to stop playing politics, pretending to agree when he didn't, and moved him into speaking up about the problem. If you're not willing to name the problem, you can't dissent about it or innovate to fix it. The more willing people are to address rather than bury the problems, the better.

In these situations, it is particularly important to remember that what you see is not necessarily what you're getting. You need to probe ("Really? It won't cause you or your guys problems?") when you run into the facile answer ("Great idea. This team stuff is the way to go."). Expect to have to do it more than once ("Art, I'm getting the feeling that maybe there's something else..."). It's hard for many people to come clean, especially if the environment has not encouraged openness to date.

You notice that Art attributed the problem to his staff. It's a typical way to raise a touchy issue. It allows Art an escape route if you react negatively since he can blame them. I bet he's really talking about himself, but it doesn't matter. It needs to be addressed no matter what.

You don't have to resolve the problem in Art's favor to encourage him to stop playing politics. But you do need to highlight your support for the risk he took in bringing it up. At the end of your conversation, you should probably say something like:

> **YOU**   *Okay, Art, I've got it about the unit's feelings, but I still think the task group is a good idea. We can make some of the changes you propose—like letting them do presentations to the group. But I want to go ahead anyhow.*
>
> **Art**   *I don't know how my gang is going to react...*
>
> **YOU**   *I know—sounds like I've put you in an awkward position and I'm sorry about that. (You apologized!) But I'm glad you brought it up. Otherwise, we would have gone around in circles.*
>
> **Art**   *Well, I thought I owed it to my guys...*
>
> **YOU**   *Absolutely.*

Depending on the trust you've established, you may not get to a resolution as quickly as depicted here. If people believe playing politics is the only way to survive, it will take some time before they'll entertain the possibility of dealing straight. But don't give up. If you are consistently aboveboard yourself and challenge what looks like playing politics, you will eventually get people to believe and trust you. And once you do, you will find people willing to disagree, debate, take risks, and innovate.

Another Way to Play Politics

Sometimes we play politics without meaning to. One well-established organization was concerned about retaining enough junior employees "in the pipeline" to take over senior positions when baby boomers retired. So young people (mainly students on work terms) were asked to recommend how to address this problem. They designed an elaborate presentation to senior management. The recommendations were adopted and the students asked to implement them. However, this initiative failed. The students didn't have the expertise or political savvy to maneuver through the politics of making a change and also didn't have the position power to ensure it happened. While the idea was a great one, the implementation left the students feeling like they'd been maneuvered into participating in a window-dressing exercise when the intent had been serious and honest. So, even if you don't mean to, it's easy to be perceived as having underground motives.

Intimidate

Shortly after he became president of the Supreme Soviet, Nikita Khrushchev denounced the excesses of Stalin before a large group of party faithful.[4] From the back of the room, an anonymous voice called out, "You were there. Why didn't you stop him?" Immediately, Khrushchev demanded, "Who said that?" Silence. After a long minute of unease, he replied, "Now you know why."

Intimidating people into agreeing with you is a well-established tradition. Dictators often use it consciously and ruthlessly. In fact, there is an old Chinese saying that you need to "kill the chicken to scare the monkey."[5] However, they pay a high price for it. At the end of World War II, Hitler was holed up in a bunker under Berlin. He had to rely on his generals' reports to deploy troops. But in the past he had punished them for telling the truth—being defeatist, in his eyes—so they lied about the true extent of the defeat. Thus he continued to move nonexistent forces against an enemy that had already won.

---

[4] Gary Hamel, "Strategy as Revolution," *Harvard Business Review* (July/August 1996), p. 79.
[5] Melinda Liu and Russell Watson, "China Kills a Few Chickens," *Newsweek* (January 11, 1999), p. 40.

Nothing so dramatic or far-reaching usually results from office intimidation but in the pursuit of innovation, even more moderate efforts are pretty successful. Especially because intimidators often don't recognize they're doing it.

I remember one incident from early in my career. I was preparing a think piece for the CEO. This was my big break, and I worked hard on the document. Finally, it was printed, bound, and distributed. It was to be discussed at the next executive committee meeting.

As I was preparing the night before the big meeting, I discovered that this mammoth piece of work, with its charts and recommendations galore, had a fatal flaw. I hadn't defined a fundamental term because I thought I knew what it meant. But the success of my recommendations depended on a fairly narrow and not very defensible view of the term. If a broader and more inclusive definition was used, my proposals were too expensive, too scattergun, and ultimately ineffective.

The sweat ran that night as I tried to figure out how to fix this problem. The more I thought about it, the bigger the hole got. The document was a house of cards. Finally, I decided to do the only thing any right-thinking corporate citizen could—I would fake it and pray nobody asked.

I think I stopped breathing about five minutes before the meeting. But the CEO opened the session with "Frances, I've read this report with great interest. It's a very thorough job. You're to be congratulated." My lungs started up again. He hadn't noticed. He opened the floor to questions.

Bernie, one of the VPs and a sharp cookie, launched right in. "Well, I agree this is excellent. I just have one question. I wasn't sure how you defined…" And he asked it. The one question for which I had no reply. My lamentably short career flashed before my eyes. I opened my mouth but nothing came out.

Then suddenly the CEO snapped, "Well, Bernie, that's kind of a stupid question. You may not know the definition but everybody else does." And Bernie, being as I say, a sharp cookie, immediately understood he needed to shut up. I closed my mouth and the report was adopted with acclaim. It wasn't until several months later, when the plan was being implemented, that the definitional problem became clear and almost all the recommendations had to be reworked.

So it's not to say that I haven't personally benefited from a little intimidation. But from the organization's point of view, this momentary lapse, this unintentional intimidation caused an otherwise flawed idea to take up resources and time that any company can ill afford.

I'm not suggesting you waste time exploring all possible dumb questions. But *how* you respond makes a difference. Instead of "Well, that's stupid," as my blessed CEO did, spending just a moment more to say something like "Really, Bernie? I'm surprised. Why do you ask?" would have cooked my goose but kept the organization on track. Even if the question turns out to be unproductive, you can avoid putting the person down by saying something like "Okay, I see your point but I think we should go with the original thought."

Organizations that, however inadvertently, use intimidation as a way to control people pay a price in innovation. Bill Gates's confrontational style of challenging ideas has been called everything from a combination of Socratic dialog and professional wrestling to temper tantrums. And despite Microsoft's vehement denials, it is not considered a particularly innovative company.[6] Generally speaking, they buy innovation, they don't grow it. In fact, research found that CEOs who are domineering and strong-willed make it harder for people to disagree with them and therefore they often stop getting bad news.[7]

I know it is not usually anyone's intent to intimidate but most managers are unaware of how easy it is to do—and, having done it, don't know how much of an impact it has on their people's willingness to dissent and innovate.

Summary

Aside from a few Hitler-like managers, no one is actually trying to suppress honest debate and difference of opinion. But dissent is a more fragile thing than most realize. It is easier to value your career over speaking up, to protect a colleague's feelings rather than point out he is wrong. And while taking care of feelings and careers is worthwhile, this desire needs to be tempered with the equal requirement to speak up and speak out. Managers can encourage this through their own actions. In fact, how much open dissent you have may be a proxy for and a predictor of good management. You can encourage dissent by avoiding actions obviously detrimental to dissent as discussed in this chapter and by sidestepping those that are more subtle. That's the next chapter.

Main Points

- Most managers don't realize they easily suppress dissent.
- *Shooting messengers* sends the signal you're unable to tolerate hearing bad news.

---

[6] Steven Levy, "Behind the Gates Myth," *Newsweek* (August 30, 1999), p. 46.
[7] Linda Grant, "Rambos in Pinstripes: Why so Many CEOs are Lousy Leaders," *Fortune* (June 24, 1996).

- *Sending mixed messages* promotes a hear-no-evil, see-no-evil culture that is anathema to innovation.
- *Not apologizing* creates a climate that drives dissent underground because mistakes are never acknowledged and their damage is not addressed.
- *Playing politics* signals that secretive behavior is the way things get done. It drives dissent underground.
- *Intimidation* decreases people's willingness to dissent.

Surprising Ways to Suppress Dissent

*There are some less obvious ways to suppress dissent
that will surprise managers who do not realize that the
road to efficiency and productivity may lead away from
innovation and creativity.*

Introduction

In the last chapter, we talked about how fragile situational dissent can
be and how desirable it is to keep dissent at that level. Some managers
act in unpleasant and unproductive ways that have the added disadvantage of suppressing dissent. But some positive things can also
inhibit dissent. This chapter will focus on them. We'll talk about the
dangers of best practices, the downsides of treating everyone equally,
the drawbacks of people with your values, and the pitfalls of designing
a process to capture good ideas.

The Dangers of Best Practices

Most organizations I go into have some kind of "best practices" effort.
Those that don't are sort of embarrassed and assure me it's next on
their list.

"Best practices" has become a catchall phrase for part of knowledge
management. If someone has already made the mistakes and figured
out the tricks of doing something, it is foolish not to build on that
experience. We all want to profit from past mistakes and avoid future

ones. But I have come to believe that the value of best practices may be more limited than we'd like to believe.

Best practices in most organizations is a fairly sterile and systematized process. Typically, part of a company's Intranet is devoted to it. Employees are exhorted to write up either how they have been successful or what to avoid. Bucks are put into making best practices widely available.

However, in my experience, after the first big fanfare, people stop contributing. They can't seem to find the time to think about what worked and what didn't. In addition, even if best practices are available, people don't use them. My experience is supported by the research. In interviews of team leaders, fewer than half (46%) regularly did any kind of in-depth, post-project analysis. Only 27% used that information to improve their own project and 13% shared that information outside the team. Obviously, if people aren't contributing ideas and not using others', best practices structures are an elaborate waste. We have a system dressed up with nowhere to go.

Why does this happen? First of all, stopping to reflect always takes more time than plowing ahead. Moreover, doing so opens up the possibility you weren't perfect—a thought few pursue with vigor. Even if you do reflect, you don't have to write it down or make it public to benefit personally—that's necessary only to help others. But do I really want to disclose I didn't know which end was up and detail how things went to hell in a hand basket? Why would I? Because my boss thinks it's a great idea? That may turn your crank but it doesn't mine. And there is a suspicion that even if you bared your soul, those reading it wouldn't take in the full value because they hadn't lived the experience. There is a learnable moment much like a teachable moment.

Is there any point to recording best practices at all? Absolutely. It is a great way to force everyone to stop and reflect on what had happened rather than running wildly to the next task. But while it's worthwhile for the group involved to reflect, are the big and complex best practices systems some organizations have worth it? Hmm, I'm not convinced.

Best practices have another downside—they may suppress dissent and innovation. Best practices are really about improvement, not innovation. Innovation is a whole new take on something; improvement is making the status quo better. While both are valuable, a system aimed at one will not get you the other. Best practices are by and large about efficiency, not innovation.

In addition, there is a distressing trend that, to my mind, shows how talented people can sometimes take a good idea so far that it turns into a crummy one. Michael Schrage, a *Fortune* columnist, reports that some companies make the use of best practices compulsory: "In practice, ... 'best practice' databases create brave new infostructures that effectively enforce employee compliance with organizational norms."[1] If efficiency was the aim, that might not be bad. After all, if there really is one best way, why not require everyone to use it? It cuts out all kinds of messing around and arguing about what to do. But messing around and arguing are needed in an innovative organization. If you always do what you've always done, you'll always get what you've always gotten. On the way to efficiency and in the wrong hands, best practices can be an instrument of conformity.

So organizations need to temper their enthusiasm for the whole-scale use of best practices. Encourage people to do it within their teams, by all means. Encourage them to share the relevant ones. Can't hurt, might help. Load them on your Intranet, even. But don't make their use compulsory, don't discourage people who think they have a better way, and don't think you're helping innovation.

In summary, best practices can be useful but their utility is probably more limited than we might wish. They are about efficiency, not innovation. You may want to hold onto them for that reason, but don't expect great new ideas to come out of the process.

The Downsides of Treating Everybody Equally

Organizations have put significant effort into making sure rules apply equally. Given their hierarchical nature, they may have one rule for one group (unlimited meal allowance limits for executives) and another for the rest (per diem), but it is still an attempt to treat people equally. You have to be senior to be eligible for the more lenient rule, but if you are, your treatment is equivalent to everyone else in your category. The intent behind treating everyone equally is an important and commendable one. Nothing creates tension more quickly in an office than unjustified preferential treatment.

But somewhere along the line, we have translated the goal of treating everyone *equally* into treating everyone the *same*: You get five parenting days a year, I don't care how sick your kid is. Everybody's performance appraisal has to be in on March 31 even if you're in your busiest period. Everybody has to come to the meeting even if it's a waste of time.

I understand how *equally* got translated into *same*. It's easier to write a rule that applies across the board than to figure out what *equally* means if it doesn't mean *same*. In the past, the one-size-fits-all

---

[1] Michael Schrage, "When Best Practices Meet the Intranet, Innovation Takes a Holiday," *Fortune* (March 29, 1999), p. 190.

approach worked more or less, and let's face it, when jobs were scarce and workers many, organizations had the upper hand. Even if you were disadvantaged by this blanket tactic, you had to accept it.

In a world where the scarcity of knowledge workers will continue for the foreseeable future, despite any blips in the stock market, we have to abandon this cog-in-a-great-machine mentality. Without leeway for individual needs or wants, people can't feel they are an organization's most valuable resource. Your capacity to retain your intellectual capital goes out the door. We need to find a way to treat people equally without treating them the same.

Interestingly enough, businesses have recognized with respect to customers that they must mass customize—that is, turn processes that produce 100,000 of the same thing into ones that can turn out one unit specially tailored for an individual. We have gone from unisex jeans to ones that fit your short torso, long legs, and ample waist.

Companies need to mass customize the work environment too, and some are taking steps in that direction in things like benefits packages. You used to get the same dental, medical, and disability insurance, no matter the need or preference. Even if your spouse already had coverage, you had to pay the premium. Now, some companies are making a range of benefits available and allowing employees to choose those that best fit their lifestyle. Here is a case of people being treated equally without being treated the same. This logic needs to be extended far further if we are to leverage the innovative capacity of our work force.

What Would It Look Like?

Even if you buy the idea that we need to stop treating everyone the same, what would doing so look like in practice? One way to start changing the culture is to question how the rules apply within your own section.

Rules are often based on the assumption that it's unlikely we could ever agree what each of us "deserved"—whether it's time off, plum assignments, or office space. So rather than get into this sticky and ultimately thankless task, we opt for an arbitrary amount (10 sick leave days a year) or doling out a scarce quantity based on objective criteria (directors and above get offices).

But at the unit level, it's not always necessary to do that. For example, if Kit's daughter is seriously ill, don't you turn a blind eye to how often she's absent? If someone's been working a lot of unclaimed overtime, wouldn't you encourage him to take a long weekend that doesn't appear on the books? I know you already do it, but I'm suggesting you take it even further. If Gary's passion is writing, would it be stretching it too much to pay for a creative rather than a business writing course? If Beth really can't work in a team, can she make an individual contribution that is then moved into a team environment? If Margery is from a culture where speaking up in meetings is rude, can you occasionally ask people to submit their ideas in writing? These types of things give people what they need rather than what they are allowed.

If you work in an environment where your protests are likely to be heard, you do everyone a favor by becoming a dissenter yourself. Of course, if your head is chopped off whenever you give what is considered questionable leeway, you are naturally going to be more careful. In that case, I'd advocate a little sneakiness. I had a boss once who didn't believe in staff meetings, which he called "14 wasted hours" (because I had 14 employees at the time). He forbade me to hold them. But they were an important way to stay connected, so every week we had an elaborate system of booking a meeting room on a remote floor and staggering our departures from our offices like terrorists on a mission.

Even in quite rigid environments, it's possible to get pretty creative. I had an employee who did wonderful things but almost never in the way prescribed. She charged lunches she wasn't entitled to, gave gifts to people not on the sanctioned list, and traveled on spec to drum up business when everyone was supposed to be watching every penny. I spent a lot of my day justifying not *what* she did—since everybody agreed she was doing a great job—but *how* she did it. The *how* just never lined up with the rules. Because she was doing such innovative work, I finally imposed only one rule: Don't get caught with the grenade pin in your teeth. That is, leave me enough wiggle room to argue that just because the grenade had been thrown, and just because she had been seen in the immediate vicinity of the explosion just before it went off—that didn't mean she had thrown it. And we were pretty successful since neither of us served time for our misdeeds.

This employee is a perfect example of what I am talking about. She would not have stayed in an environment that tied her down too much and, if she had left, we would have lost access to her energy, experience, and innovation. Because we came to an accommodation that did some damage to the rules, but not to their intent, she stayed and we made great progress.

Generally speaking, we need to create an environment in which there is a substantially wider range of acceptable behavior than now typically exists. You can start by being willing to break rules on your employees' behalf and allow them to break yours. In this way, you go a long way to creating an environment of mass customization. Instead of marching lockstep into the future, we can meander toward it in a way that best suits us individually. Like a flock of birds, we might head in more or less the same direction but that doesn't prevent short detours off the flight path. And off the path is where you find new things.

Is it favoritism?

Is there still a little niggle in the back of your mind? After all, one advantage of rules is that you can't be accused of favoritism if everyone is treated exactly the same.

Treating everyone equally means that each person feels she's getting what she needs and/or "deserves." If that doesn't happen over the longer term, charges of favoritism might be warranted. However, this is over the longer term. How long would it take you to believe that your boss can cut your budget this year with the promise of more next? That is how long it will take your employees to believe you're not playing favorites. They will use the same mechanism you do—they'll watch to see what happens.

In summary, treating everyone equally but not the same will encourage a diversity of thought, dissent, and innovation. It will require you to expand what you are doing now into new areas where you allow people to break rules that don't work for them. And if you get caught? Maybe you can use the old Chinese defense for making local exceptions to central rules: The emperor is far away and the hills are high.

The Drawbacks of People with Your Values

This principle seems counterintuitive. "You mean, I should surround myself with people who *oppose* my values?" Well, not exactly and yes, maybe.

I think it largely depends on what we mean by values. There are three categories: personal preferences, company values, and fundamental values. Let's talk about each one.

Personal Preferences

When something is called a "personal preference," it's easy to see why you should allow a wide latitude among those you work with. After all, as the name implies, preferences are idiosyncratic and have little or nothing to do with work performance. I like tea, you like coffee. I'm best in the morning, you start picking up only in late afternoon. Nobody would consciously surround themselves only with tea drinkers or night owls.

But there is a gray area between the kind of obvious and innocuous personal preferences mentioned above and values. For example, I'm an untidy-desk person. I'm really happy only if I have lots of piles of paper around me. I had a boss once who was a neat freak. It bugged him that my desk had disaster relief written all over it. Finally, he brought it up at a performance evaluation. Great work…except for one thing. My *desk* was unprofessional. Not only that, but it posed a security risk. Who knew what confidential papers were buried under the rubble?

Now you may agree with my old boss, so we're never going to get anywhere on that front. But this is not about the desk. It's about raising a preference to the status of a value. Professionalism was linked to whether you could see the top of working surfaces.

Once a personal preference is translated into a value, it's hard to challenge. We end up arguing whether an untidy desk is a sign of unprofessionalism rather than attacking the real issue—that the objection itself is based on the assumption that everyone has to do everything the same. If you do that continually and over a wide range of issues, you impose your idiosyncrasies on others. Even more importantly, it imposes a level of conformity that suppresses dissent. Dissent does not thrive in an environment in which uniform behavior is expected.

While most people (except the neat freaks) wouldn't have any problem with the example I gave, other personal preferences cause more heartache—such as how hard you work, the importance of deadlines, whether ignoring rules is kosher, how sloppy is too sloppy (in work or personal appearance), how rude is too rude.

"Wait a minute," I can hear you call out. "Those aren't personal preferences. How hard you work—that's not my personal preference—that's what's needed to get the job done."

Ah, an interesting distinction. I agree. There are always job requirements, and how hard you work may be one. However, there is a subtle but important distinction. If it's a requirement, then it just is—it doesn't or shouldn't become a value.

Let's take the not-working-hard-enough example. If your employee isn't putting in the required hours, you need to address that. However, there aren't many like that. More likely, he's a nine-to-fiver. He never stays a moment longer than he has to, never volunteers for extra work, and rather than put his shoulder to the wheel, he'll ask for an extension to a deadline. Do you start thinking, "He's lazy, uncommitted, etc.?"

But why? Because if he worked harder, your unit could get more done? True. But this is what you prefer, right? Why is he lazy or uncommitted because he isn't falling in line with your *preference*?

It's important to distinguish between personal preferences and values. Personal preferences are just that—what you would do in that person's situation. Values are more about what standard you hold yourself to and, as a manager, hold others to also.

The danger of thinking of preferences (longer hours) as values (industry or commitment) is that you tend to forget that people may legitimately differ. You can get seduced into believing that you must have people around you with those characteristics. Thus you impose a conformity on your group that, while convenient, may not be worth it, given the price you pay in suppressing different ideas. Without meaning to, you narrow the scope of diversity of opinion and approaches. And on big things, fundamental values, that's probably a good thing. But the price you pay in stifling innovation may not be worth the cost you incur to get clean desks and punctuality.

If we want an environment where many opinions, not all of them welcome, are expressed, we must start by minimizing the number of personal preferences that get turned into either requirements or values. You need some, of course, but the more you have, the less you encourage a climate of dissent and therefore innovation.

At very least, stop yourself when you feel negatively about what someone is doing and ask yourself whether it's really important. I wish he would show up for meetings on time but does it really matter in the grand scheme of things? I would prefer he was more polite to customers but is it at the unacceptable point?

I know this feels uncomfortable and even wrong but I am also convinced that if managers don't start redefining what they consider acceptable, they will drive out the innovation along with the "offensive."

Company Values

Okay, so maybe it's important to avoid using our personal preferences in either choosing or rewarding employees. But surely, you need to surround yourself with people who buy into company values. That was certainly the view of executives I interviewed. Even if every other area was open for dissent, they drew the line at them. "Something has to stay solid in an organization," they said. "If you don't have them, there's no reason for existing." You've got to sympathize with that view. If you're pursuing *service* one day and *innovation* the next, it is a chaotic world.

I agree that company values need to be stable for people to move forward because efficiency is important. But company values are rarely fundamental. They tend (with some exceptions) to be things like "Service to the Customer," "Excellence," "Responsiveness," "Innovation"—all excellent, positive ways to produce value. But there were no stone tablets associated with their creation. If you surround yourself with people who never question their worth, you are less likely to identify when they need changing.

Let me give you an example from our recent past. Schwab is an investment company that turned the financial industry on its ear by offering online trading of shares at a flat fee of $29.95 per trade. Schwab had hoped to keep two lines of business—the traditional brokerage with a commission percentage and personal service and the Internet $29.95 pricing. But customers, not being dummies, started keeping a nominal amount of money in a traditional account to access the brokers' advice and used the online service to make the really substantial trades. So Schwab decided to charge $29.95 for all its trades, whether on the Internet or through regular channels. Since the average commission/charge for a traditional brokered trade is $65, you can imagine the upheaval this caused within the company and in the industry.

Say you were VP of Important Things at the Acme Financial Services Company at the time Schwab's revolutionary approach was first announced. Acme's motto is "Service, Prudence, and Responsiveness." Schwab's maneuvers caused you concern. A bright young thing, let's call her Trish, wanted a strategy to react to this threat.

Trish *Al, we have to match Schwab's price.*

YOU *What? Even for our brokered service?*

Trish *That's what they're doing.*

YOU *I don't know how they keep up their margins.*

Trish *But online trading is growing exponentially. If we don't get on the bandwagon, the train will leave the station, if you know what I mean.*

YOU *Do you know how much we spend to keep and train a good broker? How can we recoup our investment on $30 a trade?*

Trish *I don't know, but...*

YOU *Not only that, Acme has always stood for customer service. Why, Butch Acme used to...*

Trish *Drive out to his clients' homes in the middle of the night to get them to sign off...yeah, I know that.*

YOU *Well, that's the kind of tradition we have...that's what we stand for.*

Trish *But the Internet...*

YOU   *Sure, the Internet, it's a big thing...but customers are never going to stop needing good responsible advice. Service, Prudence, and Responsiveness.*

Trish *But...*

YOU   *No, Trish, this company can't toss out everything it's ever stood for. There has to be another way.*

I don't know whether you or Trish are right but I do know your reluctance to discuss anything that goes against the company's values prevents you from entertaining ideas that, while unpalatable, may need consideration. How can you do this differently? Let's pick it up after Butch Acme and his home visits.

YOU   *Sure, the Internet, it's a big thing...but customers are never going to stop needing good responsible advice. Service, Prudence, and Responsiveness.*

Trish *Well maybe, but look at the numbers.*

YOU   *I know, I know...it doesn't look good. Maybe this is just a fad.*

Trish *Maybe it isn't.*

YOU   *I just can't believe people don't need advice.*

Trish *But look at our revenue targets. We missed this quarter, largely because of defections of existing clients.*

YOU   *You're right...*

Trish *I tell you, we need to meet their price and do it quickly.*

YOU   *Gee, I hope you're wrong...I just can't believe service isn't important anymore...but maybe I need to bring this up at the next executive meeting. At least to raise the possibility....*

Trish *Absolutely. And get them to get a move on.*

YOU   *I don't know if that's going to happen. But we need to discuss it.*

Again, for the purposes of our discussion, the issue is not whether you or Trish is right but that you have demonstrated a willingness to entertain, however reluctantly, a look at the company's values in light of a new environment.

This values discussion shouldn't happen constantly or even frequently. If they occur too frequently, it will feel like spinning wheels. And even if the discussion takes place, you may not need to change your values. In fact, in the example above, it's beginning to look like you are right. People are realizing that relying on their gut instincts and Internet research is not a match for years of the concentrated and considered experience of a broker. All you have to do is figure out is how to stay alive until enough people catch on.

Changing company values shouldn't be frequent, but it should be more frequent than in the past. Much as we intellectually understand that the only constant is change, the implications have not sunk in. Change is not just what we do but also what we believe.

In summary, you need to have people around you who believe in the same goals to get the work done and meet your targets. But you also need either a person or a climate that allows the questioning of the very values and goals you're working so hard to attain. Otherwise, when the time is right to change, you'll be so busy running down the path, you won't recognize it's no longer taking you where you need to go.

Fundamental Values

Even if I have convinced you it's not a bad thing to dissent about company values, surely fundamental values are sacrosanct—things like respect for others or a belief in democracy, non-violence, honesty, etc. Without these, life is difficult and unrewarding. It wouldn't make sense to have people around you who don't share those fundamental values. They have to be immutable. But history shows us that even bedrock values change.

Women got the vote in the first part of the 20th century in Europe and North America. From the vantage point of 100 years' experience, it's hard to imagine what all the fuss was about—it is so taken for granted today. But suffrage was a gut-wrenching attack on the values of society. Women were supposed to be in the family unit where the man of the house interacted with the outside world. Woman's place was in the home. For women to advocate that they should be allowed a voice separate from their husbands' was to shift the underpinnings of society. Order as that world knew it had to adjust.

The war in Vietnam in the 1970s provides another chance to see how our values have changed. When people first started to protest, they were often attacked, both physically and verbally, as unpatriotic, anti-American, and disloyal. "My country, right or wrong," was very much a part of the country's values. And yet today, people protest freely about the war in Bosnia and in Iraq without prompting the same visceral anger.

These examples show us that those bedrock values we once had, though of, were convinced of, and had no doubt about, have either lost currency or changed in definition so radically that our predecessors would not recognize them. We need to remember what Alfred North Whitehead, a famous British mathematician and philosopher, said: "Great ideas often enter reality in strange guises and with disgusting alliances." If we want great ideas, we need to entertain the possibility that what we've always believed might not be as true as we thought.

It's hard to question a fundamental value. And yet, you may run into a dissenter who is doing exactly that. How do you distinguish between those values that cannot change and those where listening to the dissenter might be the wiser course? Naturally, I can't answer that definitively for you but when faced with this situation, ask yourself one or all of the following questions:

- If the value you're discussing changes in the way the dissenter advocates, will I still want to work here? Would I be ashamed to admit I was employed in this company?
- If this value changes, how would I have to accommodate it? Will that make me into the kind of person I don't want to be?
- Is this value change distressing me because I will have to rethink what I *do* or what I *care about*? If the latter, do I care so much about the value under attack that I cannot allow any change or different interpretation?

There really are some values where any change is unacceptable. I don't think there are many but those there are must be held to tightly. But for the vast majority of other things that are values but not fundamental ones, you need people around to cue you when to rethink them. You don't always have to change, but being open to the possibility will encourage dissent.

So remember, the farther up the food chain an issue goes, from personal preference to company value to fundamental value, the harder it is to allow challenges to it, and fewer degrees of freedom we give ourselves to discover new truths.

The Pitfalls of Designing a Process to Capture Good Ideas

In working with clients on managing knowledge and encouraging innovation, I have noticed a trend. Invariably, as I interview the senior team, someone will say, "I know there are a lot of great ideas out there but we have no way of capturing them." Organizations do need a way to profit from their people's ideas. However, the way they express this yearning betrays how much we continue to be influenced by the manufacturing/mechanical era from which we have just emerged.

When managers talk about "capturing" ideas, there is a sense of encasing or corralling them. Like yeast and wild horses, ideas tend to resist being fenced in. But these managers would protest I'm making too much of a term—what they really mean is a process to capture (oops! there's that word again) to gain control of, nope, to *be aware of* new ideas. When I push a little more, their vision of this process usually entails something structured, all-encompassing, formal, and organization-wide.

That's how we have learned to leverage other valuable commodities in our environment. Remember when organizations had different computer systems and programs that didn't talk to each other? It was chaotic and inefficient and it was reasonable to gain control of that process. Similarly, there are a million things desirable to fund in an organization and it makes sense to corral all the items together to establish priorities and impose order. It all makes perfect sense, at least in the world we have just come out of. But in an information economy, this way of dealing with valuable commodities may no longer be valid.

Daydreaming, messing about, taking paths that don't lead anywhere, research for research's sake—all these things are inefficient but are sometimes necessary precursors to innovation. It's like you've got to keep the pot boiling with all manner of seemingly irrelevant things so that, every once in a while, a great idea will pop up. But daydreaming and messing about are typically what we try hardest to stamp out of our business processes and life. If there isn't a direct line from what you are doing to something productive, you must be wasting time— that is the manufacturing mentality. Innovation is not a linear process. You cannot command it ("You will have a breakthrough idea") or put it on a timeline ("By 10 a.m. tomorrow morning"). So trying to push the production of great ideas into a process doesn't make any sense. While total chaos isn't productive, neither is total order. A little chaos is a good thing when it comes to innovation.

However, even if you accept chaos at the idea-generation stage, there is still the question of turning the ideas that come out of the chaos into value. Back to process, right?

Yes and no. You do need a process but it's not what we normally think of. Given the unique properties of knowledge, capturing it and putting it to use may be the antithesis of what might be expected. Rather than a structured, all-encompassing, formal, and company-wide process, what is needed are relatively unstructured, somewhat random, and informal ones. I will cover these in Chapter 14, Structures and Mechanisms for Dissent.

Summary

Somewhere along the line, characteristics like being a team player, working hard, and following a vision have taken on a life of their own. They have become values in their own right. They have lost the link to the reason why organizations foster them. It is no longer so clear that they are encouraged because they help people be more productive and therefore, more valuable. And while that's a perfectly acceptable reason for encouraging these characteristics, when they lose their link to the productivity motive and become values in their own right, it's harder to see when they might actually be impediments to other higher order requirements—like innovation.

Main Points

- Some things managers think of as positive can inhibit dissent.
- *Best practices'* utility is efficiency not innovation.
- *Treating everyone equally* gets translated into treating everyone the *same*.
- *Looking for people with your values* prevents you from encouraging questioning of the very values and goals you are working to attain.
- *Designing a process to capture good ideas* may be more the random collision of ideas rather than a systemized process that, by its very existence, may distort or discourage the ideas it seeks to capture.

&o:

Who Are Dissenters?

Dissenters can be an exciting source of innovation, but they can also cause problems for managers who need to manage other people and processes. This chapter will examine the characteristics of dissenters and how to differentiate between genuine dissent and troublemaking.

The Role of the Dissenter

There are two kinds of dissenters you want in your organization. The first are those who, while generally committed to the company's direction, will speak up when things are going wrong. As we've discussed in the last two chapters, these dissenters are easy to suppress because they're often politically savvy enough to chose their personal popularity over saving the organization from itself.

But there is another kind of dissenter who is also valuable, often exactly because he's hard to shut down. They are natural dissenters, people often at odds with management. They keep raising issues everyone else would prefer to keep decently buried. Such as "Why have we priced our products so that those who need them most can least afford them?" Or "Why does Ops have the lion's share of the people when the push is on R&D"? Or "How is it that our competitors are more successful even though our managers are slave drivers"? They consistently speak truth to power even if power isn't all that interested in listening. But while difficult at work, many dissenters also have brought us great innovations.

Galileo is my personal fave because he was such a huge pain in the neck and his contribution to western science is so great. He is celebrated for his invention of the telescope, his development of the scientific method, and his support of the Copernican view of the universe. It was particularly the last that got him into trouble with the Catholic Church—the most powerful institution of his era.

For those of you whose high school science is but a faded memory, in 1543, Nicholas Copernicus published a theory that the sun and not the earth was the center of the universe. Galileo's observations led him to believe that Copernicus was right, and he began a lifelong and vocal support of the theory, so much so that he was threatened with excommunication.

Today, with science and the scientific method so entrenched in our thinking, it's hard to understand how completely unacceptable Galileo's views were to the Church. First of all, every word in the Bible was considered literally true because it was seen as divinely inspired. Thus, the sun really did stand still at Joshua's prayer and the earth was "ever immovable." Galileo's beliefs were heresy.

Not only that, but *how* he had come to his conclusions was contentious. The right way to learn was from authorities such as the Bible and Aristotle. The idea that you would bypass the wisdom of the ages in favor of your own observations and conclusions was the height of arrogance and disrespect. In addition, making your own judgments was a great threat to the Catholic Church because Protestantism—whose central belief was exactly that—was on the rise.

So it's understandable that the Church would force Galileo to toe the line. But it's fascinating to realize that two contemporaries were never prosecuted. There was Copernicus himself, who was greatly ridiculed but never sanctioned. And Jonathan Kepler, who, it has been argued, was a greater astronomer than Galileo because of his theory advances.

Why was Galileo forced to recant his beliefs while these others were not? Art Kleiner, in his book *The Age of Heretics*,[1] offers an intriguing theory. He maintains that the Church did not pursue Kepler because he ignored the Church while Galileo wanted it to change. He wanted it to "teach men how to go to heaven, not how the heavens go."

Historical research supports that Galileo did indeed continually clash with authority. He was a fierce debater who sought not merely to convince his skeptics but to ridicule and demolish them. Even *after* he was forced to renounce his beliefs in 1616, he went on to publish *Dialogue on the Great World Systems*, which not only repeated his heretical

---

1 Art Kleiner, *The Age of Heretics* (New York: Doubleday 1996).

views but also lampooned the opinions of Pope Urban VIII, who was the reigning pope, his patron, and had arranged a pension to support his research. You've got to think the man's political skills were a little fragile. Even back then, it must have been obvious that you don't bite the hand that feeds you.

Closer to today, Steven Jobs is in his second life as CEO of Apple. He was ousted in his first term in part because he was considered arrogant, mercurial, and out of touch with reality. In fact, his staff joked they were entering a "reality distortion field" when they met with him. *Fortune* magazine attributes some part of his present success to a change in his "dysfunctional style." Much as Steven Jobs was difficult for his Board of Directors and staff the first time around, Apple paid a high price for ousting him. They wandered the wilderness for many years, unable to create a compelling vision, losing market share, innovating with little success, and becoming an also-ran in the personal computer field.

Lyman Ketchum was a manager for the Topeka Gainsburger dog food plant in the 1960s. He took over a plant that was rife with sabotage and low morale and created the first major factory showplace of the postindustrial era. He involved hourly workers in the design of the plant; teams measured their own work and set their own goals; there were no special perks for managers. Productivity gains were in the order of 50%. However, when he tried to move this enormously profitable approach into the entire General Foods system, he was told he would never again be promoted, was effectively demoted, and finally lost his job. His superiors complained that he could never clearly explain what he was doing or why. When challenged, he would reply stubbornly, "This is the only way." He was seen as a zealot who wouldn't shut up and offended the powers that be.

Many other innovators have had trouble fitting in. Ted Newland, who is credited with saving Shell Oil from the worst of the oil crisis, was considered crusty and erratic. Jay Forrest, who invented system dynamics that are used to understand everything from machines to global warming, was seen as supercilious. Both Home Depot founders were fired from their first retailing jobs. In fact, when starting Home Depot, they got into such a squabble with a would-be investor that they rejected his money. The investor was Ross Perot. The CEO of catalog retailer Montgomery Ward fired General Robert Wood in part because he was "pesky" in his constant pushing for his new concept of shopping—physically setting up shop where the customer was. Sears-Roebuck hired him and he led a shopping revolution for them. Gordon Bethune, CEO of Continental Airlines, "has orchestrated one of the most effective repairs of an ailing corporate culture ever."[2] He was a high school troublemaker who flunked courses and didn't fit in. He spent 90 days doing KP in the Navy for threatening to throw a shipmate overboard.

So although these people made a huge contribution in their work, they were no picnic to be around. But Thomas J. Watson Jr., creator of IBM and considered one of the greatest businessmen of the century, said, "I never hesitated to promote someone I didn't like. The comfortable assistant—the nice guy you like to go fishing with—is a great pitfall. I looked for those sharp, scratchy, harsh, almost unpleasant guys who see and tell you things as they really are."[3]

A Package Deal

Why did Watson say that? Why go out of his way to recruit people who annoyed him? Because he knew intuitively what we are just catching on to—that dissent and innovation are kind of a package deal. The people discussed demonstrate all of the characteristics you need to be innovative: single-mindedness, persistence, and smarts. But they also have many other characteristics that are part and parcel of creative personalities.

First and obviously, they tend to be nonconformists, even to the point of rebellion. They are outsiders. This capacity to be outside the group is wonderful for innovation but tough on teamwork. Innovators also have what researchers call a "detached attitude to interpersonal relations." That is, although they may have people skills, they don't necessarily exercise them. Again, a challenging characteristic to accommodate in organizations built on consensus and compromise. Studies have also shown that innovators need a high degree of autonomy. A difficult thing to provide in a hierarchy.

In addition, their first loyalty tends to be to their profession, not the company. The respect of their peers is very important but of their manager? Not usually. In fact, because they don't understand, aren't interested in, and don't participate in organizational life, their degree of respect for their manager is often based on his technical skill. They are often unwilling to listen to managers whose technical skills are either nonexistent, inferior, or out of date. They cannot see that other skills—such as building coalitions and managing workload—are equally important.

---

[2] Brian O'Reilly, "The Mechanic who Fixed Continental," *Fortune* (December 20, 1999), pp.176–86.
[3] Thomas A. Stewart, Alex Taylor III, Peter Petre, and Brent Schlender, "The Businessman of the Century," *Fortune* (November 22, 1999), p. 118.

Finally, a study of entrepreneurs found that they often fail as leaders of start-ups because they are too arrogant. However, a big ego is exactly what's needed to have the drive and passion to persist through the setbacks that are an inevitable part of a start-up. So it is with dissenters. They need to have the passion and drive to hold onto an idea when everyone else is pooh-poohing it. They have the capacity (which Hegel called intelligence) to say no in the face of a given. They tend to put tremendous energy into getting the right answers but almost none into acquiring the power to implement the idea. They might even be proud of their refusal to "play politics." But in today's settings, this is often seen as arrogance and intransigence.

So this is a conundrum for organizations. On the one hand, we want innovators' creativity and passion. On the other hand, innovators' inability to build coalitions or even follow normally accepted rules makes them a challenge to fit into an organization. We love them because they don't fly in formation but they can also be a source of irritation for exactly that reason. The very qualities that make for great innovation—passion, drive, out-of-the-box thinking—are viewed as arrogance, unreasonableness, and uncompromising behavior by organizations bent on efficiency.

But still, someone who has no people skills, won't follow direction, has a big ego, isn't loyal to the company, has a high need for autonomy, a low interest in fitting in, and a low opinion of managers and management—makes you kind of shudder to think about supervising any of these people, doesn't it? You'd only be human to yearn for them to be more like others who play well together. And you'd be right if the primary aim is efficiency.

But if the aim is also innovation, again T.J. Watson shows us the way. He coined the phrase "wild ducks"—quirky, individualistic, highly intelligent employees who ignore procedures, shun set schedules, and resist attempts to make them more efficient. Because they were often very creative, he warned against taming them for, once tamed, they can never be made wild again.

It isn't that we can't (usually) get these people to shut up when they are proposing their risky, inconvenient, threatening or even harebrained schemes. It is that, once tamed, they will no longer offer them. And then we are left wondering why, despite our best efforts, we just can't get as much innovation as we need. Once tamed, never again wild.

The Urge to Tame Wild Ducks

But even though we know it's bad to tame wild ducks or dissenters, we seem to have an almost irresistible urge to do so. Why? One way to look at this is to think about managers and dissenters as belonging to different tribes. The manager tribe values productivity, orderliness, and consensus. The dissenter tribe values ideas, autonomy, and a touch of anarchy.

It's not that managers don't value ideas or that dissenters pooh-pooh productivity, but where dissenters would sacrifice orderliness for autonomy, a manager would be inclined to do exactly the opposite. But both sets of values are needed in an organization. The problem is that the manager tribe tends to have the power and the dissenter tribe does not. So, it's easier for productivity, orderliness, and consensus to rule than ideas or autonomy.

But because we need both to foster innovation and efficiency, we have to create an environment of cooperation that also allows for, and perhaps even encourages, people who don't cooperate. This sounds like an impossible feat but, in fact, we've already done it in society. During times of war, all able-bodied men are supposed to serve. For a long time, men were not allowed to decline except for medical reasons, no matter their private beliefs. However, gradually the idea of a conscientious objector was accepted. Thus, in most countries, there is both a rule that you must serve in war and a way to break the rule. So we must find ways to move forward cooperatively while not attempting to domesticate those who don't conform.

The next two chapters will show you how to do this but before we get to that, let's talk about how to differentiate between a true dissenter and a troublemaker.

The Problem with Too Easy Innovation

Do you read science fiction? It's a secret vice with me, and I especially like the old stuff that originally was intended for adolescent boys. Robert Heinlein was a giant in the early science fiction days. In *The Moon is a Harsh Mistress*, he describes the moon colonized by ex-cons much as Australia was. It has been a second-class satellite of Earth for so long that the inhabitants revolt. After the revolution, a wise old professor guides them, urging them to make it *difficult* to enact new laws—because new laws can lead to new tyrannies. And so it is with innovation. True innovation is a disruptive force in any organization. It changes the way you do business, it destroys markets, it dislocates jobs and people. You need to listen to dissenters while still picking those innovations whose payoff will be worth the disruption. And of course, to annoy all those innovators with a great—but not quite great enough—idea.

All That Glitters Is Not Gold. How to Differentiate between Dissent and Undesirable Behaviors

It takes a strong and committed person to be a dissenter. Strong enough (or maybe oblivious enough) to ignore or continue in the face of pressure to shut up and go along. And committed enough to try to reform rather than take his bright ideas to more congenial company. Dissenters can pay a very high personal price for their refusal to be one of the sheep. Because their dissent helps organizations be innovative, they need to be cherished rather than censured.

"Wait a minute," you are probably objecting. "You're making it sound like all the whiners and troublemakers have lily-white motives. That's not true."

Actually, I'm not saying that. Anyone who has worked long enough has seen people who are just plain unhappy. Or have had bosses who have promoted a cynicism that has encrusted their work souls. Or are driving hard for their own personal agendas. Whatever the reason, they are not dissenters, however much they might represent themselves that way. How do you tell the difference? When is it dissent and when is it whining, resistance, insubordination, or just plain pigheadedness? How do you make that differentiation without automatically believing that any dissent is bad?

I want to compare two stories, one of which you've already read. The first one is about Thinsulate. If you remember, the 3-M CEO tried five times to kill the project before he reluctantly let it through. The other story is about Sam, someone with whom I unfortunately worked. Without going into the gory details, Sam tried to kill my main project by continually going back to the CEO. I thought of him as a troublemaker, not a dissenter. But what was the difference? Is it just that I happened to be at the short end of the stick in that exchange? That obviously isn't enough reason. There must have been others at 3-M who got burned in some way as Mr. Thinsulate kept pushing his idea.

What's the difference? In both situations, somebody kept coming back to say they disagreed. In both, the complainer would have benefited personally if things went his way. That's not a reason in and of itself to toss out the idea. After all, somebody almost always does benefit from any turn of events.

As I think about it, the main difference lies in whether the dissenter/troublemaker has the good of the company at heart. That's where the two stories diverge in my mind. Thinsulate turned out to be of great benefit. But Sam wasn't proposing a better or more efficient way to achieve our goals. He didn't have an alternative vision; he was just trying to avoid losing power.

Naturally, anybody with any degree of political savvy will maintain he's acting only for the good of the organization. It would be foolhardy to maintain otherwise. So how do you know? Not an easy question. Let's run through a situation and see how you can try to differentiate between troublemaking and true dissent.

Your company has just taken over another in Israel. Both companies perform several of the same functions, one of them being portal development. Your guy, Brian, wants to talk about that.

Brian	*Hi, Linda, ready for our meeting?*
YOU	*Sure. What's on the agenda?*
Brian	*I wanted to talk about this Israeli deal. I'm getting a lot of flack from my guys.*
YOU	*How come?*
Brian	*There's a rumor you're going to move portal development to Israel.*
YOU	*Well, PorTus got into the whole thing earlier than we did. It's a possibility.*
Brian	*You realize of course that all of my guys will walk if you do.*
YOU	*Why? There's plenty of great projects here.*
Brian	*No way. It's the only thing they'll work on.*
YOU	*Really? Have you talked to them about it?*
Brian	*Not yet. I don't want to spook them. But I just know. And anyhow, I don't think we should let the PorTus guys get away with this.*
YOU	*What do you mean?*
Brian	*Come on, Linda. Portals are hot. Why give it away?*
YOU	*But they are us, now.*
Brian	*Yeah, but let's get real. I mean, after all, we bought them. Doesn't that count for something?*
YOU	*Like what?*
Brian	*Well, isn't there an old saying about he who pays the piper picks the tune?*
YOU	*I don't know about that.*

This conversation would probably go on longer, but we have enough for our purposes. It would be great, wouldn't it, if people would just say what's really on their minds? "I want to retain my status and power, I want to win, I want the other guys to lose." But that's not going to happen. Brian talks about threats to the company (his programmers will leave, the Israeli company is flexing its muscles), but they don't ring true to me. I think it's more likely he's dressed up "unacceptable" motives in clever guises. You need to listen carefully to sort them out. To confirm your suspicions, ask about his motives.

YOU	*If portals get moved, that would be tough on you, wouldn't it?*
Brian	*On me? Nah. I can go anywhere.*
YOU	*I'm sure that's true. But you've built the business from nothing. It would be tough to give it up.*
Brian	*That's not my concern at all.*
YOU	*Really? But it will affect you.*
Brian	*Nah, no problem. I'm only interested in the good of the company.*

Well, it's a judgment call, isn't it? Personally, I'm suspicious of people who don't admit that a change will impact them, especially if adversely. Your previous history with Brian will determine whether you see him as a dissenter or opportunist. If you believe him, great, then the two of you can get into what to do about the problem. But if you sense more opportunism than opportunity, you might want to handle it this way.

YOU	*Okay, Brian, I think I've got your concerns. I'll keep them in mind.*
Brian	*It's critical that we keep the portal business here.*
YOU	*I can see you feel that way.*
Brian	*It's just not going to work any other way...*
YOU	*Thanks, Brian. I think we've done all we can on this right now. I'll get back to you when I know anything else.*

Remember—saying "I'll keep them in mind" shouldn't be just a way to blow Brian off. One of the annoying things about ideas is that it is difficult to come to a hard and fast decision about their value. So keep his concerns in mind, even if you are almost entirely convinced that they are opportunistic rather than dissent.

Also, don't be tempted to dismiss this as politics. It is politics, but keep in mind that legitimate dissent can be imbedded in it. So while it's important not to play politics, you shouldn't dismiss the idea out of hand just because of the guise it comes in.

As you can see, whether a person is a troublemaker or a dissenter is a judgment call. When you are called on to make that determination, you can use the following questions to help with the decision:

- Has this person had good ideas in the past?
- Does she generally try to do what is right?
- Is she usually a turf protector?
- Is her eye always on the next promotion or way to impress the boss?
- Does she generally deliver what she promises?
- Do you fundamentally trust her?

In all of this, two things are important. First, don't automatically assume people who oppose you or would benefit from their advocacy are, by definition, troublemakers. Second, give these guys the benefit of the doubt. If you're not sure, let it run a bit. Continue to probe how their view will be better than the one currently in force. If it feels like the idea really is the driver, you might need to put up with the pushiness, the ego, and the lack of team skills. And you thought managing was hard before.

Recruiting Dissenters

Has all of this made you think, "Okay, great, I'm going to hire dissenters from now on"? Hmmm...don't think so. As we have discussed, there is a pretty fine line between dissenters and troublemakers and I'm not sure, however extensive your interviewing process is, you'll be sure you've got one but not the other.

In addition, I don't think it's necessary. Instead, look for people who have shown they have been innovative either in other jobs or in their personal lives. Dollars to doughnuts, if you get innovation, you'll get dissent. But if you do hire for innovation, remember, it's a fallacy to assume that a few of these individuals will make an innovative culture. Organizations are very skilled at suppressing them. The culture of most organizations will either mold them to its own non-innovative norms or make it so unpleasant that they'll leave. The only exception might be if innovators came in en masse and threw out the old guard. But isn't that called revolution? Not something those in power purposely whip up. The next chapter will show you how to start creating the kind of culture that will encourage innovation without overthrow.

Summary

Both dissenters and innovators are outsiders. The very qualities that make dissenters annoying, like arrogance and unreasonableness, are the flip side of the qualities—like passion and drive—that are needed to keep an idea alive. Life would be so much easier if we could separate the desirable characteristics—like passion—from the undesirable ones—like unreasonableness. But it's a package deal. We need to take the good with the bad, the wheat with the chaff, the horse with the carriage (you get the picture). Now we need to figure out how to manage these people who won't fly in formation.

Main Points

- The qualities of innovation—passion, drive, out-of-the-box thinking—cause difficulties for organizations, which see them as arrogance, unreasonableness, and an inability to compromise. You can't get one without the other.
- The trick is to manage so these people contribute their ideas while still being efficient.

The Manager as Political Handler

*Innovators/dissenters can provide valuable ideas to the organi-
zation but they rarely have the political skills to get their ideas
accepted and implemented by the organization. In fact, they
are often proud of their unwillingness to "play politics." And
yet, when playing politics means helping others understand the
importance of the idea, including them in its development, and
gathering funding and support for its implementation, these
are activities critical to success. The manager of the dissenter
can play this role and the skills he or she will need
are outlined in this chapter.*

A Cautionary Tale

A colleague consulting with a defense contractor gave me this story of innovation faltering at the last moment. Josh was a brilliant engineer who had developed a prototype for a new guidance system. He was ready to present the idea to the Board for funding. He was so excited about its possibilities that he began to believe the only acceptable outcome was total approval for full production. Anything less would be disaster.

The presentation went swimmingly. Just one small catch. To launch the system, a good deal of capital was required and it was too rich for the present. Josh was invited to resubmit his proposal at a later date. No promises were made, but a politically savvy observer could see that next time the project would probably get what it needed.

But for Josh, who was not politically savvy, this was executive incompetence at its best. They'd rejected a great idea all for the want of a little extra cash. Within a couple of weeks, he left to start his own business, taking half the engineering staff with him. This disrupted the company's plans and of course, they lost key knowledge workers. Yet I don't doubt it was a sound business decision. Could anything have been done to avoid this? Yes, and the solution has to do with understanding the role of the manager as political handler.

Manager as Political Handler

Political handler. What does that conjure up? The person behind the candidate—positioning him, getting the right people to listen, calming him down, propping him up, building coalitions, and lobbying for support, money, time, and attention. The candidate is front and center but the political handler makes it possible. This is the role managers need to play with innovators, just as leaders always have. The ancient Chinese philosopher Lao-tze said:

> *A leader is best when people barely know he exists. Not so good when people obey and acclaim him. Worse when they despise him. But of a good leader who talks little, when his work is done and his aim fulfilled, they will say, "We did it ourselves."*

The Conference Board sees the role of a middle manager as a broker of opportunities for innovation and collaboration. In fact, pharmaceutical companies' success in turning out a steady stream of new drugs has been attributed, in part, to their managers' ability to challenge the company's conventional wisdom. Thus your job is to have the political savvy to get an idea accepted so the dissenter doesn't have to.

You might be objecting. "Wouldn't it be better to teach dissenters how to handle the politics themselves? What if his next manager can't or won't play along?" Good point. I think there is value in helping the dissenter marginally more politic, as I will cover in the next chapter. But otherwise, I don't think so.

First, teaching dissenters to be political is like teaching salespeople to be team players. Salespeople are a special breed. Good ones are single-minded about getting that bonus or filling the quota. But that focus on their own success can make them bad team players or at least reluctant ones. In fact, Rod Brandvold, VP of Organizational Development at the business intelligence software company Cognos, Inc., has observed that if you try to make team players out of salespeople, you sometimes produce a kinder, gentler salesperson who doesn't fill his quota. So it is with dissenters. Being outside the group gives dissenters their capacity to see the new and different. If we force them to come closer in, we may dull that gift. In fact, Thomas Edison, one of the century's greatest inventors, was so incompetent at getting things implemented that his backers removed him from every business he founded.

I'm not against salespeople or dissenters learning skills to be more cooperative and less abrasive, but we need to be sure we aren't destroying the very quality that makes them valuable. So while it doesn't hurt to try to take the edge off the abrasiveness, if we want to spark new ideas, we don't want to turn sandpaper into vinyl.

So turning dissenters into politicians isn't a good idea but even if it were, there is another problem: It's probably not possible. The ability to think outside the box is as complex a skill as harnessing people's enthusiasm. It's rare enough to find a person with one of these qualities. To expect *both* in one person—I think we're going to wait a long time before that ship comes in. If we require that the innovator have the political skills to implement his idea, we're probably going to lose a lot of great ones, both ideas and innovators.

Much as we'd like dissenters to change, to become more politically savvy, even just to get along better, it's a non-starter for all the reasons we've already discussed. Your job therefore is not to change the dissenter,[1] but to manage him effectively. That means you do the political part of getting an innovation to market and leave the innovating to Josh.

How do you play a political handler role? I'm sure you have some tricks of your own, but the ones I think are important are gathering support; providing air cover; taking and giving credit; managing expectations; getting cooperation from the dissenter/innovator without co-opting him; and holding on to innovators.

Dissenters in Power

Every once in a while, you find that a dissenter has actually had the political savvy, luck, or sheer persistence to make it into the senior management ranks. Here, you would think, would be the perfect solution to our innovation and dissent dilemma. Make the dissenters the bosses. Then they can keep the organization hopping while still having the position power to make things happened. I've had the fortune (or misfortune) to work for two such bosses.

My first boss was wonderfully inventive and was even able to manipulate a fairly hidebound financial system to squeeze extra money out of it regularly. He was very well respected in the industry. But he made powerful enemies internally, often because of

---

[1] Although truthfully, you may need to do some smoothing of the edges. I'll cover that in the next chapter.

these financial shenanigans—which are too complicated to go into but trust me, were pretty neat. He was so completely focused on doing his thing that he did not see the storm clouds gathering, and when they broke, he had no protection inside to keep him from being let go. So while his position allowed him to accomplish great things, it also exposed him to political players with a lot more skill and interest in playing than him. And that led to his downfall.

The second boss also had that quality of great ideas and persistence but was a disaster as a boss. I thought of him as having a thousand good ideas, a hundred great ones, and one stroke of genius. The problem is he couldn't differentiate one from the other and wanted to implement them all immediately. Because he was also very charismatic, he could easily get us caught up in the romance of conquering his latest Everest. We'd stampede up the mountain when he yelled "charge!" But halfway up it, another peak would attract him. He'd convince us that that one was really Shangri-La. We'd race down the first mountain and up the next. Halfway up that one...well, you get the picture.

Even if you could get dissenters to learn the political skills to get into positions of influence, I'm not entirely sure it would be a good idea for them or for the organization. But I got to see a lot of scenery.

Gathering Support

Your innovator may have a great idea but he's not aware that the rightness of the idea is not enough to get it implemented. You need to have the support from all parts of the organization. Certainly your bosses, but also marketing and sales, production, and any other key players. If you don't, any one of them can stop the project in its tracks. You need to sell them on the value of supporting the innovation so it will have as smooth a path as possible from idea to implementation.

To do this, meet with each key organizational player. The easiest way is to hold these meetings on your own. But don't. Take the innovator along. He needs to know that people identify him with the breakthrough. Otherwise, he'll start to believe he's been left out of the loop or, worse, that you're stealing his idea. However, he may be a bit difficult. You need to coach him on what to say, or more importantly, what not to. But keep taking him.

There is a hidden agenda. The innovator is likely to find the meetings torturous. He'd much rather be back in the lab or at the computer coming up with the next great idea. If you're lucky, at one point he'll ask you to go without him because the meetings are such a waste of time. You're now free to go ahead with your coalition building. Updating him frequently on your progress is probably all you need to do.

Potential supporters will probably want changes to your plan. They may be improvements or just ego-driven tinkering. Either way, you know the likelihood of success is lowered without the imprimatur of the people whose support you need. You need to change the plan *and* get your innovator to buy in. However, changing anything to "pander" to somebody whose importance he cannot see will be difficult. Here your skill as a political handler comes in. Let's use Josh from the previous example to see how the conversation might go.

YOU	*Hi, Josh, got a minute?*
Josh	*I'm pretty busy...*
YOU	*Just wanted to let you know what happened in the marketing meeting.*
Josh	*Better you than me. Sure, what did the stuffed shirts have to say?*
YOU	*They're pretty excited about the whole thing. Very enthusiastic.*
Josh	*Of course. It'll make the company a bucket.*
YOU	*They just had a small thing. The project name. They think there are too many products on the market called "strategic." They're afraid we'll confuse buyers.*
Josh	*That's stupid. The guys buying the system aren't 15-year-olds choosing lipstick. They know their stuff. They're not going to be fooled into spending 10 million because they got the name wrong.*
YOU	*I don't think marketing was saying that. Their concern was getting buyers' attention initially. If the name sounds too much like our competitors,' it'll take longer to penetrate the market.*
Josh	*Well, that's not my problem, is it?*
YOU	*I guess it's ours, though, because we want this to be a success.*
Josh	*Come on, Sam. This is stupid. It's just marketing flexing its muscle.*
YOU	*Maybe, but you know, Josh, Tom has Aveno's ear. If he doesn't like a product, it's harder to get funding. I think we need to pay attention.*
Josh	*Politics!*
YOU	*You're right. But your product is too good to get derailed by a silly thing like a name, don't you think?*
Josh	*Of course, but if the dorks in marketing would just...*
YOU	*I know, I know. But does it really matter? I mean, in the big scheme of things?*

Josh *I guess not.*
YOU *And it makes them think they've helped.*
Josh *Ha! Like a name's gonna make a difference!*
YOU *I'm with you, but it probably doesn't hurt to let them have this piece, does it? If it means they'll support us?*
Josh *I guess not. Yeah, why not? They can call it a Tootsie Roll if they want.*
YOU *Well, I think Tootsie Roll's already taken.*
Josh *Ha! Yeah.*
YOU *They'll come up with some names and run them by us. Okay?*
Josh *Sure. Whatever. Lookit, could you get lost? As I said, I'm pretty busy.*

Josh is likely to react to any changes to "his" project negatively, perhaps even in a knee-jerk way. Innovators often have great ownership of what they produce. And usually, that's an excellent quality—it makes them the passionate, committed people they are. However, it can be problematic when you know that small concessions can make a big difference. If you continue to emphasize the smallness of the concession compared to the importance of the project, he is more likely to acquiesce.

Similarly, although Josh knows politics are operating ("It's just marketing flexing its muscle"), he doesn't think they're worth paying attention to. You're unlikely to convince him that there is merit in worrying. But he can be brought around to being content to let things happen as long as his work is not affected.

You notice Josh uses the first person a lot—"That's not *my* problem." As we know, he doesn't necessarily see himself as part of a team. Use *we* a lot to emphasize, however subliminally, that he is part of a team—or at very least, is dependent on others to be successful. You don't need to hit him over the head, but the use of *we* may eventually get him both to use the pronoun and pay attention to what it means.

Finally, you're not going to convince Josh of all the changes others want, even if they make sense. Some may have to go through without his consent. If you've helped him to recognize that these changes up the chances of success, he may go along, however grudgingly. If he doesn't, the last section of this chapter will help.

Providing Air Cover

If our dissenter were a poster boy, we wouldn't need this discussion. He'd be the perfect employee if he knew when to speak, what to say, and when to keep quiet. But he isn't and doesn't. You will need to provide air cover when he ticks off the powers that be.

Josh is the kind of employee who might seize the opportunity in an elevator or a corridor to let the CEO know how stupid turning down his idea was. He might even, like one dissenter I know, take the CEO on at an all-staff meeting. Let's say he did. The CEO has called a meeting to announce the takeover of another defense contractor—Dedalus Inc. You were traveling the day of the announcement. When you get in the next morning, your boss is in your office.

YOU	*Oh, hi, Phyllis…I was going to see you later…I got some great stuff in Boston.*
Phyllis	*Forget Boston—do you know what Josh did?*
YOU	*I haven't seen him yet.*
Phyllis	*He took on Aveno at the staff meeting!*
YOU	*Took him on? How?*
Phyllis	*He called him an idiot. In front of everyone!*
YOU	*Oh, god, no!*
Phyllis	*And told him he couldn't recognize a great idea if it bit him on the nose.*
YOU	*Oh, no!*
Phyllis	*The word came down. Aveno's ticked. He wants to get rid of him!*
YOU	*We can't do that, Phyllis! We need him!*
Phyllis	*And how long do you think he'll last calling the president names? Who does he think he is?*
YOU	*I know, I know. He was upset about the executive committee. I didn't have a chance to talk to him after the meeting.*
Phyllis	*That's no excuse.*
YOU	*I know but it sort of helps to explain, doesn't it?*
Phyllis	*No way. I want you to come down hard on Josh—I want a written apology.*
YOU	*Wow—slow down, Phyllis. Let's think about this.*
Phyllis	*We don't need to—just do it!*
YOU	*Okay, but you know Josh. He'll walk before he'll apologize.*
Phyllis	*You can't humiliate Aveno in public and expect to get away with it!*
YOU	*Agreed, but couldn't we find another way to make this right?*
Phyllis	*Like what?*
YOU	*Well—you got me…Couldn't you explain why Josh was so upset?*
Phyllis	*And that's supposed to make it okay?*
YOU	*No, but if Aveno knew that Josh thought he'd axed Josh's project—maybe he wouldn't be so upset.*

Phyllis	*So he can get away with it?*
YOU	*No, no. I'll talk to Josh but can't we try the explanation? We can't afford to lose Josh, not over something like this.*
Phyllis	*You know, there's going to be a point when he's more trouble than he's worth.*
YOU	*Maybe, but not over this. Not this time.*
Phyllis	*No, I guess not. Okay, I'll try but I'm not sure I can make it work.*
YOU	*And I'll talk to Josh.*

Sometimes the only and best thing to do is buy time. Try to create a space where everybody can calm down and think about what's at stake. You have to do that first with Phyllis. If you keep her talking long enough, you can usually get her off the first wild demands ("I want a written apology!") and to the point that she will consider how likely it is that would happen ("He'll walk before he'll apologize.") and then to an interim solution ("Can't we try the explanation?").

In addition, there is of course the problem of the CEO. It's understandable he's upset at being taken to task in public, especially for something he didn't do. It was inappropriate, and if you can get Josh to stop doing things like that, it would be great. You need to talk to Josh; I'll discuss how to do that in the next chapter.

But say you're not able to prevent Josh from saying things the reverse of polite to those in power? What can you do? If you continue to believe in his innovative talents, you need both to work with him on smoothing out the rough edges and provide air cover.

Actually, what often happens is that people—after the initial shock—get resigned to the idea that people like Josh are never going to successfully grace a drawing room. If you can get them to the point of saying, "Well, that's just Josh," you will have won the battle. Start by saying it publicly whenever you can, coupling it with "But he's the best guidance man in the business. I guess you can have brilliance or you can have etiquette but you can't have both." If you say it often enough, people will begin to see that maybe it's not the end of the world when somebody isn't as polite as they should be. Annoying and even disrespectful but not catastrophic.

Protecting Yourself

I've asked you to take a lot of guff from both above and below you to encourage innovation, but it shouldn't be unlimited. There are two ways you need to protect yourself.

The first is from bosses or others who could do you harm. As long as you are seen as an effective buffer between the dissenter and the powers that be, you're probably fine. However, if you can't totally "control" the dissenter, as of course you can't, you may see blame wending your way. Make sure your boss is clear how valuable the dissenter is and how hard it is to keep that balance between dissent and order. The harder those above you know you have to work at this, the more tolerant they will be of what they perceive to be lapses in control.

You may also need to protect yourself from the dissenter himself. We have already discussed the dissenter's lack of social skills, and who better to practice on than you? While managers need to tolerate more than they have up to now, this isn't carte blanche. I had one employee who seemed to continually have problems getting his check direct-deposited and asked me to intervene. I discovered from Payroll that various institutions were garnishing his wages and, thus his check had to be specially processed almost every time. Hence the delay. As we were trying to sort through a solution, the employee started to attack me verbally. I finally said, "John, do you think I'm to blame for this?" He stopped short in his rant, blinked a couple of times, and said, "No." I said, "Then please don't speak to me as if I were." He calmed down and we were able to solve the problem amicably.

So while I am asking you to tolerate a wider range of behavior than is typical, it is appropriate to draw the line sometimes. You aspire to be a political handler, not a doormat.

Taking and Getting Credit

We've already discussed the most important way to give credit—by keeping the innovator identified with his idea while building the coalitions to get it implemented. However, there is one particular part of taking and giving credit I want to focus on. At some point, there is usually one big make-it-or-break-it presentation. Often the choice of who does the presentation comes down to the innovator or his manager. Josh or you.

You know the executive committee is a hard-nosed bunch, very dollars and sense. Investment is a word they know but don't like to use too often. Throwing in Josh, with his—shall we say—free-flowing style is a risk. He may not be able to focus his presentation on what ExComm needs to know. You may be tempted to do the presentation yourself. And that may make sense since, realistically, some people are better presenters than others, often because they are sensitive to their audience's needs. I had one brilliant employee who consistently started his presentations where his thinking left off. No context, no history, just a sort of public thinking out loud. Not only did it confuse his listeners, it annoyed them, too, since he made it clear he thought they were stupid because they couldn't follow when he started in mid-sentence.

If you're lucky, the innovator will want you to make the presentation because he knows he isn't strong in this area. But I wouldn't count on it. Just because they're not supersensitive to other people's needs doesn't mean they themselves don't require care and feeding. Doing this presentation is recognition. And, as the political handler, you don't want to be grabbing the spotlight anyway.

But if you think Josh will have a problem, strike a deal. You will let him make the presentation (after all, it is your decision) if and only if he will work with you to prepare it. He'll find it a huge pain in the neck but if he wants it enough, he'll probably agree. Then you can insist he consider everybody's motivations, possible stupid questions, what aspects to downplay, and which to highlight. One of three things can happen at this point. The first is that he listens to your advice and you have a fair level of confidence he'll do a good job. The second is that all this fussing makes him realize it is taking too much time away from his "real" work and he will hand the whole thing over to you. Then you can do the presentation with a clear conscience. Make sure he's in the room and give him credit but go ahead. The final possibility is that he won't listen to your advice and still wants to do the presentation. Keeping him happy is important but it doesn't supercede the need to effectively represent the project to the Board. You may need to do the presentation yourself. It will be difficult to tell him that but the essence of the discussion isn't that different from ones you have already had with him. You already both agree that getting the project approved is paramount. He knows (he doesn't like it, but he knows) that the political side is important and can sink it. He doesn't have to like that you are taking over the presentation but you may need to do it.

Managing Expectations

In our original situation, Josh's manager didn't help Josh have reasonable expectations of the executive meeting. Because people like Josh have little political savvy, they are unable to read the signals or even, as in this case, know when they have won.

In working with Josh on the executive committee presentation, you realize he thinks the only acceptable outcome is getting his proposal adopted exactly as stated. You need to talk him down so he is prepared for less than a home run. Let's see how that might roll out.

YOU	*Hey, Josh. Ready for the big presentation?*
Josh	*Almost. I still think 20 minutes is stupid. I need at least an hour.*
YOU	*I know but I've seen Aveno cut people off in mid-sentence when their time is up so we need to make our points quickly.*
Josh	*That's ridiculous. I mean, sometimes you have to take the time.*
YOU	*True—but if you hit the high points like we discussed, you should be fine.*
Josh	*I wish I had more time.*
YOU	*I hear ya, but there you are. Any thoughts about what Aveno might say?*
Josh	*You mean, like objections?*
YOU	*Yes—but I was thinking more about outcomes.*
Josh	*Yeah, we want the money to move into production.*
YOU	*That's possible, of course, but we've kept this pretty close to our vests. It'll be the first time ExComm has had a chance to look at it.*
Josh	*So what? Once they see it, they'll love it.*
YOU	*I hope that too. But it's a big whack of dough—they may be more cautious than we'd want.*
Josh	*More cautious—you mean, like they'll tank it? Hey, they can't...*
YOU	*No, I'm not saying that...but what if they want to proceed more slowly—do another prototype, for example?*
Josh	*Lookit, this one works fine. Sure, I want to fine-tune some of the initiation sequences, but it's all doable.*
YOU	*Well, say they want to see that before they'll give the go-ahead?*
Josh	*That would be stupid.*
YOU	*I'm not saying they would, but say they did?*
Josh	*I wouldn't buy that.*
YOU	*What does that mean?*
Josh	*Do you think I'm going to be second-guessed by a bunch of stuffed shirts?*
YOU	*Is it second-guessing to want to be sure their money is going to the right place?*

Josh	*No, but I tell you, we don't need another prototype.*
YOU	*It might not be a prototype, Josh. They might want more test results, more market surveys, anything.*
Josh	*I tell you, we're ready to go into production.*
YOU	*I know we are. But sometimes people don't see things as we do, so...*
Josh	*Then they're stupid.*
YOU	*Not necessarily—anyhow...I just wanted to talk about what the upshot might be. Just so we're prepared.*
Josh	*For what?*
YOU	*For anything. From full-steam ahead to go back and try again.*
Josh	*They've got to approve this, Sam. They've got to. Do you know how many years I've put into this?*
YOU	*I'm not saying they won't, but sometimes it's a win just to get to keep trying.*
Josh	*But we're ready to go.*
YOU	*I know, I know, but even if we don't get everything we need right off the top, we can still finish ahead.*
Josh	*No way—I need everything I'm asking for.*
YOU	*I'm sure you do. But what if they gave us what we want over five years rather than three?*
Josh	*Stupid. It would delay getting to market that much longer.*
YOU	*But not the end of the world, right?*
Josh	*I guess not.*
YOU	*See, that's all I'm saying. We need to be ready to roll with the punches, if there are any. The main thing is to keep the project alive.*
Josh	*True, although they'd be fools not to buy it.*
YOU	*But the main thing is to keep us alive, right?*
Josh	*Yeah, I guess so. But they'd still be stupid.*

As in other conversations, Josh shows his fierce ownership of the project ("Do you think I'm going to be second-guessed by a bunch of stuffed shirts?"). He has trouble seeing any other point of view except his and that's where you are invaluable. I doubt you can get him to agree that others should have a say, but you may be able to get him to view it as a necessary evil.

Also, Josh immediately keyed into one of the possibilities you floated (doing another prototype) and was prepared to argue that one into the ground. He missed the point you were making—that things might not go exactly as expected. Don't be sidelined into these types of discussions. They will probably get him even more upset and more importantly, will obscure the main point ("Sometimes it's a win just to get to keep trying."). Instead, keep coming back to the need to roll with the punches and keep the project alive.

You can't expect Josh will become a model corporate citizen or that this conversation will have him bowing and scraping to the higher-ups. But you've accomplished what you needed to. Josh is entertaining the idea that less than 100% can still be a win and that's all you need for now. It's an important preventive measure.

Getting Cooperation without Co-opting

As I mentioned earlier, there may be points you must move ahead even though the dissenter does not agree. How can you get his cooperation without shutting him down completely?

Make it clear you're going ahead despite his opposition and that you require him to carry out his part with enthusiasm and judgment. In addition, the dissenter's public disagreement may be detrimental. He needs to agree on how he will express his disappointment. In return for all of this, you will listen—actually listen and not just keep silent until he is finished—when he finds new evidence (as he will) that you've made the wrong decision.

Sound like a tall order? It's doable. Let's use a different example. You're a director in Eduware, a software company developing products for the education market. Katie is your manager of multimedia programming and is excellent technically. But, in your view, she has allowed the programmers to run wild. Delivery of software is consistently behind schedule. The marketplace is going to stop believing Eduware is viable if you keep missing deadlines. You have been discussing bringing in a project manager.

YOU *Hi, Katie—why don't we finish up our conversation from yesterday?*

Katie *Sure, Rick.*

YOU *I've thought about what you said—that you can't put development on a schedule.*

Katie *Right—the programmers will walk if we try.*

YOU *I understand you don't think it will work, but I'd like to try.*

Katie *Rick, we've been through this—you can't put a creative process on a schedule.*

YOU *I understand your arguments but I am very concerned about the missed deadlines. We have to do something.*

Katie *This isn't going to work...*

YOU *Maybe not. But I feel we have to go ahead. I know you don't agree but I need your support so I'd like to talk about what we can do to make this as palatable as possible.*

Katie *That's easy. Don't do it.*

YOU *I'm of a different mind. Can I make a deal?*

Katie *What kind?*

YOU *If you'll try to make it work with a project manager, I'll promise to listen if things are going off track. I'm not promising to change my mind, but I'm promising to listen seriously.*

Katie *But you don't need to do this—lookit, if the schedule thing is all that important, let me give it a go.*

YOU *We've been trying that for the last couple of months and it isn't working.*

Katie *Okay, I'll put more energy into it if that's what it takes.*

YOU *You know, Katie, I can see you're great with the programmers. They respect your experience and you can get them enthusiastic about the project. Those are important skills.*

Katie *Well, I believe in the product.*

YOU *That comes through. But we all have our strengths. I don't get the impression you enjoy the management side of the job.*

Katie *Well, no, who would?*

YOU *A project manager would let you offload something you don't like and leave you more time to do what you're good at.*

Katie *But it's not going to work.*

YOU *You may be right but we're not going to know until we try, are we?*

Katie *Sure, we can. I know it won't.*

YOU *Okay, I hear you but I want to go ahead. So, it's really a matter of whether you can buy into the bargain I'm suggesting.*

Katie *You mean if I go along, I can tell you when it's not working?*

YOU *Yes, but it's more than go along. I need your help to make it work. The programmers set great store in what you think. If you're doubtful, they'll be too.*

Katie *So you want me to fake it?*

YOU *No, but could you see your way clear to giving it a try, really trying to make it work for a while and see where we are?*

Katie *I suppose so. But for how long?*

YOU *What about three months?*

Katie *I guess I could stand three months.*

YOU *Well, great. And I'm willing to listen to any problems.*

Katie *I bet I'll be in here a lot.*

> **YOU** *Could be. Can I ask one more thing?*
> **Katie** *What?*
> **YOU** *Could we discuss how you talk about this?*
> **Katie** *Well, like I said, do you want me to fake it?*
> **YOU** *No, but when they ask you about it, would you be willing to say, "Well, I have my doubts but I'm willing to give it a shot"?*
> **Katie** *I guess so.*
> **YOU** *If you want to talk more about why you object, that's up to you. But would you be willing to end with "But I'm willing to give it a try for a couple of months"?*
> **Katie** *I guess it wouldn't kill me. Okay. But this isn't going to work, Rick.*
> **YOU** *But you're willing to give it a try for a couple of months?*
> **Katie** *But I'm willing to give it a try for a couple of months.*

This dialog assumes you have spoken to Katie at least once or twice before about the missed deadlines. If you haven't, this would be completely unfair to spring on her. It is quite likely Katie assumed or hoped these previous conversations were just so much hot air that would dissipate if she ignored them. She starts to pay attention only when you raise the possibility of a project manager ("If the schedule thing is all that important, let me give it a go."). But you need to have had those conversations anyhow. Otherwise, you haven't given her a chance to change of her own accord.

You notice that you summarized her arguments right at the beginning. This helps her realize you understand them—you just don't buy them or believe others are more compelling.

You will probably need to reiterate more than a couple of times that you are going ahead. However, your objective is not to get Katie to like it or even agree. She's not going to and that's okay. You should not require her to fake agreement or pleasure. It isn't possible to always be in agreement and we should abandon the myth that it is. In fact, it's a good thing if your persuasive powers don't razzle-dazzle her into submission. It's not in your long-term best interests to encourage people to ignore their own internal promptings if you want to keep dissent alive. Instead, simply make clear that you are moving forward, that you need and expect her support, but that you will continue to listen.

The rubber will hit the road when Katie has an objection. Let's say the project manager started a couple of weeks ago to get things organized.

	Katie	*Rick, I told you it wasn't going to work!*
	YOU	*Hey, slow down! What isn't working?*
	Katie	*This Lew guy—he's a menace!*
	YOU	*Why, what's he done?*
	Katie	*He's got my programmers all up in arms.*
	YOU	*Why?*
	Katie	*He wants them to agree to objectives for SpellBound.*
	YOU	*And that's bad?*
	Katie	*Well, of course!*
Make sure she's not doing an end run around Lew.	**YOU**	*Have you talked to Lew about this?*
	Katie	*Yeah, but I didn't get anywhere with him.*
	YOU	*What did he say?*
	Katie	*Some junk about everybody having their own vision of SpellBound.*
	YOU	*Is that true?*
	Katie	*Well, maybe, but don't you see, that's where the creativity comes from—from people mucking around. Sometimes we can't decide what we want until we've tried different cuts.*
Is it possible Katie has a point? Don't judge too soon—keep asking questions.	**YOU**	*So you think having a firm objective would stifle creativity?*
	Katie	*Of course.*
	YOU	*I don't think I understand. How does it do that?*
	Katie	*Rick, an objective puts blinders on people—they stop looking for the great effect or the killer visual.*
	YOU	*Really? How come?*
	Katie	*You've hemmed them in—they can't get really creative.*
You may not agree but are you sure you're right?	**YOU**	*Hmmm—I guess I don't see how that happens but I think Lew has a point. If we can't agree on what SpellBound looks like, it's going to be hard to get a product.*

	Katie	*We've gotten great products in the past.*
	YOU	*Yes, you're right. But the problem has been the deadlines.*
	Katie	*Well, you know the old saying—you can have it on time or you can have it right.*
You don't need to change your mind about what you need.	**YOU**	*Yes, but you also know that first to market wins the day. Getting out a dynamite product doesn't do us much good if we're also-rans.*
	Katie	*But neither is a crummy product.*
	YOU	*I don't think your guys would ever do a crummy product. But let's get back to the main point. Is there some way we can have a firm objective while still letting the programmers experiment?*
	Katie	*No, no way.*
	YOU	*What about this? Could we specify a period of experimentation and then set an objective?*
	Katie	*How long?*
	YOU	*I don't know—you'd need to talk to Lew about that. But what about it? People could fool around on their own for a bit, then come together and decide what the look will be.*
	Katie	*I dunno. It still means their creativity gets stifled in the actual production.*
	YOU	*How do you see that?*
	Katie	*What happens if they get a great idea that takes them off in a completely different direction?*
	YOU	*I guess they'd have to call everyone together to discuss it.*
	Katie	*What a bureaucratic answer!*
Ignore the slur.	**YOU**	*How would you handle it?*
	Katie	*I'd just let them take it on the road and see where it led but I can see that that's not going to fly...so well, maybe agreeing isn't all that bad. But I'd want my guys to run the meeting—not Lew.*

YOU		*Sure—although shouldn't we get Lew in on this discussion so we're all on the same page?*
Katie		*I suppose—but I'm not having Lew run the meeting.*
YOU		*Let's talk to Lew about it.*

There is a problem with dissenters (well, beyond the ones you already know about). If you have promised to listen, they may use you to sidestep conversations that really should take place with their colleagues. However, since we know dissenters don't necessarily have the interpersonal skills to successfully conduct these conversations, you may have to mediate as you will be doing in the case above. But nothing you do should encourage the dissenter to tattle on his colleagues. We will cover more of this in the next chapter—Coaching Dissenters.

In addition, you notice that when you asked Katie for a solution, she didn't have one. I think this is pretty typical. Dissenters can see the problem but are often so wedded to their solution ("Let the programmers have complete freedom."), it's hard for them to go farther afield. However, if you can come up with a viable option, most dissenters are at least willing to listen if you have been returning the favor. But don't look to them for ways to make it work. They can usually only gradually be nudged into compromise.

Katie has raised a point that may need attention. Are you going to lose innovation for the sake of efficiency? If it were completely possible to schedule innovation, we'd have done it a long time ago and I wouldn't be writing this book. Is it possible you need to take her position into account?

You may not agree with the way the conversation was resolved and that's fine. Everyone has to apply their own judgment. The most important thing is not thinking "There she goes again." If you do, you've defeated the purpose. Remember, dissent can have an effect only if people continue to listen. I realize there is a repetitive nature that is exasperating. This is a downside of keeping dissent alive. You may have to repeat yourself more than you want to.

So, much as it is a pain in the neck, you want Katie to continue to be the guardian of her group's creativity. She may not be able to see how creativity can be merged with efficiency but hey! that's your job anyway.

Institutionalizing Dissent

You need to draw a fine line between getting the dissenter to cooperate and domesticating her. You don't want her, on particular issues or in general, to believe she should not dissent. You want an environment in which she feels valued enough to raise the red flag when a new danger comes along.

There is a temptation to try to strike a balance between off-the-wall dissent and order by providing the dissenter with an "official" role. This might be a "customer advocate," a sort of court dissenter. Assigning dissenters to a strategic planning unit also seems to make sense. After all, strategic planners are supposed to be looking out and seeing a different path.

But once a dissenter is part of the mainstream, her position is explicit and predictable, she and it can be discounted. Worse, the dissenter may start to believe that if she can influence the organization even the tiniest bit, she has to play the assigned role. This is taming a wild duck.

Fundamentally, I don't think it works to institutionalize dissent. The creative need to be an outsider drives dissenters and thus institutionalization may kill the very property you are trying to retain and manage. Mainstreaming dissent may be an oxymoron. It's best to allow dissent to occur, as it typically does now, all over the organization. Life would be easier if they came when called, but that's not how you find new lands.

Holding onto Innovators

As an experienced manager, you know that you can't win every time. But the innovator doesn't necessarily know that. Your challenge when you lose is both to help the innovator understand it isn't the end of the world and to keep him continuing to contribute.

Let's go back to the situation with Josh. Say things had gone as badly as he had thought—ExComm has expressed doubts that the guidance system will work or be profitable. You have come back with your tail between your legs and, in addition, have a mad Josh. First off, it's important to recognize that while Josh sounds angry, he's really hurt and offended. Rejecting dissenters' projects is rejecting them (just like authors, as it turns out). Keep that in mind when you're talking to him.

In addition, you obviously think Josh and Josh's ideas have merit, or you wouldn't have put so much effort into trying to get his project funded. So you also need to try to ensure that Josh isn't going to take his marbles and go home—or worse, take them to another kid's place to play.

Josh	*Can you believe those guys! I told you they wouldn't know a good idea if it bit them on the nose!*
YOU	*It was pretty disappointing.*
Josh	*Well, that's it! Catch me ever giving them another idea!*
YOU	*They didn't see the potential.*
Josh	*'Cause they're stupid! What did I tell you?*
YOU	*But we still need their support to go into production.*
Josh	*I don't see why. I'll just take my idea to StarTech.*
YOU	*Okay, Josh, I know you're mad and I'm mad too. But you know you can't. Because of your employment contract.*
Josh	*Do you think all the know-how is in the prototype? If I walk, you'd be dead in the water. You couldn't get it into production if you had a billion bucks!*
YOU	*I know that's true. That's why I hope you'll stay. We need you.*
Josh	*They have a funny way of showing it!*
YOU	*I know...I wish it had turned out better. But they didn't close the door...we just need to prove it's different from what's already on the market.*
Josh	*But it is! They're just too stupid to see it.*
YOU	*I can't prove it to them without your help.*
Josh	*We shouldn't have to prove it at all!*
YOU	*Granted. But this is too good an idea to die here. We need to keep plugging.*
Josh	*I don't know...maybe I should just go off on my own.*
YOU	*I'd be sorry if you did. And it probably would mean the project would die. It would be a shame.*
Josh	*Damn right.*
YOU	*Well, I know you need to think things over but can I put in my two cents? You could leave and I'd hate to see you go. But you'd have to leave the prototype behind. And you wouldn't be able to work on anything like it for the next two years. But if you stay, maybe we can turn this around.*
Josh	*Fat chance.*
YOU	*You never know. This really is too good an idea to die, don't you think?*
Josh	*Of course.*
YOU	*So, you'll think about it?*
Josh	*Yeah, yeah.*

After a major setback, everybody thinks about whether they have a future in the company. You may be thinking that yourself. Understandable. It's not surprising that Josh is threatening to leave. And of course, he may. But you can lower those chances. First, you need to let him vent, as you did. He's mad and perhaps justifiably so. So let him go for a while.

Although you can't determine whether he will stay, you can point out the realities of his situation. Most employment contracts today have stringent non-competition agreements. Josh knows, as you do, that the most important thing is Josh's brain power and that is the major loss if he leaves. However, he may not realize that non-competition agreements usually prevent the person from developing the idea he was working on when he left. Thus, Josh might be willing to hold on so he can keep working on his brain child.

Having said that, however, handcuffs do not make a committed and eager knowledge worker. Even if Josh decides to stay, you need to pay particular attention to showing how valuable he is to the company, even given the setback. That doesn't necessarily mean money, although it may be part of the package. Remember, knowledge workers get a thrill from working on new things, from being on the leading edge, from having control over their work. So, if you can, give him some time and money to work on a pet project that has been on his back burner.

In fact, doing that will give *you* time to change the focus and approach of the old project so it can pass muster next time. It may also be that his idea is so far ahead of its time that you actually need to wait for the right moment. The trick is to hold onto him until the climate is ready for him.

You can do some things to help get the climate ready. You can step up your coalition-building activities. Do a postmortem with anyone pivotal to the decision. Find out what you need to do to make it work. Do you need some outside world expert to give credibility to the idea? Do you need to accommodate underground forces? I once was in a situation where the head cheese was having a long-term affair with one of his managers. The only people who thought it was secret were the couple involved. Nothing got through unless the manager approved even though she was not on the executive committee. So we all managed to just casually mention the benefits of whatever we wanted approved to her. Shouldn't have had to do it, but there you are—organizational life in the raw.

If you can't resurrect the old project, putting Josh on the most prestigious or newest project you have might be a way to get him committed and engaged again. If you treat him well, he is less likely to follow through on his threat to withhold his intellectual capital from the company. If he finds the new project as intellectually challenging as was the old, he may be willing to give you and the company another chance.

Summary

Innovation has two aspects—the great idea and the ability to turn it into something of value. The latter is probably unfamiliar territory to the innovator. You can help move the idea to reality but you need to do it in a way that will keep the innovator front and center. If he thinks he is sidelined, you will either lose him or find he has parked his brain even if his body is showing up for the paycheck. It's a fine line, but keeping in mind that you're a political handler will focus your role. However, being front and center sometimes requires more skill than the dissenter has. The next chapter will cover how to coach him.

Main Points

- Innovation is both a great idea and the capacity to get it to market.
- This requires an ability to build coalitions, which innovators are not good at.
- Managers should be political handlers.
- Critical skills are gathering support, providing air cover, taking and giving credit, managing expectations, getting cooperation without co-opting, and holding onto innovators.

CHAPTER 9

୭୯

Coaching Dissenters

The manager is a valuable political buffer between the dissenter and the rest of the organization. However, dissenters can be so single-minded that they damage themselves and their projects. The manager needs to convince them to acquire some rudimentary political skills and to help them do so. This chapter provides tips on how to do this.

Introduction

In the last chapter, I discussed being a political handler for your dissenter/innovator. This is an important role managers should continue to play but sometimes you need a little more from the dissenter. While you can try to substitute your political acumen for his, you probably can't be a total replacement.

Her lack of skill may have you working at cross-purposes. If you're busy building coalitions for her idea while she's ticking off the very people you're cultivating, you're going nowhere fast. A dissenter who is too far outside the norms can threaten your effectiveness. But forcing her out or into the fold will lead to less innovation. You need to walk a fine line.

Two Problems

You know that a modicum of working well with others can help enormously. Research on emotional intelligence shows that this quality is twice as important to success as raw intelligence or technical know-how.

Of course, this argument is unlikely to hold water for dissenters. Since much of their view of themselves is tied up with their pride in their technical competence, they are not going to give much credence to anything that questions its preeminence.

So while you don't want to kill the goose that lays the golden eggs, you need to encourage her not to attack the other geese while she's doing it. Remember Josh from the previous chapter? You promised your boss, Phyllis, that you would talk to him about telling the CEO off in public. Let's see how that might go.

YOU *Josh, I just had Phyllis in my office.*

Josh *Oh yeah? What did the old battle-ax want?*

YOU *She was kind of upset about the staff meeting yesterday.*

Josh *You mean when I went toe to toe with Aveno?*

YOU *Yep, that's what she was talking about.*

Josh *Yeah, it was great. I really nailed him. And in front of everyone, too. It was excellent.*

YOU *That's what I wanted to talk to you about.*

Josh *Oh yeah? Are Phyllis's knickers in a knot?*

YOU *She's upset.*

Josh *Ah, let her stew. It was about time somebody told it like it really is.*

YOU *What do you mean—like it really is?*

Josh *You know perfectly well—if they think I'm hanging around after they tanked my project, they've got another think coming.*

YOU *That's not what I got out of the meeting—the opposite in fact. They loved the idea but funding was a problem.*

Josh *They had enough money for Dedalus.*

YOU *It's because they bought Dedalus that they don't have the capital right now.*

Josh *That's just a ploy. They wouldn't know a great idea if it bit them on the nose. I told Aveno that.*

YOU *So I heard. But, Josh, they do want to fund it. It's just a problem right now.*

Josh *Picking up a second-string contractor is more important than this guidance system. Do you know what this system could do for us?*

YOU *Yeah, Josh…we've discussed that. But Aveno wants to fund it— otherwise, why did he ask us to come back next quarter?*

Josh *That's a lifetime!*

YOU *But we have interim funding—that means he's serious.*

Josh *Well, the interim funding—Yeah, that was good.*

YOU *Honestly, I think you were a bit hard on the guy. I mean, he wants to go ahead but it's a timing thing.*

Josh *Well, maybe. But I was ticked.*

> **YOU** *Sure, I could see that if he'd turned you down. But he didn't.*
> **Josh** *Well, maybe not. Maybe not.*
> **YOU** *So what do you think we can do?*
> **Josh** *What do you mean?*
> **YOU** *I think you were pretty hard on him.*
> **Josh** *Isn't that what he's paid for?*
> **YOU** *To be taken to task in public for something he didn't do? I dunno. Doesn't sound right to me.*
> **Josh** *Well, what do you expect?*
> **YOU** *I don't know...what do you think would make it right?*
> **Josh** *I'm not apologizing!*
> **YOU** *I'm not suggesting that. But what about an e-mail, explaining what you thought?*
> **Josh** *You mean, that I thought he'd turned me down? I suppose that wouldn't be impossible. But I'm not apologizing!*
> **YOU** *Nope—but explaining you hadn't understood him correctly, that would meet him halfway, don't you think?*
> **Josh** *Possibly. Let me think about it.*

Will he send the e-mail? He might, he might not. If he does, you've successfully navigated this one. If not, you and Phyllis will have to put your heads together on what else might be done. Even if he doesn't send it, you need to continue working both sides of the fence—calming down and keeping happy both the higher-ups and your dissenter.

This conversation illustrates how different your views are from his. He thinks taking on the CEO was a little piece of fun; you see your career and his project fading into the sunset. Because he is so uninvolved, unaware, and uninterested in small "p" politics, he doesn't realize the jeopardy he has put the project in.

It also points out that you have a double problem in helping the dissenter smooth out rough edges. He needs to acquire and use different skills. But even before that, you have to convince him it's necessary to learn them. He will see the skills you're talking about as playing politics, bureaucratic meddling, brownnosing, etc. Also, he is probably convinced he has nothing to learn from you—or that what you have to teach him isn't worth learning.

Sort of daunting, isn't it? But not an excuse to give up. It is reasonable to demand a minimum level of functioning in an organization. You don't expect Josh to run the charity drive for Thanksgiving baskets, but neither should you have to spend all your time cleaning up in the wake of destruction. It is doable. Read on.

Teaching Smart People

One of my favorite management writers is Chris Argyris. He always makes such sense. One of his classic articles is "Teaching Smart People How to Learn,"[1] published in the *Harvard Business Review* almost a decade ago. However, what he says hasn't lost currency just because we've changed centuries.

He points out that smart people are often very vested in their smartness—that is, they are used to always having the answers, always being in control. To maintain this fiction (you do know it's a fiction, don't you?), they may telescope their lives only to those areas where they are already top of the class. They convince themselves that if they can't do it, it's not worth doing. Thus, it is easy for them to believe that the need to relate well to coworkers is so much foo-foo dust kicked up by HR types to keep themselves occupied. So although they believe the skills you want to coach them on are stupid, useless, or irrelevant, be aware they may really be trying to avoid an area where they are, at the moment anyhow, incompetent.

Preparation for Coaching

Preparing for coaching is probably the most important part of the whole shooting match and the one least or most poorly done. You're dying to let Josh know how he's doing and coach him to do better. I understand the urge. But don't go in unprepared. Spend some time thinking about the exact nature of the problem, what the desired change would look like, how far you want to push this, how Josh is likely to react, and even your opening lines.

1. *Define the problem precisely*

What is the problem that has got you bent out of shape? On the next page are some things that concern managers about dissenters.

This is not an exhaustive list—there may some unique ways your dissenter annoys the life out of you. The farther down the list the behavior is, the more doubtful the wisdom of trying to change it. Intimidation and belittling others? Absolutely. Pushiness and questioning sacred cows? Probably not. Almost no matter how annoying, dissenters need these qualities to maintain their out-group status and

---

[1] Chris Argyris, "Teaching Smart People How to Learn," *Harvard Business Review* (May/June 1991), pp. 99–109.

Problem	Description
Intimidation	• *The dissenter uses his superior thinking and verbal skills to browbeat others*
Belittling others' contributions	• *No idea can be as good as his* • *Feels defensive if someone else has a good idea*
Attacking superiors verbally	• *Criticizing those in power as if they had no feelings* • *Often phrased like "You're weak-willed, you have no influence, you're too slow, you have no vision, you're letting them push you around."*
Sabotaging efforts	• *Actively trying to slow, distort, or stop others' work*
Uncooperative	• *Not sharing information critical to others' success* • *Dragging his feet*
Not listening/ ignoring	• *Not complying with rules, requests, orders*
Questioning sacred cows	• *Speaking out when people are engaging in cover-up, reinventing wheels, playing games, duplicity, one-up contests, hidden agendas, holding grudges, protecting turf, blind spots, or complacency[2]*
Ignoring direction	• *Doing what he wants rather than what is mandated*
Pushiness	• *Pushing his ideas no matter what, even if—or especially if—no one is listening*

capacity to come up with new and fresh things. Successfully tamping down those attributes may also successfully dampen innovation.

But it's not hard and fast. You'll notice I've put "attacking superiors verbally" fairly high on the list because pragmatically, bosses are less likely to support those who call them idiots. Both you and the dissenter

---

[2] My thanks for this compendium to Sharon VanderKaay, VP Strategy at X-Design Inc., a firm that assists organizations to take a contrarian view of their business opportunities.

know this. The difference is that you accept it and the dissenter rails against it. You need to temper some of his behaviors simply because they fast-track your dissenter into the wilderness even if he doesn't know it. As a rule of thumb, dissenters need to be coached on making the distinction between trashing the idea and trashing the person. We'll cover more about this later.

Once you've picked the problem, make sure it is defined precisely. Not: "He's too rough on people; he isn't polite." Define the *behaviors* at issue: "He calls people idiots behind their backs and to their faces"; "His tone is sarcastic when he disagrees." Have examples of when it happened and why it was a problem. "At the last meeting, Dave had some interesting things to say but he shut down when you made fun of him. We're losing valuable ideas."

2. Decide how far you want to push

Even as a boss, you need to think about how many brownie points you'll use up to get your way. You want the dissenter to change but also to continue to work effectively. You don't want a successful operation where the patient dies. *How* you do the coaching will go a long way to accomplishing this but also ask yourself whether this is a plant-the-flag-on-the-hill issue. If he must change, you need to go the whole nine yards of the process I outline later. You will use up a lot of good will, but if it's critical, you have to do it. If it isn't, decide whether you want to do it at all. Is it worth the investment of your time and the consumption of the brownie points you've built up with Josh? I don't know the answer but I think the question is important.

3. Define the desired change in behavioral terms

You know the problem and how much you want to push for change. Now you need to be as precise about the change you want.

We get sloppy about this step. "I want him to be better, kinder, more humane, less intimidating, more god-like." All worthwhile, but not too specific. Also, keep the desired change within the realm of possibility. Asking Attila the Hun to become St. Francis of Assisi isn't likely. Define the change so someone else watching could see the difference before and after: "He can make it through an entire meeting without yelling, sarcasm, or belittling." If you can't be specific (and it may be difficult with attitude or values), understand it will be vague for Josh too. Even if he changes, the new Josh may not look exactly like you expected.

Finally, be clear on next steps. Will you be doing other things such as monitoring or further coaching?

4. Identify the likely defensive reaction

I would be astonished if the initial reaction to your coaching *isn't* anger and defensiveness, no matter how careful you are. Dissenters and innovators often have an inordinate belief in the rightness of their views, their exceptional knowledge, and their general superior thinking capacity. They simply don't believe others have much to teach them. Given this, it's going to be a shock to hear differently. And naturally, they'll display some defensiveness. This is not a reason to avoid the conversation—quite the opposite. People often use anger to stop others from discussing uncomfortable topics. So you need to push through.

The figure below gives you some examples of what people say when defensive. Which ones are your dissenter likely to use?

Defensive responses aim to sidetrack you from the main point. If you get caught up in a long and protracted argument about whether your take on things is correct, correction it can be avoided. The trick is not to engage. State whatever data you have and/or your views but don't argue whether your concerns are true, accurate, or appropriate. If he says, "You're making a mountain out of a molehill," you just need to say, "I don't agree. I think it's important to talk about how you deal with the technicians." See, not all that hard, is it? Just keep being a broken record whenever a defensive reaction comes up.

However, don't automatically assume every objection is a defense. Some may be legitimate. You'll lose valuable ground if you're on automatic pilot and lower the effectiveness of your coaching by discounting valid reasons for the problem. Say Josh says, "It's Marjorie, isn't it? She's such a troublemaker. She's complained about me to every boss we've ever had." Did you know this? Is it possible he's right? I'm not suggesting he is, but his "defensiveness" may actually be a different slant on a problem you thought you understood.

What defensive reactions might look like

The problem doesn't exist	*It's not true*
	I question the data
	Your perception is wrong
Even if it exists, it's irrelevant	*It doesn't matter*
	I don't have time for this
	What's the big deal?
	You can't tell me what to do
	Does it really matter?

Even if it exists, I have no choice	*I need this for the project* *Your deadline forced me to*
There's something wrong with you	*You're making a mountain out of a molehill* *You're misreading the situation* *You're oversensitive*
There's something wrong with the others	*You're pandering to him* *She's asking too much* *They should grow up* *This is mollycoddling* *If _____ would just do her job, I wouldn't have this problem* *He's taking it too personally* *She shouldn't feel that way* *They should sit up and fly right*

5. Get your opening line down pat

As I mentioned earlier, your first task will be to convince the dissenter he needs to change at all, so your opening lines will be critical. Here are some possibilities that you could apply to a variety of situations:

- Implementing the idea is just as important as the idea itself. Otherwise, it's a waste of creativity.
- You know what politicians say their first duty is? Staying elected. It kind of makes sense. If nobody is listening, you can't influence them. That's true here, too. If people have turned off, they won't hear the great idea. We need to stay elected too.
- We're asking people to take on a really tough challenge. I know it's worthwhile but we need to pace how much we ask of them.
- This is too great an idea to lose—but if we don't have senior management's confidence, it'll go nowhere.
- You know, your idea makes marketing look bad. I know that shouldn't make a difference but it does. We don't want to lose the whole shooting match just because someone's nose is out of joint.
- You know and I know that this idea is important. It's ripe for us. But it hasn't ripened on the tree for everybody. We've got to be smart about how we get them to see what we see.

Once you have the opening line, list the points you want to cover: state the problem and why it's important to talk about it; the data you have to support your view; what needs to be different; how you are willing to help.

Avoid the Word "Coach"

Although I've used the word frequently in this chapter, I almost never do so in the conversations. "Coach" has too much baggage attached to it, too much "I-know-best-you-should-listen." Instead, use substitutes such as the following:
- throw some ideas around
- brainstorm options
- get a different perspective
- be a sounding board

However, even though the words are less prescriptive sounding, you still need to do the coaching. If the dissenter resists, you may need to move to expressions that make it clear there is an imperative or urgency about the matter. These might include:
- need to work through the problem
- decide how to avoid the problem
- resolve the concern

And remember, although you would prefer the dissenter to want to be coached, there may be times when you have to do it even if he doesn't.

Coaching the Dissenter

As I mentioned in a previous chapter, despite their willingness to sound off quite freely about others' faults, dissenters may not do so in the person's presence. They have trouble—as many people do—confronting work issues head on rather than in corridors and behind backs. The dissenter is not necessarily being underhanded. He literally may not know how to handle the situation differently. But since he can be quite vocal, this will cause much bad feeling if allowed to continue. The following steps will help you to coach him.

1. Surface the problem
Josh and his lab technician have been in a running battle ever since you took over. She complains he never takes any of her suggestions; he thinks she's too slow and mouthy to boot. Both need coaching. You're going to start with Josh. You have done the homework outlined above. The technical meeting is just winding down.

> **YOU** *Okay, Josh, anything else?*
> **Josh** *Nope, I'm done.*
> **YOU** *I have one more thing. How are things going with Marjorie?*
> **Josh** *Same as ever. I wish you'd get rid of her.*
> **YOU** *Her skills are pretty scarce. She'd be difficult to replace.*
> **Josh** *Surely we could get someone who wasn't constantly bitching and complaining.*
> **YOU** *Even if we could, it would throw off our schedule to get the new person up to speed. I think it makes more sense to get your working relationship on a better footing.*
> **Josh** *Well, great. Talk to her.*
> **YOU** *I will, but in these matters, Josh, I think it takes two to tango.*
> **Josh** *Huh?*
> **YOU** *When things are going badly, there can be a lot of tit for tat.*
> **Josh** *You think I'm just going to put up with her? I give as good as I get.*
> **YOU** *But that's the problem, no? It's hard to make things better if everybody is just trying to get back at each other.*
> **Josh** *She started it.*
> **YOU** *You know, it's kind of like peace in Northern Ireland. I mean, how could anything happen unless somebody decided to make a fresh start?*
> **Josh** *Fine, I'll wipe the slate clean. Now are we done?*
> **YOU** *Well, I'm glad to hear that, but I think it takes more than good will to resolve a problem like this.*

In opening the conversation, make sure you state why you feel it's important to have the discussion ("I think it makes more sense to get your working relationship on a better footing") and what impact not resolving the problem will have ("it would throw off our schedule"). Josh probably has an inkling of where you want to take this conversation and tries to cut you off at the pass. This is a type of defensive reaction and is to be expected. However, you can't stop here because as soon as Marjorie annoys him again, the vendetta will be back in full swing. You can't take his assurance that the hatchet is buried.

You will also notice Josh tries to deflect the conversation to Marjorie's role. This is understandable. From his point of view, Marjorie is the problem. You want to acknowledge that there is a problem from both sides ("I can talk to Marjorie"), but keep focusing on Josh's responsibility to resolve the issue.

2. Coach
Josh had a defensive reaction to your attempt to open the subject. Don't let it deter you. Keep moving on to the crux of the matter—helping him modify his behavior.

YOU	*What could you do differently to make things better?*
Josh	*Whoa! I'm not the problem.*
YOU	*Josh, if it takes two to tango, both people need to work at it.*
Josh	*Well, if she would just do what I say and not argue…*
YOU	*Josh, I'm asking what you can do, not Marjorie.*
Josh	*Sam, it's Marjorie…*
YOU	*Sorry, Josh. I just don't buy that. I think there's always something we can do.*
Josh	*Like what?*
YOU	*For example, you said Marjorie argues with you…*
Josh	*Constantly.*
YOU	*What if, rather than sloughing off her suggestions, you explained why they wouldn't work?*
Josh	*I don't have time to explain her job to her.*
YOU	*Which is what?*
Josh	*To do what I tell her.*
YOU	*No, Josh, that's not right. Marjorie is a skilled technician. She can tell us when things are going wrong.*
Josh	*Nothing would go wrong if she would just do what she's told.*
YOU	*Josh, I need you to resolve this situation in a way that works for everyone. A start is to listen to her.*
Josh	*But Sam, they're stupid suggestions.*
YOU	*All of them? Didn't Marjorie point out that the tolerances on sub-system B were out of whack?*
Josh	*Okay, lucky break.*
YOU	*How do you know she hasn't got more of those?*
Josh	*I tell you, it was just a guess.*
YOU	*Come on, Josh. You know that's not true. Marjorie saved our bacon. And might be able to do even more if she got listened to.*
Josh	*Sam, I don't have the time.*
YOU	*How long does it take? What did you say last time?*
Josh	*When she made a stupid suggestion? I told her so.*
YOU	*That the suggestion was stupid?*
Josh	*Of course.*
YOU	*But why was it stupid?*
Josh	*Sam, you wouldn't understand. It's way beyond your capabilities.*
YOU	*Maybe so, but would Marjorie?*

Josh	*Might have.*
YOU	*So what is the problem with explaining?*
Josh	*It's a waste of time. Why bother?*
YOU	*Because the more she gets it, the better she can do for you. And she finds that out by understanding why her suggestions won't work.*
Josh	*God, this is a huge waste of time.*
YOU	*But isn't it also a waste of time fighting with her?*
Josh	*Well, yeah, that's why you need to get rid of her...*
YOU	*Josh, will you try something? Just for next week, try explaining why something won't work. Just try it and see if it makes a difference.*
Josh	*I don't see...*
YOU	*Josh, I need you to try this out. Will you?*
Josh	*Oh, all right, if it's such a big deal to you.*

This conversation could have gone on a lot longer, depending on how defensive Josh was and also how good he is at throwing up smoke screens. I made him not all that sophisticated on both counts to save a couple of trees. But you get the drift. Expect the coaching to be larded with continual objections about doing it at all.

It's always a good idea to start off with asking the person what he suggests could be done to resolve the problem. If he suggests something viable (i.e., *not* "if she would just do what I say"), you are already ahead since it's more likely he'll implement a solution he has generated.

But don't be surprised if he can't or won't. You can force him into the conversation but you can't make him want to solve the problem. You will probably have to come up with a suggestion for the change yourself. However, also expect that as soon as you make it, Josh will reject it out of hand. You may have to spend more time than you think reasonable explaining why it's important to explain the *why* of his actions.

Expect to come back to this discussion several times. It's unlikely Josh will do anything the first time you talk to him. You'll probably need to have the conversation a couple of times before it even hits his radar screen. Because of his resistance, progress will probably be slow.

Once he has started listening better, he may see there's something in what you're saying. Don't expect him to acknowledge it ("Gee, Sam, you've completely changed my life. I don't know how to thank you!"), but if, deep in his little heart, he knows things are better, he may be less resistant to further interventions. Not eager, just less resistant.

However, there could be a point where getting him to change would be a Pyrrhic victory. That is, the damage to your relationship would be so great that you end up worse off than when you started. Obviously, you don't want it to get to this point. So, be aware when the resistance is so great you must back off.

Luckily, with people like Josh, the signs of resistance are unlikely to be subtle. He will argue vehemently. As he is doing so, gauge how strongly he feels. If forcing the change, or even the discussion, will increase the chances he will leave or stop contributing, decide whether the risk is worth it. If not, find a way to exit gracefully out of the conversation. Agreeing with the last thing the dissenter says usually works, as in:

"Sam, this is stupid. Lab technicians are born whiners. If you just ignore them, they either quit or shut up."

"Uh-huh. So that's how you think it works best."

"Absolutely. Don't give it another thought."

Then you withdraw. But remember you back down only if the cost is becoming greater than the potential benefit. You have to expect some resistance and defensiveness. It is only when either gets to a crisis point that you withdraw to fight another day, all the while remembering that Rome and relationships aren't built in a day.

The Use of Memorable Metaphors

Your dissenter may use his smarts to come up with very inventive ways to criticize his opponents. I have found, through grievous trial and error, that it is significantly more difficult to mend fences if there have been memorable insults. For example, early in my career as a manager, I told an employee that all he ever did was complain. I likened it to dropping cow pucks in the road and leaving. Note to those from southern climates: Pucks are what hockey players push around the ice. What cows leave on the road freezes in the winter and sometimes kids use them to play hockey. I told another person that giving her anything to file was like consigning it to the black hole of Calcutta. Neither of them ever forgot the phrasing. So encourage the dissenter to use unmemorable words when he's talking. Believe me, it's better.

3. Require change

In the previous stages, you supported change. Sometimes that's enough. When it isn't, you have to *require* it. Changing is difficult. For Josh to do what you want, he'll have to ignore his gut reactions and take the high road. While it's the more productive route, it's not the obvious one in the midst of finger pointing nor is it, let's face it, the most emotionally satisfying. Scoring off an enemy is more attractive than struggling with personal change. But if it is causing a major problem, you need to address it. You need to not simply support the change, but require it.

	YOU	*Josh, got a minute?*
	Josh	*Sure.*
	YOU	*How're things going with Marjorie?*
	Josh	*Could be better. She's up to her old tricks.*
	YOU	*I thought you were going to try something new.*
	Josh	*I thought about it. It's not going to work. I mean, Marjorie's not going to stop making stupid suggestions, is she?*
Remind him of your agreement.	**YOU**	*Let's stick to your part. Have you tried explaining why her suggestions don't work?*
	Josh	*Nah...it's useless.*
Don't let him off the hook.	**YOU**	*How do you know if you won't give it a try?*
	Josh	*What's the use? After all, you're born with what brains you have.*
	YOU	*How do you know helping her understand won't make her better on the job?*
	Josh	*Oh come on, why should it?*
	YOU	*But if you don't try it, how can you know?*
	Josh	*Sam, I don't have the time...*
Keep focusing on his behavior.	**YOU**	*Josh, I'm really serious about this. Marjorie is too valuable to lose just because nobody's listening.*
	Josh	*I'm not holding her hand.*
Make the requirement clear.	**YOU**	*I'm not asking you to. I don't want to do this, but unless I see an improvement, I'll have to agree to the transfer she's asked for.*
	Josh	*Fine. Then we can replace her with somebody better.*

	YOU	*No, I don't think so, Josh. First of all, her skill set is pretty scarce. And if you can't get along with Marjorie, I can't see you doing any better with somebody else.*
	Josh	*You can't do that! Who's going to do the grunt work?*
	YOU	*Good question.*
	Josh	*You can't do this to me!*
	YOU	*Josh, all I'm asking you to do is explain your decisions. How hard can that be?*
	Josh	*It's a waste of my time.*
	YOU	*It's going to be an even bigger waste to have to do her job as well as yours.*
	Josh	*You can't do that to me!*
	YOU	*Will you give it a try?*
	Josh	*All right, all right. If you promise I can keep Marjorie.*
Don't give away the prize before the behavior change.	**YOU**	*Nope, if Marjorie wants to leave, I need to do all I can to keep her. If that means a transfer, that's what I'll give her. Unless she decides she wants to stay on with you.*
	Josh	*This is blackmail!*
	YOU	*Come on, Josh. Just tell her why her suggestions won't work. Honestly, it's not going to be that hard.*

These conversations are never easy, especially with someone who is quite convinced he has no part in the problem. You may have to resort to hardball just to get him to try out the new behavior. You're between a rock and a hard place. You can't afford to lose Josh but neither can you keep losing lab technicians solely because they are treated shabbily.

If you are at this stage with Josh and have decided you must insist on some behavior change, however minor, don't expect he'll like it. I know this sounds ridiculous, but managers often keep arguing endlessly in the hopes that something they say will suddenly make Josh exclaim, "Gosh, I never thought of that. You're right. I've been terribly difficult and I'll mend my ways." If you strive for that, you'll be waiting a long time for that puppy to grow up. As long as you've made it clear why you need the change, what the change is, and allowed him sufficient time to vent, you've done your duty.

If you have to push him down this path, expect he will complain all the way down it. Even if he gets quite proficient at the new skill and possibly even sees its benefit, he will not stop railing against a manager who forces him to do something he doesn't want to. On this, you'll just have to suck it in and accept that management is not a popularity contest.

By the by, don't threaten Marjorie's transfer or any other sanction unless you are willing to follow through. If you don't when push comes to shove, Josh will rightly see you're all talk, no action. And that will make it even harder next time you have this kind of discussion. So bring out only those hammers you are actually willing to nail with.

4. Follow through

Follow-through is another thing managers hate to do and aren't typically good at. There is an understandable reluctance. So much of management is getting along—I give a little, you give a little. It's uncomfortable to keep coming back to an issue. Following up can be simply repeating your expectations. It doesn't have to be negative. It can be praising the effort Josh is making. But it usually isn't fun. However, once you have required the behavior, you need to make sure it happens. Otherwise, you confirm you really were making a mountain out of a molehill.

And anyhow, isn't it better to know there's a problem than merrily gathering daisies, assuming all is well? You'll be forgiven if you're tempted to answer, "Let me think about it."

Another Example

This is pretty tough stuff, so let me give you another example. Josh again. This time, his memorable encounter with the CEO. Let's say he didn't send the e-mail to Aveno, explaining that he had misunderstood what had happened. But things have calmed down and nobody's talking about apologies and such any more. However, you know that you have to speak to Josh about how he refers to senior management. He does it too frequently and too openly not to have some repercussions eventually.

Let's do the prep work:

1. **Define the problem precisely.** This one at least, is easy. Josh criticizes senior people as if they had no human feelings. Phrases like "idiot" and "couldn't recognize a good idea if it bit you on the nose" make it less likely the senior people being criticized will fund the project. This may be obvious to you but may not be to Josh.

2. ***Decide how far to push it.*** Is this a to-the-wall thing or a I-wish-you-wouldn't-do-it thing? You know your senior executives better than I do. If they would take revenge because of a personal slight, you might have to go to the wall. If they could rise above the occasional insult, it's still worth talking but you needn't go as far in requiring the change.

3. ***Define the desired change in behavioral terms.*** What does Josh need to do differently? Not calling the CEO names, certainly, but are you asking for more? Do you want him to be polite (which may be tough), or listen better (still a challenge) or help you sell the idea (great, but how likely is that?)? Each possibility will result in a different conversation. Keeping in the realm of possibility. Let's say you'd be happy if he just refrained from bad-mouthing the senior people, both to their faces and behind their backs.

4. ***Identify the defensive reaction likely.*** Josh thought the confrontation with Aveno was pretty neat. So his defensive reactions and your responses could be:

Defensive Reaction	*Possible Response*
"What's the big deal?"	"He holds the purse strings. So if he thinks it's a big deal, it's a big deal."
"You're pandering to him."	"Maybe so. But it would be a shame to lose all you've done just because of a few words."
"He's taking it too personally."	"Possibly. But neither of us can control that. If he's going to take it personally and it's going to affect our funding, isn't it worth paying attention?"

5. ***Get your opening line down pat.*** How do you want to open this can of worms? Let's see by launching into the conversation.

	YOU	*Hey, Josh, got a minute?*
	Josh	*Yeah, I guess so. I'm waiting for a test run.*
	YOU	*Great. You know, we have to go back in couple of months to re-present the project.*
	Josh	*Yeah, I hope they develop some brains before then.*
	YOU	*Hmmm…you know…what you just said…that's what I wanted to talk about.*

	Josh	*What?*
	YOU	*The crack about developing some brains.*
Defensive reaction. Let it run its course.	**Josh**	*Ah, Sam, it was just a joke. Don't get all bent out of shape.*
State the problem.	**YOU**	*I know, but others don't see it that way. They can get pretty ticked.*
	Josh	*Well, that's their problem, isn't it?*
Explain why it's important.	**YOU**	*I think it's our problem, too. We need their support. We don't want to lose it just because someone took offense at a name.*
More defensive reaction.	**Josh**	*Well, what do you expect me to do? Brownnose?*
	YOU	*Not at all. But there is a difference between being a brownnose and not offending people.*
	Josh	*Ah, come on, Sam. I tell it like it is. These guys are earning the big bucks. They should be able to take it.*
	YOU	*I'm not disagreeing, but what if one of them decides not to?*
	Josh	*Like I said, that's his problem, no?*
	YOU	*Even if it means he decides not to support the funding?*
	Josh	*He can't do that! That would be stupid!*
Convince.	**YOU**	*I agree but why take the risk?*
	Josh	*There's no way he should be against me just because he can't take a few home truths.*
Broken record is effective here.	**YOU**	*Agreed, but again, why take the risk?*
	Josh	*You think anybody would be stupid enough to tank a great project just because his nose was out of joint?*
Again, broken record.	**YOU**	*I'm not saying anybody would, but is it worth running the risk?*
	Josh	*Boy, is that stupid.*
	YOU	*But is it?*
	Josh	*Well, maybe not. So you want me to brownnose?*
Coach.	**YOU**	*No, but would it be all that hard to stop calling them idiots?*

Josh	*But it's true!*
YOU	*I'm not sure I agree with you. But even if it is, lots of things are true without needing to rub people's noses in it. You're carrying around a couple of extra pounds. Do you need someone continually reminding you of that?*
Josh	*I guess not. Okay, okay, so maybe I can tone it down a bit.*
YOU	*Great. What would that look like, do you think?*
Josh	*Okay, I'll lose the idiot jokes.*
YOU	*Sounds good. Do you think you might even be able to see your way to thinking that they're not stupid but just have different priorities?*
Josh	*Whoa! I don't buy that! I'll stop saying they're stupid but I won't stop thinking it.*
YOU	*Okay, just thought I'd give it a try.*
Josh	*Nice try but no cigar.*

You notice Josh thinks there are only two options: brownnosing or saying what he thinks. If that were true, we'd probably make the same choice he did. You are trying to help him see the gray, the other possibilities that allow him to stay true to his values without attacking your bosses.

You also need to help Josh understand that how he affects others makes a difference. The great thing about people like him is they are so internally focused. They don't need to be motivated or cajoled to work on issues they care about. But because their drive comes primarily from the inside, they may not find much value in assessing the impact of their actions and words on others. He may need you to point out the effect he's having before he can even entertain the idea of changing it.

In the dialog, you act like a broken record several times. This can be very effective. You keep repeating the important point, no matter what the other person raises. The broken record phrase is important. If it's "Do it because I said so," your chances of success are dim. However, a phrase or an argument that makes a dint in Josh's armor ("Is it worth running the risk?") may get you somewhere.

As I have mentioned earlier, you may not get the agreed-upon behavior at first. You may need to cycle back and do the requiring change stuff. However, you have introduced the topic in a way that didn't get Josh's hackles up, or at least not for long. This will make it easier for follow-up conversations.

Summary

Coaching people who don't want to be coached has got to be one of the toughest things for a manager. Its difficulty is exacerbated when the person doesn't think there is a problem and, moreover, is too valuable to lose. But it is also one of the most important things you do, not only for the smooth running of the section but also for the person being coached. She may not thank you for it but your coaching widens her skill set. It gives them other ways to deal with problems. It makes them more valuable as employees. Difficult though it is, it has a payoff both in the short and long term. And difficult though it is, it's nothing when compared with dealing with underground dissent, the subject of the next chapter.

Main Points

- A dissenter too far outside the norms can seriously threaten your effectiveness.
- You need to convince the dissenter he needs relating skills.
- Preparing for coaching entails identifying the exact problem, specifying the desired change, deciding how far to push, anticipating likely defensive reactions, and even practicing your opening lines.
- Coaching the dissenter includes bringing the problem to the surface, requiring change, and following through.

CHAPTER 10

୧୨

Identifying
Underground Dissent

*It's not always easy to know whether an organization or unit
is getting along well or actually suppressing dissent. On the
surface, both look the same. This chapter gives the
manager a test to determine whether there is
underground dissent in the workplace.*

Is Silence Consent?

Have you ever been in a meeting where the boss says, "So does anybody disagree?" There is silence. Then he says, "Okay, silence is consent, you know," and proceeds to other business.

We know what happens. Three months later, he's pounding the
table, "Why isn't this happening? We discussed it last quarter." People
don't say anything, but he's ticked enough to keep pushing. "You,
Andy, customers were supposed to get samples. What happened?"

Andy shifts in his chair and looks for support. But everyone's eyes
are fixed firmly on the table, so he says, "Well, Brian, the samples—
they were kind of tatty. And anyhow, I never thought customers would
go for them, even if they were free."

Brian shifts his laser focus to Andrea. "Tatty! How come they were
tatty?"

Andrea clears her throat. "Brian...we couldn't get the silk blend the
prototype was made of...we had to go with a polyester that
stretched..."

"Enough! If there were problems, why didn't somebody speak up
at the time? Now we've lost three months!"

Brian's right. If Andrea had pushed the production problems or Andy the customer reaction, a different decision might have been made or they would have gone ahead with a better understanding of the problems. In either case, the group would not have wasted time going nowhere. Why don't people speak up? Because if I say it's not going to work, my boss, who obviously is deeply in love with his idea, will slam me. And why do I assume that? Because he's done it before.

The phenomenon of silence when dissent would be appropriate is well documented. Warren Bennis, leadership expert, found that 7 out of 10 employees say nothing rather than correct their superiors—up to and including allowing them to make mistakes.[1] The past provides us with similar data. A study of the decision-making in the Kennedy Administration during the Bay of Pigs invasion concluded that the disaster went forward *because* the group was very cohesive and John Kennedy was a strong leader. This produced pressure for a uniformity of thought and silenced those like Dean Rusk and Arthur Schlesinger, who had considerable doubts about the undertaking.[2]

Silence is not necessarily consent and may even be an indication of underground dissent.

The Three Faces of Underground Dissent

Underground dissent. This is the stage that gives a bad name to all dissent and is what managers understandably fear. The signs are subtle.

Your boss is a micromanaging control freak, so you inundate him with details. You tell him everything; he just can't figure out what he needs to know. You provide off-the-wall options so your boss will have to reject them, leaving only what you wanted anyhow. You admit that some piece of information he absolutely must have once existed but now can't be found, probably due to the server crash six months ago.

Underground dissent doesn't have to be active. It could be knowing a machine will break down and doing nothing. Or "forgetting" to tell the boss that the meeting across town has been canceled. Or omitting to mention that this too-good-to-be-true price is available only if she makes the decision by close of business today. There is even the story of a boss who was always looking for a pen. A disgruntled employee systematically removed them. When the employee left, a huge stash of pens was found behind a supply cabinet.[3]

---

[1] Charlan Jeanne Nemeth, "Managing Innovation: When More is Less," *California Management Review* (Vol. 40, No. 1, Fall 1997), p. 65.
[2] Ibid.
[3] Carol Vinzant, "Messing with the Boss' Head," *Fortune* (May 1, 2000), pp. 329–31.

Underground dissenters vary in their sophistication. Some are the Tiger Woods of this sport and others duffers. Here are three levels.

The Underground Dissent Duffer

The least sophisticated underground dissenter isn't usually very successful because it's pretty easy to see that he's trying to sabotage things. In a meeting, he might say something like "Even if Tom is right, we should still implement the recommendations" or "It won't work and I'll do it just to prove it." Notice the straight-out approach. On the one hand, he's telling you he doesn't agree and on the other, he's trying to have it happen anyhow. He wants it to fail. Easy to see through. Not a sophisticated player.

The Sophisticated Underground Player

The next level is more savvy. He knows that if an initiative is run up the flagpole, he needs to salute even if he disagrees. To express his discontent, he usually expresses variations on the following two statements:

"Think the objective is great. Love it."

and

"Just some concerns about the process to get there."

The group then spends all its time tweaking *how* to make the decision (need mountains of background information, not everybody who should be involved is at the table, need to rethink decisions already made). If you spend enough time massaging the process, you don't actually do anything. This player doesn't question the end—he just mires the road to get there.

The Master Underground Dissenter

The top-of-the-line underground dissenter is very sophisticated. This approach is subtle, so I'll give an example by way of explanation. The CEO of a large multioffice, multiregion organization decided to break up the centralized decision-making and evolve power out to the regions. He put together a group of people from across the organization to recommend how to do that. Roger got himself appointed to this team.

Roger was VP of Operations and had been with the company his entire career. He knew the political ins and outs and where all the skeletons were buried. He had seen CEOs come and go, some who agreed with him that power should be centralized and others like the current one who preferred it closer to the customer. For years, he had scared off CEOs by prophesying typhoons, tornadoes, and all manner of natural disasters if power was decentralized (mostly out of his area). Previous CEOs, not being technical experts, bought it. However, the current CEO had more meteorological expertise and vision. Nope, he'd chance the weather disasters and move decision-making to the regions.

Roger was too savvy to use either of the other underground dissent approaches described above. After having gotten himself appointed to the team mentioned above, he played his cards carefully. He supported any status quo leanings by other team members (and let's face it, unless we assume our predecessors were absolute boobs, there are always good arguments for the way we used to do things). But he didn't support the status quo himself. Quite the opposite. Everything he said was completely supportive of the CEO. Nobody could accuse him of resisting change or not being a team player.

His true brilliance as an underground dissenter showed up in a seemingly innocuous change. He got the team to agree that some national consistency was desirable. After all, where would McDonald's be if in Milwaukee you got crispy, julienned preppie French fries and in Toronto you got the dark, thick, hand-cut ones that make you salivate at the thought? Sorry, I got carried away.

Some national consistency. After all, customers in Region A had a right to expect the same type and level of service as those in Region B— so some national consistency was required.

"Some" is such a loose word, isn't it? You may think "some" French fries fit into the palm of your hand; "some" to me is falling off the sides of the dish. Roger, needless to say, had the latter definition. By the time he was finished—well, I'm pretty sure the regions could decide how many cafeteria staff to hire and I'm positive they had control over office layout, but beyond that—national consistency kicked in. See how sophisticated that is? Roger can say he loves the objective and is crazy about the process. Just a couple of unimportant implementation details that nobody needs to worry about.

Although I'm making rather light of this (and you have to admit, it has its amusing side), there are some very real consequences. Roger managed to look supportive while fossilizing the status quo. He appeared to give the CEO what he wanted but it was in name only.

Underground dissent can be played at various levels, and the more sophisticated the player, the harder it is to catch and combat.

Why Does Dissent Go Underground?

If you remember, the first and second stages of dissent can be important and positive contributions to innovation. The first is *situational dissent* when someone who is normally pretty content has a bone to pick. The second stage, also positive although more difficult to deal with, occurs when people take on a *dissenter role*. They are more likely to protest past the point when efficient organizations want them to shut up and go along. As we have discussed, organizations that tolerate both types well are more likely to recognize and leverage innovative ideas.

However, if managers start to value efficiency too much over innovation, they can push employees into underground dissent. They do this by treating legitimate objections ("We can't do this unless we kill ourselves for the next eight weeks") as if the dissenter were betraying some sacred trust. In an environment that suppresses dissent, people who point out plain truths are considered disloyal, not team players, and troublemakers and treated accordingly. Thus, dissent is suppressed.

But a manager who labels dissenters this way often confuses the truth of the dissenter's statement with the manager's ability to do anything about it. It may be that people will to have to work insane hours to meet a deadline. The manager may not be able to do anything about it. But because he can't do anything about it, he will sometimes actively discourage people from bringing it up at all. He doesn't realize that by being unwilling to acknowledge the truth of something that is plain to everyone, he sets up conditions for that discontent to go underground. If he does it enough times, people will know that they cannot raise legitimate beefs without being labeled as troublemakers. But neither the truth nor the wish to be heard go away. Instead, they go underground and in that process, become distorted into the kind of destructive force we fear.

Underground dissent is "a way of communicating when you can't, or when you're afraid to speak up for yourself," says William Lundin, co-author of *When Smart People Work for Dumb Bosses*.[4] And fear is why 70% of people surveyed don't speak out. Underground dissent is a way for those who feel downtrodden to express their discontent without reprisal. For those without power, it is a weapon.

---

[4] Ibid.

Why Worry About Underground Dissent?

So what? Really, aside from some inconvenience and game playing, so what if people go underground?

The American Society for Industrial Security found that employees are the leading conduits for proprietary information leaks.[5] It is estimated that two-thirds of all intellectual property losses can be traced to this source. In our massively competitive environment, the enemy within is much more dangerous than any outside our gates. And are leaks more likely to come from the happy and fulfilled employee or the one who feels unappreciated or unheard? Disgruntled employees cost you money.

In addition, underground dissent is lost innovation. Marc Spooner, a University of Ottawa professor, studies creativity and deviance. He has found that creativity requires nonconformity and risk-taking but so does deviance.[6] You can see that in the examples we've already discussed. You have to put as much creativity into finding the exact thing that will frustrate your boss (love the pens!) as generating that which will thrill her.

Worse, Spooner found that once you start down one road, it snowballs. People who initially choose to be deviant tend to do it more and more. They run into or seek out like-minded people. Through these associations and practice, they get better and better at expressing their deviance (which means getting better at putting a spoke in the wheel without getting caught). It is also easy to get the negative cycle going. The good news is that this cycle works either way. You also tend to be more and more creative once you start expressing it. If you can get people onto the innovation track, they're more likely to stay on it.

So people in organizations are going to be creative. Whether its expression is negative or positive can be the difference between an innovative company and one in constant trouble.

The final reason to worry about underground dissent is the most insidious and dangerous. I once worked in a company where things were not going well. It was decided to do a team-building exercise. We were split into two groups, both with the same task. But the exercise was set up so that the only way both teams could succeed was to cooperate. Donna was a very sharp cookie and saw this immediately. She quietly pointed that out. Her group listened politely and then proceeded to plot a competitive strategy. We went on for a little while longer, not getting anywhere. Donna again made her suggestion. A

---

[5] Tim Carvell, "By the Way…Your Staff Hates You," *Fortune* (September 28, 1998), p. 202.
[6] If you remember, creativity is having new and different ideas. Innovation is being able to turn the ideas into something valuable. And deviance is actions that are not socially acceptable.

polite silence. She made one more attempt. Finally, time ran out and neither team succeeded.

In the debrief afterwards, the group realized it had missed the teamwork boat. If I had been Donna, I would have been beating my chest, yelling, "I told you so!" But she didn't (which possibly explains why she was more popular than me). Rather than point out that the problem stemmed not from not knowing the answer, but from ignoring it, she participated in the debrief as if she was having the same revelations as the rest of the group. She joined in the discussion about the value of teamwork and vowed, like the others, to do things differently next time.

I mulled over this strange behavior that evening and then it came to me. The company placed a very high value on consensus—well, not exactly consensus but at least the appearance of agreement. Donna demonstrated why she was successful in the company. She knew it was better to let the group fail and be with them to lick their wounds than to stand out and lead the way. In a culture where harmony was everything, it was better to lose *with* your colleagues than battle *against* them.

This story illustrates what Milos Forman, a film director who fled his native Czechoslovakia, understands. Forman has become well known for his controversial films, one of which was *The People vs. Larry Flynt*. Some people charged that he portrayed *Hustler* publisher Larry Flynt much more sympathetically than his occupation or lifestyle warranted. On being asked why, Forman replied, "This country is the strongest in the world not because it's the richest or biggest or smartest, but because it's the freest. Censorship is bad enough, but even worse is the self-censorship which it provokes. Because you start to tamper with your own honesty. And subsequently you are not who you are."

He understands that true censorship comes when repression of dissent becomes internalized. It's not simply that it goes underground—it is that the person himself no longer has dissenting thoughts. It is the greatest danger of all—that little by little, piece by piece, without meaning to, you can create a climate where people censor their own thoughts. They must not even think the different idea, the new thought, the radical departure. The real danger in not paying attention to how your actions affect dissent is that you may never know how successfully you've censored it. Now that's a scary thought.

Underground Dissent Quiz

The biggest problem with underground dissent is that organizations don't know they have it. Things seem pretty calm on the surface, people look like they get along. But funnily enough, targets are missed, deadlines slip, nobody is available to put on that little extra push. Not only do you lack innovation, you have trouble getting the regular work done. So the first step is knowing whether these problems are due to underground dissent. The quiz below will help. It's not the be-all and end-all—that is, it's not one of those battery of tests you get at a career counseling session. It is based more on my observations of the symptoms and signals of underground dissent. It has four sections. The first is about organizational culture; the second, about your relationship with your boss and colleagues; the third, your unit; and finally, how you view dissent.

For each statement, check "agree" or "disagree." I know some items are the kind where you sort of agree and sort of disagree, depending on the circumstances and the time of year. Lighten up. This is just an estimate, so go with your first reaction.

Underground Dissent Quiz		
The culture of the organization. In this company,	**Agree**	**Don't Agree**
You don't want to stick your neck out too far—it might get chopped off.		
It's wrong to be wrong—i.e., failure is not acceptable.		
The high flyers are best at agreeing with the boss.		
You've got to watch your back.		
Troublemakers are ostracized.		
Mistakes are a source of embarrassment.		
People who identify problems are troublemakers.		
A team player does not question policy or party line.		
People who object too much are whiners.		
Somebody always has to take the hit for a mistake.		
Subtotal		

How my colleagues/boss act	Agree	Don't Agree
There is a lot of backstabbing.		
Behind-the-scenes deals are common.		
It's more important to look like we agree than surface real issues.		
People are often reluctant to say when something won't work.		
Most of us wait to hear what the boss thinks before expressing an opinion.		
We keep doing strategic plans that don't lead to anything really new.		
I worry about my relationship with my colleagues if I am seen as a troublemaker.		
Loyalty means giving the boss what she wants, regardless.		
I don't really trust my boss.		
I can't trust my colleagues farther than I can throw them.		
Subtotal		

How my employees act	Agree	Don't Agree
When I ask to have something done, sometimes it just doesn't seem to happen.		
When I ask why, the excuses are vague.		
There is little or no disagreement with official pronouncements.		
My employees tend to agree with what I say.		
My guys don't ask a lot of questions. They just find out what needs to be done and the meeting's over.		
I think there's a real stinker in the group but I haven't been able to catch him at anything yet.		
Sometimes I feel like I'm the only one who cares about our unit's goals.		
I have to be constantly vigilant to keep things on track.		
Nobody will tell me bad news or they dress it up so much, I can't figure out the problem.		
I don't know who is opposed to any given project.		
Subtotal		

What I believe. There's no point in dissenting because:	Agree	Don't Agree
It won't do any good.		
My boss won't change.		
I'm not sure I'm right.		
I don't want to cause trouble.		
No one else is doing it. Why should I?		
I'm not good at confrontation.		
Things might get ugly.		
People will be hurt.		
I'll be disliked.		
I worry about reprisals.		
Subtotal		
Grand Total		

Scoring

Compute the subtotal for each of the four sections. Generally speaking, the following ranges apply:

1–2 Agrees in each section	Dissent is probably in the open
3–4 Agrees	There may be a problem
5–6 Agrees	Dissent is probably underground
7 plus Agrees	Dissent is tunneling throughout

Add up the subtotals for each of the four sections. The total number of agrees can be assessed against the following table:

1–10 Agrees overall	Dissent is probably in the open
11–20 Agrees	There may be a problem
21–30 Agrees	Dissent is probably underground
30 plus Agrees	Dissent is tunneling throughout

Analysis

How did you do? Are you and your organization at the lower or higher end of the scale? If you are at the lower, congratulations—looks like you don't have a lot of underground dissent. It would be astounding, and a bit suspicious, if your total score was zero or anywhere close. Organizations always have a little bit of underground stuff. Your group may be reluctant to hurt other people's feelings or be suffering the effects of a previous boss. In addition, some descriptors could be innocuous. If you have a new group of employees, you might have to be vigilant because they lack the experience to make the right judgments. But if your score is in the lower range, it's usually a good sign. You can go directly to Chapter 13, Kickstarting Your Innovation Culture.

But for those whose scores are approaching basketball numbers, let's look a little deeper. When you look at the subtotals, where are most of the "agrees"? Is it in the culture, with your colleagues and boss, with your employees, or with yourself? It's not atypical for the problems to be pervasive. How your group acts has something to do with how you're managing but is also influenced by what you have to do to survive with your boss and among your colleagues, and with the pressure put on all of you by the culture.

Even if the assessment of your own group has turned up relatively few "agrees," high scores in other areas mean your group is likely affected by working in an environment that favors the underground even if they themselves are pretty aboveboard. So even if your group is okay, you need to be mindful of the wider culture in which you are operating.

The next chapter will address how to surface underground dissent in yourself and in those around you—when it's possible and when it's not.

Summary

Underground dissent is that destructive way of dealing with problems that has given all forms of speaking truth to power a bad name. As we have discussed, other types of dissent—the ones that have not gone underground—need to be fostered in organizations to increase their innovative capacity. But some companies have yet to put a foot on that path. They are still mired in a culture of underground dissent. They are that ulcer-producing, high turnover kind of place everyone hates, isn't very productive, and certainly isn't innovative. You'd need to address this problem even if innovation weren't the imperative it is.

Main Points

- Dissent is destructive if it goes underground.
- Underground dissent actively and covertly works against the goals of the company.
- The more sophisticated the underground dissent, the harder to catch and to combat.
- A quiz helps managers identify sources of underground dissent.

CHAPTER 11

ဆင်

Surfacing Dissent in and around You

Even if the manager identifies underground dissent, it's not easy to surface. Managers need to help employees and colleagues be more open and also to question their own motives. This chapter shows how.

Changing the Culture

In the last chapter, you used a quiz to identify the sources of underground dissent in your organization. This is an important first step since companies that don't know they have the problem attribute phenomena like missed deadlines and failed projects to other causes when underground dissent may be at the root.

To address this issue, you have to change the culture. Whenever I say that, managers throw up their hands. "I can't change the culture," they protest. "I'm just a cog in a big machine."

Changing the culture is such a big, amorphous, and vague thing. Everybody agrees it needs to be done, few people know how to do it and everybody thinks it's somebody else's job. Middle managers wish senior managers would do it and senior managers say, "if only those managers would sit up and fly right." Thus we have a perfect system to maintain the status quo, with each side waiting for the other to act. And, in fact, feeling helpless in the face of the other's inaction. And yet wise men (see the sidebar) have always known that change, no matter how big, begins with the individual.

Changing the Culture Begins with You

No change, however large or small, can succeed unless each individual decides to begin. Structure and processes and senior managers all have an effect but so does the individual as many before us have known.

Let him that would move the world first move himself.　　Socrates

We must be the change we wish to see in the world.　　Gandhi

One man with courage makes a majority.　　Andrew Jackson

He who cannot change the very fabric of his thought will never be able to change reality, and will never, therefore, make any progress.
Anwar Sadat, President of Egypt and Middle East peacemaker

It is true senior managers have a particular responsibility for the culture. There are some structural and other things they need to do to promote a more innovative culture, which I will cover in Chapters 13, Kichstarting Your Innovation Culture and 14, Structure and Mechanisms for Dissent. However, culture is not some cloud floating "up there" that no one can touch or affect. Culture is what you do when no one is looking, when no one is standing behind you with a rulebook. It is how or whether you involve people in decisions, how or whether you tolerate dissent, whether you use a carrot or a stick to motivate. All of these things are under your control to a great extent.

It is more difficult to change the culture from a middle level in the organization and even more difficult if that culture is dysfunctional. You have the weight of those above you restricting your action. You need to proceed carefully and quietly. But you need to proceed. Even if your ability to change your boss's mind or shape the culture is slow or even nonexistent, you can, at very least, change how you think and feel and influence how your direct reports think and feel.

In the last chapter, I listed four areas where underground dissent can flourish and therefore, where you need to try to effect a change: in yourself, in your employees, with your boss, and in the culture. In this chapter, I'll suggest how to surface underground dissent with your peers, your employees, and within yourself; a discussion of doing it with your boss and in the work culture will follow. The order of discussion is from easiest to hardest, which is not the say the first is easy— it's just not as hard as the later ones.

Surfacing Dissent with Yourself

If you had a fairly high number of "agrees" when you assessed your willingness to dissent in the quiz in the previous chapter, you may feel close to giving up. Disagreements with your boss or the company are kept under wraps, taken out only when there is safety in numbers or with trusted friends, never expressed when it might do the most good—when you're the only one who sees the emperor has no clothes. This daily grind of having to pretend you believe what you don't, support what you oppose, like what you hate, has taken its toll. It may show itself as hopelessness, doubt, diffidence, self-preservation, or fear of getting hurt or of hurting. However it presents itself, it is the worst thing about a bad job—it saps your confidence in yourself.

This state of affairs can't continue—not if you want to stay sane and healthy. You need to ask yourself the following questions:

a) Is it time to leave?
b) If I want to stay, should I speak up?
c) If I decide not to dissent, can I change my attitude about what is going on?

Let's talk about each one.

Is It Time to Leave?

It's hard to know, isn't it? You have an investment in your workplace. You know the people and even if you don't like them all, you value some. At the very least, you know how things work. And there's no guarantee things will be better elsewhere. Finally, financial, lifestyle, or other reasons may make leaving unappealing. All perfectly reasonable.

However, one reason for staying needs a second look. I have seen people stay in a situation well past when they should have left primarily because leaving would mean They had won. You're not going to let Them drive you out. You're going to get your revenge. If your situation has got you thinking this way, consider the story below.

I worked with a colleague some years back who was quite brilliant but constantly took offense, saw enemies where there were none, and attacked first rather than be caught unawares. She was let go because she was unable to work with others. Some time after she left, she contacted me and asked me out to lunch.

When we sat down, she said, "I'm having a problem at my new job. You seemed to get along with everyone, so I wanted your advice." I was flattered and immediately willing to show off this expertise.

She thought her supervisor was a jerk. When she described his actions, it did sound at very least, as if, he was an inexperienced or not very talented manager. They battled over a series of issues and later events often proved her right. However, he had given her a bad evaluation and she was determined to get back at him. She wanted to complain to his boss, the director, and "expose his incompetence" as she put it. I agreed it was standard practice to go to the next level if you disputed your evaluation and we discussed what she might say. All of that was fine.

As we were winding down, I said, "You know, Julie, if the director agrees with your supervisor, even if you are right, you need to think about whether you have a future in the company." She immediately flared up. "No way," she vowed. "I'm going to get him if it's the last thing I do." I found out later that she did go to the director, he did agree with her supervisor, she stayed on, and was fired three months later.

I wish it were different. I wish I could believe that being right was enough or that all situations, no matter how bad, can be salvaged. But in most organizations today, position power usually wins, no matter how righteous the cause or persuasive the argument. If part of why you are staying has to do with not letting Them have the satisfaction of driving you out, I admire your fortitude but I don't think much of your chances. There are times when discretion is the better part of valor and leaving may be the best thing you can do for you.

If I Want to Stay, Should I speak Up?

You may decide you want to stay in this job. Perhaps you love the work, or your specialty is so narrow that other opportunities are few. Fair enough. But continuing to be silent in a situation that makes you feel hopeless, doubt yourself, or be constantly on your guard is not good for you. You need to do something. One option is to speak up—to become a dissenter. If you remember, one type of dissent is situational—dissenters made by the circumstances rather than natural inclination. You probably fall into this category.

This is not an easy decision. If the job has affected your feelings of confidence and worth, it's probably quite a destructive environment—one you disturb only with the greatest care. On the other hand, as you know, prolonged periods of stress can be very deleterious to your physical—not to mention mental—health.

If you decide to dissent, you should be clear on your objective. It's about speaking up but it's not about revenge. Dissent rooted in a need to get even will not be seen as credible nor will it advance your cause.

Equally important, the speaking out should be more about needing to fight than needing to win. At one point, I applied for a promotion within a large corporation. After the interview, I realized some of the questions would allow the interviewers to discriminate against me. When I didn't win the job, I went to my union rep. Her eye (as I found out later) was on running for political office so she wanted to fight only cases she could win. She didn't think I had enough proof, so I dropped it. I have regretted that decision to this day. I realized too late that sometimes it's important to fight even if you don't expect to win. It is not the winning but the fighting that can restore what has been lost.

So it is with dissent. There are times when standing up and saying, "I'm not going to take this anymore" is more important than winning. If speaking out is integral to recapturing the person you were, whether you do it should not be driven by the chances of success.

In difficult work situations, this is without a doubt an act of courage. And realistically, you need to be careful how you do it. If your dissent concerns your boss, I'll deal with *how* in the next chapter.

If I Decide Not to Dissent, Can I Change My Attitude?

You may think it's not possible to dissent. It may be a wise survival move, since others may have tried and been punished. But the problem doesn't go away. Negative feelings about work gnaw at your soul and spread to all parts of your life.

One solution may be not changing the situation but how you feel about it. We can make assumptions that lead us to feel negative when it is equally possible to feel positive.

If a colleague is not devious but simply doesn't realize she has to let you know when her work and yours overlaps, it causes less stress. If your boss is a poor manager rather than being an underhanded so-and-so, it is easier to overlook his mistakes.

I'm not suggesting you sugarcoat what's going on. If things are bad, there is a limit to what you can reframe. However, if you have decided to stay in this job, you need some way to cope with the stress. If you can't do it by speaking out, reframing may be a way.

Another is to refuse to play the game. I worked with someone who was intensely competitive. Win-win was simply not in his vocabulary. If someone is out to win no matter what, he sees any attempt to compromise or work together as a weakness and therefore an opportunity to exploit—which this guy did. Every time we both agreed to give a little, he'd renege but only after I'd done my part.

I tried to tell my boss but my nemesis was a master at managing upward, so all I did was make myself look like a whiner. The final straw came when I heard (through the grapevine, of course) that Percy had convinced my boss I should report to him. I would be effectively demoted. I decided to leave but didn't have the luxury of the grand gesture, the I'm-taking-my-marbles-and-going-home move. I had to stay until I found another job.

I thought hard about how I wanted to act for the remaining time. One option was to circle the wagons and give as good as I got—reneging on agreements, hoarding information, going behind people's backs, and lying by implication and omission. It would no doubt be satisfying. But then I'd be playing by Percy's rules—what I had objected to to begin with.

I decided instead to tell him what he needed although he continued to withhold information. I raised problems directly with him while he complained behind my back to the boss. When I left the company, everybody thought he had won and I had lost. And perhaps, given the rules of that company, they were right. It was a hard pill to swallow.

But I realized that while you can't always win, you can always refuse to play. It's not easy and may look like you have failed to the rest of the world. But you can retain your self-respect while others are tossing theirs to the wind.

I don't wish to suggest this option is preferable. Much as I believe that how you feel is determined internally, having to constantly protect yourself from destructive influences is energy draining and stress-producing. Frankly, I'd always prefer leaving or dissenting.

If you feel negative about your situation, you have three options. Leave, speak out, or change how you feel. None are easy but of the three, the last is the most damaging over the longer term but may be a way to cope in the shorter term.

Surfacing Dissent with Your Colleagues

One source of underground dissent may be your colleagues. In fact, if the atmosphere is bad, calling them colleagues is kind of a joke since they are in no way collegial. For example, your peer manager's unwillingness to require his people to meet deadlines means your people don't have enough time to do their part well, but quality problems are laid at your door. In an organization schooled in underground dissent, you might whip your people onward to get the product up to spec and out on time. Or have a private conversation with your boss, to let him know where the real problem lies. You might set up a situation where your peer manager can fail and be tagged with it. All these may work but they also keep conflict underground and unresolved.

How do you improve this uncomfortable and unproductive environment? You want to be able to speak directly and honestly about problems currently buried or ignored. Since that isn't happening, you need to break the logjam. But it's not necessary or wise to launch a wholesale attack. You want to target your intervention.

Although as a group you may not want to bring your colleagues home to dinner, they're probably not uniformly difficult. Some may be more amenable to change than others. Spend a few minutes assessing them against the following chart. Each category represents a type of relationship. Of the people you are working with, decide who falls where.

Category	Explanation
FAMILY	• *Totally supportive no matter what. You could murder and they'd provide an alibi.* • *Usually few in number and may have little credibility because they're known fans.*
FRIEND	• *Usually supportive, but has own needs and issues that must be addressed.*
FOREIGNER	• *Is neutral.* • *Won't hinder but probably won't help either.*
FOE	• *Is opposed to you or the raising of dissent.* • *Will fight.*
FOOL	• *People who regularly and enthusiastically adopt new ideas (flavor of the month).* • *Her support might harm the credibility of what you want.*

If you have *family* among your peers, you probably already deal openly and honestly and problems don't fester. However, there is a danger in *family* if underground dissent is rife. It is natural to ally yourself with them, and you may look like you're plotting against the others. Even if you aren't, they'll think you must be because that's what they'd do. However, a *family* ally can be invaluable if she will join you in improving relationships.

Friends and *foes* are obvious. *Friends* are willing to deal with you directly, are not likely to double-cross you, and are willing to listen to what you have to say. However, they have their own needs and wishes, fears, and concerns that must be met if they are going to support you in swimming against the tide. Similarly, you know where *foes* are. They are least likely to support and most likely to try to do damage—not the place to start off with something risky.

In underground dissent, *foreigners* may have made peace with the situation by keeping their heads down and noses clean. They won't work against you but neither can you expect them to take up a banner and lead the parade.

Fools is an interesting category. Unfortunately, there are people in organizations who have boundless but undirected enthusiasm. They can always be relied upon to be on top of the latest thing but are often seen as impractical. These people, while genuinely committed, are not usually credible with co-workers and you should avoid engaging their support. Their involvement is likely to lessen your credibility, not increase it.

Categorizing your colleagues identifies both the opportunities and realistic expectations. If a colleague is a *foe*, it's unlikely you can move him to *friend*. The most you may be able to achieve is *foreigner*. You may be able to move a *foe* to *foreigner*, *foreigner* to *friend* and *friend* to *family*, but it's probably baying at the moon to think you can move a *foe* to *family*. The most you can usually achieve is a level up from where they are (except for *fools*, who are a category unto themselves.).

Just a note—*foe* and dissenter are different. *Foes* have an element of the personal or malicious—they might oppose something simply because you suggested it. Their objections are not about helping the company get stronger.

Now that you have situated your colleagues on this scale, decide what help, if any, you want from each. It would be ideal if everyone enthusiastically embraced dissenting openly but if that were the case, you wouldn't be in the collective pickle you are now, would you?

There are three possibilities. First, you'd like your peers to tolerate dissent. They wouldn't necessarily actively support it but they wouldn't damage its flowering, either. They need to be convinced that there is no advantage in opposing open dissent, even if they don't do it themselves. This is the position you would optimally convince *foes* to adopt. Secondly, you can ask people to encourage dissent. Not just tolerate but promote it. *Friends* might do this. Pay special attention to their information needs and help them understand the risk involved. Finally, people can be encouraged to dissent themselves. If they are going to embark on this, they will need information ("This is how our silence is adversely affecting both our operations"), skills development ("You might tackle it by saying…"), and support ("Can I help you think through talking to Jed?"). Likely only *family* will take this leap with you.

Doing this analysis allows you to have realistic expectations. It also points out that you have work to do even with *foes*. It is not effective to stick only to *friends* and *family*, much as it is more comfortable. *Foes* who are not transformed at least into *foreigners* can be dangerous.

Now you know who is likely support you and what you need from each. But how do you start? The first challenge is probably getting a *friend* to deal with you openly.

You are responsible for designing training for salespeople on new products. Wendy sets prices, decides market positioning, etc. You both report to Matt, as does Henry who does product development. Matt has to approve Henry's product before it is turned over to Wendy for the sales position. Matt then has to approve Wendy's approach before you get to develop a sales training package. Because you are the end of the chain, your people never have enough time to do a good job. Salespeople regularly complain that they get the training after customers know about the product or that the training doesn't have enough detail. Your request for more time has fallen on deaf ears. But Matt still blames you when the salespeople aren't as effective as they could be.

Matt approaches everything in this controlling way. He always has to approve one step before going onto the next. Even in very small things, he gets angry if people try to "usurp his authority" as he sees it. You know asking him to let go of some control is probably a non-starter. But you have to do something because you are an this untenable situation. You decide to raise the issue with Wendy who is a *friend*.

Remember, this is an underground culture. You're pretty sure Wendy is aware that Matt's controlling tendencies make it difficult for everyone but you've never discussed it. You need to help her identify how both of you suffer under this regime. In addition, Wendy will be worried about being perceived as a troublemaker. She may feel trapped between doing what is right and possible sanctions. If you don't discuss this, it won't go away and may decrease her ability to stick to any agreement. Finally, keep in mind this is not about building secret alliances or deals. Instead it is trying to, slowly and person by person, bring dissent into the open.

YOU	*Hi, Wendy. Got a minute?*
Wendy	*Hi, Frank. Sure. Pull up a pew.*
YOU	*I was talking to Janet this morning. She's ready to roll on the sales training design but we don't have your piece yet.*
Wendy	*Yeah, well, I should have something into Matt by next week.*
YOU	*But that only leaves my guys a week to put a training package together. It isn't enough time.*
Wendy	*I don't know what I can do, Frank. My people are working as fast as they can but Henry took four weeks longer in product development than anticipated.*

YOU	*I know you have the same problem I do. We're both stuck until Matt signs off on the previous unit's work.*
Wendy	*Well, what ya gonna do? That's just Matt.*
YOU	*True, but I was wondering whether you'd let my guys in on some of your discussions now. It'll give them a head start on the training if they understand your thinking.*
Wendy	*You know I can't do that, Frank. Matt would have a bird.*
YOU	*I know Matt needs the final word on your sales approach and he'd still get it. But a preview would let us fix the problems we've been running into.*
Wendy	*I dunno, Frank. Matt wouldn't like it.*
YOU	*You may be right. But this is causing you as much problem with Henry as I'm having. Maybe we need to help Matt rethink what he's doing.*
Wendy	*Easier said than done.*
YOU	*True. But if we could, would you work together on this?*
Wendy	*I guess so.*
YOU	*We could go in and talk to him.*
Wendy	*Wow! No way! You know how Matt gets if you question his decisions.*
YOU	*Okay—what about just going ahead and cooperating? Let my people get a preview of what you're planning so they can begin the training design.*
Wendy	*But he might find out…*
YOU	*We could say we realized we'd get a better product if we worked together. I don't see how he could object.*
Wendy	*But what if he just pretends to be okay? What if he's really ticked?*
YOU	*Yes, it's a risk. I guess we won't know until we try. But I think it's worth it if we can turn out a better product. If the salespeople don't get good enough training, we all suffer.*
Wendy	*Well…okay, but I'm still worried.*
YOU	*I understand. Me too. But I think this is worth the risk, don't you?*
Wendy	*Well…yeah…I guess so. I hope it works.*

If you have not been involved in underground dissent, you may find this conversation practically incomprehensible. What boss wouldn't want his people to cooperate? How could anyone see that as a risk? But in environments where authority cannot be questioned, there is a lot of second-guessing. Because you feel you cannot directly ask your boss's preferences, you can get into the equivalent of reading tea leaves—trying to figure out what is expected from very subtle cues. And it is a risk to stray from that reading.

Even though Wendy is a *friend*, she either hasn't or doesn't want to think about how things could be better ("What ya gonna do? That's just Matt.") It's a survival stance that is understandable but not good for dissent or innovation. She may have made this accommodation to protect herself against Matt's vagaries. But because she is a *friend*, she is willing to at least entertain the idea of trying to change things.

Notice you also pointed out how your crusade might help her in the long run ("This is causing you as much problem with Henry as I'm having."). Because she's *friend* but not *family*, Wendy needs to have the what's-in-it-for-me question answered, however obliquely. If you don't, you may strain the work friendship beyond the breaking point.

In the conversation, you did not try to reduce Wendy's risk to zero. You can't do it for Wendy or for yourself, and there is no point pretending you can. If you have to come up with a totally safe way to change things, you'll never take action. On the other hand, if it's too risky, Wendy won't do it. It makes sense to talk about how to minimize risk. If speaking directly with Matt is too risky, quiet cooperation may be the best first step.

The danger with this conversation, as you probably know, is if you have misread Wendy. If she is less of a *friend* than you thought, she may scurry off to Matt and tell him what you said. You need to be prepared. The next chapter will help you do that. But people are usually pretty close to how they present themselves. If you thought she was a *friend*, she probably is.

Once you are successful with Wendy, you can move on to other, perhaps less friendly, colleagues when the need arises. It is wise to proceed slowly and pick your spots. Remember there are some colleagues you may never be able to blend completely into the fold, but you may be able to neutralize them. That is a big step in the right direction.

Conflict and Dissent: A Reprise

The previous situation might have left you thinking, "Wasn't that just about managing conflict? What has that got to do with dissent?" Quite a while back, I made the distinction between managing conflict and managing dissent. Conflict is about *I don't like you, you don't like me, but we have to work together*. It makes sense to try to smooth over, minimize, or get rid of conflict. If your objections about Matt are seen as a personality conflict—you can't be a team player or you always have to have your own way—*who* needs to do the adjusting and whether it should even be brought up would differ than if it is seen as dissent—a wish to make things better. If it is conflict, you might just conclude that you and Matt have different styles and to learn to temper what you want to suit Matt. You might opt for getting the information you need in a more roundabout way that would not ruffle feathers. But because this is about trying to make the organization better, you actually need to go out of your way to raise issues that will cause tension and discomfort. While the techniques of managing conflict are useful in surfacing dissent, the objectives of the two are fundamentally different. You want to minimize conflict but maximize productive dissent.

Surfacing Dissent with Your Employees

Underground dissent among your employees is often hard to pick up. It may be evident in projects that are not done on time, are done poorly, or have to be redone. It is there in those who won't share their knowledge or sit in silence at staff meetings. It may be felt when you know you are the only one who cares whether the unit meets its goals.

A colleague consultant told me a story of underground dissent in operation. He was helping a company develop its marketing strategy. Because the company was quite dysfunctional, he proposed a good number of internal changes. But every time he submitted a draft to his client, the VP asked him to soften parts, to fuzzy up who had not been doing what. After the second or third go, my colleague asked whether there was a problem. The VP admitted he suspected his marketing manager (to whom my colleague copied the correspondence) of distributing drafts to managers singled out for comment in the strategy. These managers insisted that the report be changed. The VP felt he had no choice since the strategy depended on everyone's cooperation. What could the VP have done? Here's one option.

VP	*Bill, I just had Sandra in my office. She was pretty upset. She has seen the draft marketing strategy.*
Bill	*Oh, really?*
VP	*Did you send her one?*
Bill	*Well, yes. I didn't realize it was secret.*
VP	*It isn't exactly secret. But it's causing a lot of problems.*
Bill	*Really?*

> **VP**   *If people see the report before it's final, they might get the*
> *wrong impression.*
> **Bill** *Really?*
> **VP**   *I'd like you to stop distributing it until it's in final form. Of*
> *course, you need to see it. But nobody else.*
> **Bill** *Okay, sure.*

Exactly the wrong thing. The VP is sending the signal that he doesn't want people to disagree. To avoid that possibility, he'll keep the plan secret. Nope, this is not going to surface the dissent but help it go deeper. To surface underground dissent, you must begin to confront it wherever you find it. Let's see how the VP might have handled it differently. We'll pick up the conversation halfway in.

> **VP**   *If people see the report before it's final, they*
> *might get the wrong impression.*
> **Bill** *Really? So are you telling me to stop*
> *circulating the drafts?*
> **VP**   *Well, no, but made me wonder why you were*
> *doing it.*
> **Bill** *I believe in sharing with my colleagues.*
> **VP**   *Fair enough, but incomplete drafts don't give*
> *a full picture.*
> **Bill** *I thought they needed to know.*
> **VP**   *Know what?*
> **Bill** *What was in the report.*
> **VP**   *But they would know when it came out. Why*
> *was it important now?*
> **Bill** *Come on, Len, people should know when*
> *they're being criticized.*
> **VP**   *The consultant is supposed to analyze*
> *what we need to do. He has to name areas.*
>
> It's not unusual to **Bill** *And people should know.*
> have people repeat
> their argument to
> avoid the real issue. **VP** *They will when the report is final. What's*
> *important about now?*
> **Bill** *By the time the report's final, it's too late.*
> **VP**   *Not if something is incorrect.*
> **Bill** *Incorrect! Well, that's kind of in the eye of*
> *the beholder, isn't it?*

Rather than continue to argue, get back to basics.	**VP**	*Bill, I don't know what to do. Do you think it's important to have a marketing strategy?*
	Bill	*Of course.*
	VP	*I don't get that impression.*
	Bill	*I'm sorry you feel that way.*
	VP	*What's sticking in your craw, Bill? What's going on?*
	Bill	*I just want to keep everyone fully informed.*
	VP	*No, there's more here than that. There's something else. What is it?*
	Bill	*Well, if you must know, I don't see why we went outside.*
Ah, ha! Pay dirt.	**VP**	*Gerry has great credentials.*
	Bill	*He can't know our business as well as we do.*
	VP	*Granted. But there's value in an outside perspective.*
	Bill	*If you say so.*
Arguing your point doesn't work.	**VP**	*No, I need to understand. What's the problem with bringing Gerry in?*
	Bill	*We could have done as good a job internally.*
	VP	*But you said yourself this isn't a market you know.*
	Bill	*And how am I supposed to learn if you don't give me a chance?*

We can leave it there because I think we're at the root of the problem. For whatever reason, Len (the VP) didn't involve Bill in this strategy development. Rather than say anything, Bill went underground and tried to tank it by stirring up bad feeling before the strategy was even out.

If things are really underground, trying to raise them to the light may take more pushing and prodding than I showed. However, this conversation illustrates that people are often unwilling to raise issues for fear of what they might hear. If Bill asked Len why he went outside, Len might tell him he wasn't competent or that Len had lost confidence in him. Equally, Len contributed to the problem by not explaining why he outsourced this task.

In some ways, it's a perfect system. The boss's actions can be interpreted in a variety of ways. There is a strong but unspoken rule that you can't ask. Instead, you make up what you think is going on. And using that, you protect yourself—in your mind—from an unfair and underground boss. It is easy for both boss and employee to inadvertently cooperate in keeping dissent underground. Somebody has to break the logjam and usually, because you have the position power, it needs to be you.

Even if you are willing to allow dissent, it's possible underground dissent is a well-established practice in your group, encouraged by previous bosses. Even if you want to operate out in the open, employees may not be willing to. However, that doesn't absolve you of the responsibility to be open. You must model the behavior you want. If you are unhappy, speak up. Of course, given your position, you need to do it carefully. If you want to give an employee feedback, do it in private. But do it. You should not in any way participate in how the group does business—that is, complaining behind people's backs, keeping quiet when there is a problem, or even trying to "get" someone.

With Whom to Start

As with your colleagues, you need to start somewhere and with someone. Doing the analysis of *family* to *foe* may help. However, there is one caveat when using that system for this situation. You need to think about whether it is better to first work with the most influential in the group or with those who are victims of how things currently operate.

In a dysfunctional group, there is usually a leader who is often very strong. Her relationship with the group may be benevolent or negative but in some way she holds sway. These leaders are often very resistant to change because they have positioned themselves on top even in this bad situation. A new regime doesn't guarantee their continued success.

Also in dysfunctional groups are those who aren't doing well. They may be excluded by the informal leader who has created an in-group and an out-group, or be the butt of jokes. They are more likely to be friendly to your endeavors because they have little to lose. But you may be treading on shaky ground if you work first with the victims of the current culture, however welcoming they might be. Although they will understand the advantages of change, they also, fairly or not, have the least credibility with other group members. While they may not be *fools* as in the formulation above, they may nevertheless not be able to help you bring dissent to the surface among the others. In addition, you don't know how strong they are. If they take a stand that helps you, they will come under fire, particularly from the informal leader. If they back down, it will damage the ability of the group to see the value of surfacing dissent and will set back your initiative. Thus, although it is by far the harder course, the best people to focus on are those with most influence.

What It Might Look Like

It's important to point out that what works with most groups and with most people is the consistent and steady application of good management practices. That is, the regular involvement of people in decisions, communicating well, fair and respectful treatment, and patience. Even in underground dissent situations, most people will start to come around if they see the manager as consistently trustworthy. So before you undertake any of the things I suggest below, you should have had a long period of using regular good management practices to address the problem.

For example, even if you suspect sabotage, for the first few times, take the excuses ("The supplier should have checked his parts," "I didn't know the deadline was Wednesday") at face value. Then try to ensure the problem doesn't happen again. ("What do we need to do to make sure our parts are always up to spec?" "How can we make sure everyone knows about deadlines?") For the majority of people, this will help move them in the right direction. If they start to trust you, they will eventually be more willing to tell you what they really think. At that point, you are just trying to encourage continued dissent, which is covered in a later chapter.

However, if you continue to have problems, you may be running into the dynamics of a dysfunctional group. A dysfunctional group can be as cohesive in its own way as a well-functioning one. But it coalesces around destructive norms. A norm may be to tell the boss nothing he doesn't specifically ask for. People who—as a result of your good management—start letting you know when things are going off the track will be ridiculed or ostracized. They might be accused of being a "management stooge," and suddenly nobody will take breaks with them. If this continues, all your good work will be for naught. Much as some people might want to change, they will be pressured by the group to maintain the old.

This is when you may need to confront the informal leader of the group directly. You can usually tell who she is because she speaks for the group ("That's not the way we used to do things") or she is the one to whom people go for advice. They are often very competent, talented people.

With the informal leader, wait for an opportunity that focuses on what she isn't doing to help dissent. Say you have a retail bookstore. You can't compete on price with the mega discount places so you want to increase service. Sandra reads voraciously. Customers often come in specifically to get her advice. You want her to write these assessments down so other salespeople can use them and you can post them on your Web site.

You've asked Sandra to do this several times but it hasn't been done yet. You had already decided that is something rotten in the state of Denmark and that Sandra is one of the informal leaders. This might be an excellent opportunity to raise the issue. Remember, you need to have a private talk and leave enough time so that neither of you is pulled away at a crucial moment.

YOU	*Sandra, how are we coming on those book reviews?*
Sandra	*Gosh, Rob, I just haven't had a moment.*
YOU	*You know I'm willing to pay overtime for them. If you can't get to them during the day, I mean.*
Sandra	*I just can't seem to find the time. But I can get something to you next week—end of the week at the latest.*
YOU	*That's what you said last time and you weren't able to do it. Or the time before. What's going to make it more possible?*
Sandra	*I guess I'll just have to find the time.*
YOU	*Is there a problem doing them?*
Sandra	*No, no, of course not. Just got to find the time.*
YOU	*But, like I said, what's going to be different this time?*
Sandra	*I don't know, Rob. I guess I'll just find the time.*
YOU	*Are you sure it's just the time?*
Sandra	*What do you mean?*
YOU	*Well, a couple of times I saw you restocking shelves.*
Sandra	*It has to be done, you know.*
YOU	*But one of the others could have done it. You could have gone into the back and started the reviews.*
Sandra	*I wasn't in the mood.*
YOU	*Sure, but I'm wondering whether this is a pattern we need to talk about.*
Sandra	*A pattern?*
YOU	*Yes, this seems to be one thing you can't get to.*
Sandra	*What kind of pattern is that?*
YOU	*Lookit, Sandra, I don't know whether it's a pattern or not, but when I think something is happening, I like to mention it right away. That way, if I'm wrong, we can clear it up.*
Sandra	*I have no idea what you're talking about.*

YOU	*Well, like the fact I've asked you three times to do the book reviews.*
Sandra	*I told you, it's a time thing.*
YOU	*But every time I've asked you to make it a priority. Doesn't sound like it is to you.*
Sandra	*Okay, fine. So now it is.*
YOU	*Well, great, but I guess I'd like to know how we got to this point.*
Sandra	*Rob, aren't you making a mountain out of a molehill? Okay, so I couldn't get to this as fast as you wanted. Now I know it's a real bee in your bonnet, I'll get right on it.*
YOU	*That would be great.*

I suspect you won't get any farther right now. Sandra's obviously very good at dodging direct discussion of problems. Let it go and see what she turns in. If you are right and she is a leader in the underground dissent movement, she will probably do something to sabotage the effort. For example, say she turns in a review but it's flat—nothing like the sparkle and sharp wit of her verbal ones. Not only that, but because the style is very formal, you check and find she has taken the text verbatim from the book jacket. No original work at all. You need to talk to her again.

YOU	*Hi, Sandra, got a minute?*
Sandra	*I'm pretty busy.*
YOU	*Just take a minute—let's go into my office.*
Sandra	*Okay.*
YOU	*Pull up a chair. I was just reading the review of* Manhunt on the Hill.
Sandra	*Oh yeah? Well, I got it in finally.*
YOU	*Un-huh. Kind of different from what you say to customers.*
Sandra	*What do you mean?*
YOU	*It's more formal—less funny.*
Sandra	*Sorry, I guess I don't write as well as I talk.*
YOU	*And very similar to the dust jacket—in fact, identical.*
Sandra	*Oh, you caught that, did you?*
YOU	*Yes.*
Sandra	*I just didn't have the time—so I took a shortcut.*
YOU	*Well, this is what I mean about a pattern.*
Sandra	*What?*

YOU	*That you didn't have time to do it initially and then when you do it, it's not what I asked for.*
Sandra	*How is that a pattern?*
YOU	*Feels to me like you didn't want to do it to begin with.*
Sandra	*Well, you didn't give me much choice, did you?*
YOU	*Sorry, I didn't realize you felt that way. I thought of it as a compliment—to get a wider audience for your thoughts.*
Sandra	*It wasn't.*
YOU	*Sorry—why was it a problem?*
Sandra	*I put in the work—doing the reading. I think about the book and the kind of customer who would enjoy it.*
YOU	*Right.*
Sandra	*So why should the others get away with cribbing from me?*
YOU	*Cribbing? That's what you think the reviews would be?*
Sandra	*Well, yeah. If the others want to look good to the customers, they should read the books themselves.*
YOU	*I see your point. But yesterday Karen asked you to tell her customer about* Memoirs of a Geisha *and you did. What's different?*
Sandra	*Yes, but they have to ask me—they can't just get it from a crib sheet.*
YOU	*Oh, I see, and pass it off as their own.*
Sandra	*Exactly. Why should they get credit for work they didn't do?*
YOU	*I see. And it doesn't make any difference that your name would be on the review?*
Sandra	*Well, they're not going to show that to the customer, are they?*
YOU	*They'll just pass off your thoughts as theirs?*
Sandra	*Sure. They do it now. They ask me once about a book and then they use it from then on. As if they'd actually read the book.*
YOU	*I see. So it's important to get credit for your work. Makes sense to me.*
Sandra	*It does?*
YOU	*Well, sure. I'd probably feel the same way.*
Sandra	*Oh.*
YOU	*I'm really glad you told me. Means we can try to figure out a way that will work for both of us.*
Sandra	*Oh.*
YOU	*For example, what if we printed up flyers with a banner on it like "Sandra's Picks"? Something like that. Put them out at*

> the counters, maybe even with your picture next to the banner. Then people would know whose recommendation it was.
>
> **Sandra** Well, that sounds okay.
>
> **YOU** I think it would be great for the customers, too—to know there's someone in the store they can talk to.
>
> **Sandra** And we could do a new book every couple of weeks.
>
> **YOU** Sounds good. Could you look into how we could set that up? Maybe do some costing on those stand-up sheet holders? I think it could look really good at the registers.
>
> **Sandra** Sure, I've got a friend in printing. I can call him.
>
> **YOU** You know, I think we're on to something. And I'm really glad we were straight with each other. I think we ended up with a better idea.

Even though Sandra is the informal leader of the group, there are still tensions among group members. This is typical of a dysfunctional group. While Sandra might lead the group in an attack on or defense from an outside force (i.e., you), the internal workings of the group are likely to be fraught with just the kinds of tensions illustrated in this conversation.

Expect Sandra to be very adept at avoiding the issue. She's had a lot of practice. And for her to challenge you ("You didn't give me much choice, did you?"). Remember, she has a power base of her own. She sees you as an equal since she knows she's got the group on her side. I don't think there is any problem with accepting that relationship except that it is also legitimate for you to ask her to do work. After all, that's what a paycheck is about.

Don't go into the meeting with vague impressions or hunches. You need to have data ("You didn't have time to do it initially and then when you do it, it's not what I asked for."). Using that data, draw the conclusion you want to talk about ("Feels to me like you didn't want to do it to begin with."). You need to put the cards on the table—Sandra certainly will not.

If she is extremely underground, Sandra will continue to deny that your perceptions are correct. She will cite coincidence, paranoia, or any other factor that will allow her to avoid addressing the root issue. If she is very skilled, you probably won't be able to even to agree on the facts. But that shouldn't deter you. If she leads you down that blind alley, simply say something like, "We obviously don't agree on what happened but I still think we have a problem," and then proceed on with the discussion you want to have.

I don't think you need to, or should, push surfacing the issue too hard initially. You may be able to convince her by your actions that speaking up gets better results than working feverishly underground. However, it is important, as you did, to praise her subtly for being willing to talk about the issue at all. This will register even if she doesn't admit it openly.

So you can deal directly with the informal leaders but it is usually best to wait until you have an issue that affects them personally. Appealing to their better self and asking for their cooperation in the abstract is unlikely to have much effect if the group is used to being underground in its dealings.

Requiring Change

Surfacing dissent is, in and of itself, a difficult thing to do. If you can do it, you are to be congratulated. But unfortunately, a one-time coming up for air isn't enough if you really need to clear out underground dissent. You need to spend a lot of time helping people understand why they should be more open and inviting them in various ways to do so. One way was illustrated above—by challenging underground behavior.

For most employees and for most situations, the invitation will be enough. But for some, you will need to require the change. That is, to insist they operate in a more open way. I don't want to repeat what I have covered in some length in other material,[1] but suffice to say that you need to strike a balance between requiring people to adhere to the new way and allowing them to make this difficult change at their own pace.

I learned the latter lesson from a manager who used to work for me. He was from a culture with a very traditional view of authority. His North American employees constantly complained about his dictatorial manner. The manager realized some personal changes were in order. He was trying, but I was annoyed by the continuing complaints. He pulled me up short by saying, "Do you believe I'm trying?" Nonplussed, I answered, "Well, yes, but not fast enough." He shook his head. "Frances, you know sharing power is new to me. I'm changing as fast as I can. I need some time to make the adjustment."

If I had decided that this manger's rate of change was substantially jeopardizing what needed to happen, I would have had to remove him. If not, I had to suck in and accept exactly what I'm telling you. You can't make personal change go faster because you want it to, or even because you need it to. You can force overt compliance. But the change of heart will happen on the timeline that changes of heart take.

---

[1] Frances Horibe, *Managing Knowledge Workers: New Skills and Attitudes to Unlock the Intellectual Capital in Your Organization* (Toronto: John Wiley and Sons, 1999), p. 177.

Even though his employees were legitimately upset, he was making progress and that's all I could require.

Troubled Employees

One word of caution. In the course of surfacing dissent, you may find that a person is manipulative or underhanded not primarily due to the stress and strains of work life (although they may have contributed to it). There may be an underlying and deep-seated problem. I had an employee who, while very competent, was very destructive to the productivity of the group. If they didn't do things her way, she ridiculed them, to the point that they were afraid to make suggestions or demonstrate any initiative. When I realized what was going on, I pointed out how important it was to allow others to do things their way. After a long discussion, she finally agreed. However, as she stood up, she said, "And anyhow, when they do it wrong, I can just get them to do it again." I don't think she got the point.

She was incapable of recognizing that work can be useful and valuable and still not be exactly as she would do it. While many people have that problem, she was unique in her inability to even understand, much less empathize with, how intimidated and humiliated she made her co-workers feel. Without that understanding, which I could not coach, train, or motivate into her, she could not successfully change her behavior.

These types of employees need to be encouraged to seek professional help from the employee assistance counselor or another health care professional. Once you recognize that the underground activity comes from a troubled person, step away from trying to mediate it. This is not to say you allow the dysfunctional behavior to continue. You must still require that the person act appropriately, but if she does not, then in consultation with the health care professional, it may be a case of giving her sick leave or transferring her out of the unit.

Does This Always Work?

I'd love to say it does but you'd know I was lying. Whether this works depends on how invested the group is in its dysfunctional behavior. If the group has been dysfunctional for a long time and, in addition, has clever, manipulative, and influential informal leaders, you may be in for trouble. Unless you can establish yourself as having equal influence (and remember, the informal leader's influence is not derived from the privileges of being boss), it will be difficult to make a dent.

It is certainly worth trying first to work with the informal leaders of the group. However, if you have done that conscientiously and for long enough (and it may take about three times longer than you think it should), you may have to take other action.

One way, although radical, is to break up the group in some way. That may entail assigning part to another manager or adding new people whose values and outlook match yours. Another way is to let the most dysfunctional people go. This will be covered in Chapter 16: Knowing When Enough is Enough. If you are serious about surfacing dissent, it may be necessary to significantly disrupt the social patterns of the group.

Summary

As you can see, once dissent goes underground and especially if it is a situation of long standing, bringing it to the surface can be difficult and even risky. However, there is an equal risk in doing nothing. Tolerating the status quo can cause health problems for you—both physical and mental—and health problems for the company in the continued inability to innovate.

The next chapter will discuss how you can dissent with your boss.

Main Points

- To raise *dissent in yourself*, ask yourself: Is it time to leave? or Should I speak up? or Can I change my attitude?
- To surface *dissent in colleagues*, categorize them on a family-to-foe continuum and decide what help you need from each.
- To surface *dissent with employees*, focus on the informal leaders.

෨෨

Surfacing Dissent above You

*Even if a manager is successful in surfacing dissent in himself
and with his employees and colleagues, if his boss continues
to operate in an underground manner, it will be difficult
to innovate. This chapter will discuss how a manager
can influence his boss to surface dissent.*

Surfacing Dissent with your Boss

The previous chapter asked you to undertake some difficult actions to
surface dissent. But these actions are easier than what we will discuss in
this chapter. In surfacing underground dissent with your employees,
you have the advantage of position power. With your colleagues, you
are at least on a level playing field. But with your boss, the balance of
power shifts against you. Your boss has more power and is typically used
to wielding it. We will need to approach raising dissent with even
greater caution.

   If there is a lot of underground stuff with your boss, you know it's
more important to look like you agree than discuss real issues. People
won't speak up if there are problems: they wait to hear what the boss
says. Loyalty is the top priority, even if it means slowing the group's
ability to move ahead or come up with anything really new. If you want
to surface dissent with your boss, you must raise issues directly with her,
not fake agreement when you don't, or enthusiasm when you aren't.

There are times it's not worth doing because of the personal risks involved. But you know the effects of being forced to operate in an underground culture, even if your section is functioning openly. If you have to sniff the wind to get information, you are less effective in guiding your people. If you can't raise issues that trouble your staff with your boss, they become frustrated and eventually will blame you for your inability to be heard. Much as they may like you, they will eventually lose their respect for you. So although surfacing dissent with your boss is risky, you need to at least consider it.

There is a kind of kamikaze feeling even thinking about it, isn't there? You would actually point out to your boss he is suppressing dissent? Do shivers run up your spine? If so, listen to these promptings. Most of us have been around long enough so when our skin crawls, it crawls for good reason. There are bosses who will not change and punish those who suggest the possibility. However, one needs to distinguish them from the normal human beings like you and me who almost never welcome negative feedback and are likely to react emotionally rather than logically at first. So ask yourself a question.

Is He Worth Helping?

What you are about to undertake could put you at risk, so it is only reasonable to first ask whether the person and organization are worth helping. But you shouldn't answer too quickly. Let me tell you a story to illustrate.

I know a CEO who consistently ignored his direct reports' urging to rethink the company's target markets. For several years, the CEO insisted on aggressive revenue projections that the VPs knew were impossible. The monthly close meetings became nightmares. The CEO yelled about under-performance. By now, the VPs knew that mentioning the changing market brought more vituperation, so they were silent. The CEO began issuing edicts of the run-faster-and-harder variety. The whole organization was under the whip, doing everything it could to pursue a dollar they no longer believed was there.

At the CEO's insistence, the executive team put together a plan for turning the company around still based on the assumption that working harder would do the trick. Since the CEO suspected the VPs weren't communicating his message (which was true), he called an all-managers meeting to announce the plan himself.

The managers, fed up with the constant pressure and deaf ears, staged the corporate equivalent of the Storming of the Bastille. They rose up as a body and refused to support the plan. The CEO, shaken by this, quickly adjourned the meeting. The VPs saw a chance to go at it again. Managers, they said, weren't going to buy any plan until there was some serious talk about the underlying problems. The CEO reluctantly agreed.

The executive group ran focus groups with managers and asked them to really participate. So they did. They were brutally frank. A couple were particularly articulate about the shortcomings of the executive team.

The executive group was horrified. The CEO was especially offended. He was angry and hurt that his (as he saw it) single-handed efforts to keep the company afloat were not only unappreciated but also widely criticized. In particular, the articulate managers' comments rankled as he felt he had nurtured their careers by assigning them to high-profile projects. To avoid having to deal with them, he switched the projects to less competent managers who hadn't spoken out. The articulate managers saw this as retribution and soon the whole company felt the CEO was not only incompetent and secretive but vengeful too. With the best intentions, this attempt at change left the organization worse off, with people even more entrenched and bitter than before.

You may be thinking, "Well, it was obvious from the start. The guy was a jerk. The signs were all there." Frankly, I'm not sure. What I've described is not all that different from what goes on in organizations every day unfortunately. The CEO was certainly insensitive, didn't listen, and was a proponent of command-and-control. Sound like any boss you've had? Sure. But these are not faults of the soul (necessarily).

Nor was the CEO's reaction to the focus group. It doesn't suggest he's evil but rather human, with feelings that can be hurt. The truth of the complaints is not the issue. I can be hurt as easily by a lie as a home truth.

When I ask if he's worth helping, I'm not talking about personal idiosyncrasies that can be annoying or even hurtful. I'm not talking difficult. Your boss may be short-tempered, petty, impatient, hard-driving, demanding—all human characteristics that we'd prefer to be without but hey![1] He may still be worth helping even with all of these.

What you're looking for is a core of decency, a deep-in-the-gut wish to do well (however incompetently expressed). If that's there, you're in business. If he practices command-and-control because that's the way he's been successful, that's one thing. If he does it because he delights in having people under his thumb, that's another.

So don't judge too quickly or too harshly. Try to distinguish between someone who doesn't currently engage in optimal behaviors and someone who can't. If you're not sure, give him the benefit of the doubt. It may be worth the risk of being wrong.

---

[1] Although being willing to look at how these behaviors reduce the leader's effectiveness will be required.

You may not buy the distinction between someone who isn't behaving optimally and someone who can't. After all, if you're not doing the right thing, why not just sit up and fly right? It must be because you don't want to. But one possibility rarely considered is that the boss is acting, not through maliciousness or underhandedness, but because she truly doesn't know how to do it differently. The information age has played a terrible trick on managers. They have spent most of their managerial lives being rewarded for being tough, delivering on time, and winning. An era of collaborative innovation leaves them in the dark. They may scoff (as many do) that what you need today—trust, partnership, respect, and risk-taking—are just common sense. And they are. But though it is common sense, it is not common practice. And it is not common practice because managers don't know how.

Also, given the pressure managers are under to be in control, they often fear looking weak if they admit they don't know how to do what are now pivotal requirements of the job. Rather than ask for help, they stumble along, doing the best they can. Little wonder many don't do very well. If you assume your boss is underskilled rather than underground, it is easier to decide to help. Addressing a skill deficit, while not simple, is easier than addressing one of the soul.

What You Need to Consider

Even if you decide your boss is worth helping, sometimes trying to surface dissent is still not a good idea. To decide whether to do so, consider the following.

First, your skills. Are you good at phrasing things diplomatically? Can you say unpalatable things in a way to which people respond well? Can you keep your temper when others lose theirs? Are you intimidated by outbursts of anger? You don't have to be ambassador level in diplomacy or the Dalai Lama in serenity. You just need enough so you don't shoot yourself in the foot.

Second, what's your relationship with your boss? Well, obviously not good, given that you want to speak to her about such a big topic. But how does she see your work? Does she value you? Bad bosses often make their subordinates feel worthless. A friend had a boss who kept giving her new assignments and more money while belittling how well she did things, how quickly, and how cheaply. She thought he didn't value her when he did. You may be more important to your boss than you realize. And therefore, she may be more disposed to listening to you on other topics.

Third, your boss's past history. She has suppressed dissent in the past; otherwise, you wouldn't want to talk to her about it. But does she also take revenge first and ask questions later? Has she the capacity to understand the problem she is creating? I don't mean, is she smart enough. Most managers are. I mean, does she have the emotional intelligence to get what you are saying. If she has little empathy or concern for staff, she will have trouble understanding what all the fuss is about. You can usually tell by how guilty she seems when she is doing destructive things. If she is completely unconcerned, that's a problem. If she avoids talking about it and shuts down those who try, that usually means she knows she's doing something she shouldn't.

Finally, is this the right time? There will never be a good one, but some are worse than others. If she is fighting an unusual number of fires or the operation is going down the tubes, she may not be able to hear what you are saying. That's true even if the reason things are going down the toilet is *because* she suppresses dissent. Picking a time of relative calm will up the chances she can really listen.

You need good interpersonal skills, and a boss who values your work and has some realization that things are not operating optimally. If one or all of those are lacking, you may want to reconsider whether the time is right to raise the issue.

However, even if not all the ducks are in line, sometimes you need to surface dissent with your boss to keep your self-respect. That's a worthwhile reason. You just have to be realistic about how successful you're likely to be. I'm not saying you will fail, but you need to be okay with that possibility. As we discussed previously, this may be more about fighting than winning.

What to Say

As you can imagine, trying to surface underground dissent is a difficult conversation and it is worth thinking about how your boss might react and how to respond.

In the previous chapter, you remember you and Wendy decided to cooperate even though Matt prefers obedience over innovation. You turned in the training design and just got an e-mail from Matt, asking you to see him in half an hour. You check with Wendy. She has not been invited. You fear the worst. Matt is going to call you on the carpet for disobeying him. Of course, you may be wrong but better to be prepared. In the half-hour you have, spend some time thinking about what might happen.

Let's assume Matt is angry you didn't wait until he had okayed Wendy's work before designing the sales training. You could deny you did that or make some excuse and apologize. Or you could take the bull by the horns and address the way Matt is acting.

As you know, the first options, while temporary expedients, will do nothing to address the underground climate. If Matt really is a vengeful, troubled person, you may need to opt for one of them. But let's assume you decide both you and Matt have enough going for you to risk it.

Think through the possibilities. What's the worst that could happen? Matt is furious, wants revenge, and completely loses it. Another bad outcome would be if he won't discuss the issue. But what's the best? He will discuss what is really happening. Let's run through how to handle each.

Matt Loses It

	YOU	*Hi, Matt. Ready for our meeting?*
	Matt	*Yes, come in. Close the door.*
	YOU	*Sure.*
	Matt	*I got the training design.*
	YOU	*Yes, I think my guys did a pretty good job.*
	Matt	*I notice on page 4, you tell the sales people to let potential customers trial our Web site version for a month.*
	YOU	*Yes…*
	Matt	*That was in an old edition—I changed it to two weeks just before I gave you the go-ahead to start the training design.*
	YOU	*Oh…*
	Matt	*What do you have to say for yourself?*
This is a crossroads. Either you surface the dissent or you run for cover.	**YOU**	*Matt, Wendy and I thought…*
	Matt	*Don't bring Wendy into this. I'll deal with her later. Don't try to hide behind her.*
	YOU	*I wasn't trying to…but I realized we needed early access to the sales approach to have enough time to do a good training package…*
	Matt	*And since when do you decide what you work on and when? Last time I looked, my job was filled.*

It would be easy to apologize now and slink out, but keep going.	**YOU**	*I wasn't trying to do your job but I was trying to do mine well. I think my people need early access to the product and sales views to do a good job.*
	Matt	*You think! You think!*
You need to keep calm even if he's losing it.	**YOU**	*That's what you pay me to do.*
	Matt	*Not when it means not doing what you're told.*
	YOU	*Matt, I'm sorry you're angry but have you looked at the product?*
	Matt	*I flipped through it.*
	YOU	*Was it good?*
	Matt	*That's not the point!*
	YOU	*But isn't that exactly the point? If it's good, that's all that should matter.*
	Matt	*That's not the point.*
You need to stay focused.	**YOU**	*But it is. I think it's excellent—and it's because my guys had enough time to do a good job.*
	Matt	*Even if that was true, you still didn't…*
	YOU	*Yes, you're right. But I know you're very focused on results…*
	Matt	*Of course.*
	YOU	*Exactly. And a good training product will mean better prepared salespeople and more sales.*
	Matt	*But..well…I need to look at it more closely before I decide.*
	YOU	*Okay. Do you want Wendy and me to come back when you've had the chance?*
	Matt	*Yes, I guess so.*

When people "lose it," they do it in a variety of ways so how your boss does it might not correspond to the way Matt did. However she does it, there are some things you need to watch out for.

You notice that when you made a reference to "Wendy and I," Matt reacted very negatively. If Matt is the bad manager he seems to be, he's likely to divide and conquer. Any suggestion of ganging up will be quashed. So, initially, talk only about your part. However, since you don't want to encourage Matt in his divisive tactics, when he is calmer, suggest speaking together about the problem is more useful.

You will also notice that at one point I say don't apologize and at anothe, the dialog has you saying you're sorry Matt is angry. These really aren't contradictory. You shouldn't apologize for what you did. However, you can regret that this has made Matt angry. After all, you probably are sorry. Not enough to back down or change anything, but you regret that an action of yours has created a negative reaction. It's like lancing a boil. You can regret the pain you are causing but you still do it. They are not mutually exclusive.

Staying calm while Matt is flying off the handle is critical. If you react, becoming angry yourself or shrinking from it, he will succeed. If you can stay calm, you can keep the conversation focused.

You will also notice that you kept insisting that the quality of the product was the issue, while Matt was stuck on the fact you disobeyed him. It is often necessary to keep restating your view in the face of considerable anger. If you do, Matt will either lose it completely or calm down and focus, as he did in this conversation. If Matt goes out of control, bring the discussion to an end. You will not be able to continue productively.

Finally, don't assume you have completed your job of surfacing dissent with Matt. You have opened the door but have yet to step through. In fact, Matt may feel tricked. You backed him into a logical corner. He wanted to tear a strip off you and ended with the possibility he might have to change his mind. While he should be grateful that you pointed out his faulty logic, that is unlikely. More frequent is a kind of lingering resentment that you forced him to back down. When things are calmer, you need to go back in and talk about the underlying issue. This is covered in the third of these conversations.

Matt Won't Discuss It

Although some people avoid confronting the boss because they fear an outburst, I think it more likely Matt will continue to try to shut you down. Let's see how to deal with that.

YOU	*Hi, Matt. Ready for our meeting?*
Matt	*Yes, of course. Come in.*
YOU	*You wanted to talk about the sales training?*
Matt	*Yes. How did you get your sales information?*

	YOU	*Wendy and I worked together.*
	Matt	*What does that mean?*
Again, your moment of truth. Raise dissent or bury it.	YOU	*Well, my people need to get the information as soon as possible. So, I convinced Wendy to let them preview some of the sales material.*
	Matt	*Even before I signed off?*
	YOU	*Yes, but...*
	Matt	*And even if it means giving the sales people the wrong information?*
	YOU	*Wrong?*
	Matt	*Yes, like listing the trial period as a month when I changed it to two weeks.*
You can fall on your sword and ask forgiveness or try to get at the real issue.	YOU	*But those details can be caught before the training is released.*
	Matt	*Details! You may think they're details but try telling that to sales when we miss our quarter.*
	YOU	*I didn't mean they're unimportant. I meant that the package will be vetted before it goes out.*
	Matt	*But we wouldn't have to do that at all if you waited until I gave you the go-ahead.*
You are being side-tracked into a minor issue. Try to introduce the root problem.	YOU	*That may be, but I wonder if this project isn't a symptom of a bigger problem.*
	Matt	*Like what?*
	YOU	*We seem to have a recurring problem. There are delays in product development, delays in sales, and then I don't have enough time to do a good training program.*
	Matt	*Oh really?*
Make your pitch.	YOU	*Yes...I was thinking that if we could all work together from product inception to training, we would have a better overall product.*

	Matt	*Are you questioning the way I manage?*
Well, you are, but don't get sidetracked.	**YOU**	*Not at all. But I want to give you what you need. I really think a joint project team would be a better way.*
	Matt	*So you can spread the accountability around.*
	YOU	*Sorry?*
	Matt	*You heard what I said. Well, it's a clever idea but it won't wash.*
There's something else going on. Try to get at it.	**YOU**	*Are you saying you have a problem with my work?*
	Matt	*No, no. I just think it's a pretty clever way to obscure who's on the hook for what.*
	YOU	*Is that what you think I'm doing?*
	Matt	*No, no. Of course not. I'm just saying I want to stick with the way we do things.*
Try once more.	**YOU**	*You know, I'm pretty thick-skinned. I'd rather know if something I'm doing bugs you.*
	Matt	*No, no, not a thing.*
	YOU	*So, you and I are okay?*
	Matt	*Oh, absolutely.*

Hmmm—do you believe Matt? I don't. It seems like he does have a problem with your work but he won't say it, even though you asked him to be straight with you. In addition, he sees your attempt to suggest a better way as self-serving, a way to avoid getting the blame for failed projects. Matt did not come clean with you and chose to keep his true motives and motivations a secret.

In addition, Matt tried to sidetrack you into a discussion of the details of the training. He would have been quite happy to argue you into the ground about its minutiae rather than allow you the opening to raise the larger issue. He may not even be aware he's doing that. He may think he's just proving himself right and you wrong. So keep focused on what you want to raise and keep coming back to the fundamental issue. Don't let Matt lead you away from the crucial points.

Since Matt will not be straight with you, you are unlikely to get a definitive answer about what's going on and, moreover, you are starting down the path of reading tea leaves and looking for signs in the entrails of organizational sheep. It makes for paranoia. If you work for a boss who can't be straight even when you bend over backward to get the feedback, you need to think about whether you have or want to have a long-term relationship with him. Whatever the problem, it's going to bug him, and given his track record, he'll likely try other ways to get what he wants without confronting.

Matt Will Discuss His Behavior

The final likely scenario—Matt will discuss why he is operating in this underground way. Although it may not seem all that likely right now, there is a good possibility he will, especially if the issue is not malice but lack of skill.

	YOU	*Hi, Matt. Ready for our meeting?*
	Matt	*Yes, of course. Come in.*
	YOU	*You wanted to talk about the sales training project?*
	Matt	*Yes, I notice there were some errors. Like the length of trial. Who gave you that information?*
	YOU	*Wendy and I worked together—she let my guys preview the material.*
	Matt	*Yes, and you see where that gets you— with wrong information.*
	YOU	*Sorry, I'll have sales vet it again.*
	Matt	*Well, if you hadn't gone off half-cocked, you wouldn't need to.*
Ignore the "half-cocked" comment.	**YOU**	*I did it so my guys would have enough time to do a good training program.*
	Matt	*How good can it be with errors like that?*
	YOU	*But they're details. Being privy to the sales thinking early gave us the time we needed.*
	Matt	*They're not details.*
Stop dancing around issue. Bite the bullet.	**YOU**	*What's the problem, Matt? Is it the because Wendy and I worked together?*
	Matt	*No, I don't care about that.*

	YOU	*Well, then what is it?*
	Matt	*Ah, lookit, forget it. It's not worth it.*
This is uncomfortable for Matt so he's avoiding it. Keep pressing.	**YOU**	*But there's something bugging you.*
	Matt	*Okay, since you asked. This training product is just like all the others.*
	YOU	*Meaning?*
	Matt	*Not good enough. Just like the last two.*
	YOU	*But the last two were problems because we didn't have enough time…*
	Matt	*And this one is full of errors.*
Don't argue about the specific example. Stick to the bigger issue.	**YOU**	*I don't agree. I was trying to get my guys more time so we could avoid the problems of the past.*
	Matt	*But it didn't seem to make any difference.*
	YOU	*I don't agree. We do have a better training package.*
	Matt	*With errors.*
Okay, we've been around the mulberry bush already on this. Try to get back to the root.	**YOU**	*Matt, it's obvious there's something bigger than this training sticking in your craw. What is it?*
	Matt	*Well, with this kind of product, I don't see why we need you guys.*
Say this even if you don't feel it.	**YOU**	*I'm glad we have this out in the open. Why don't you think we're needed?*
	Matt	*I just don't see how your section adds value.*
Don't jump to the defensive too soon.	**YOU**	*Really? So you don't buy that time was the issue before?*
	Matt	*Not when you hand in something like this.*
	YOU	*Okay, well, I'm glad to have the chance to discuss it.*

For our purposes, we can leave the conversation. You have managed to raise the hidden issue—that Matt has for some reason decided your unit isn't valuable.

This is hard to hear and it would be natural to immediately jump to the defense of your people. But remember, this must be difficult for Matt. Otherwise he wouldn't have used these elaborate and inefficient ways to avoid a confrontation. So, hard as it is to hear, keep your cool. It's the only way to get to the bottom of the whole thing. If you fly off the handle, he's likely to do so too and you'll get nowhere.

As with the last conversation, it's important not to get sidetracked into arguing details. You can spend all your time debating whether the errors in the package are or aren't major and no time on the real issue—that Matt sees this project as another example of bad work.

That is not to suggest you don't argue. But wait until Matt has completely unloaded his complaint. Once he's done and you're sure you understand it ("Okay, let's make sure I've got this. You aren't sure my guys are value-added because of the problems we've had in the past. Right?"), you can deal point by point with his perceptions. If you're feeling really steamed (and I'd be surprised if you weren't), you might schedule another meeting later when you've had time to calm down and marshal your thoughts.

However you handle the situation, make it clear that, hard as it was to hear what Matt had to say, you appreciate it. ("Well, thanks for being straight with me. I guess it was pretty tough.") Praise him for raising the issue so he will do it again. Otherwise, he'll revert to his underground way when another problem arises. I don't underestimate how hard this will be. But doing it will lay the foundations for a relationship with Matt that is characterized by openness rather than secretiveness.

As you can see, whether you can surface dissent with your boss depends not only to some extent on your skill, but also on his willingness to speak about uncomfortable issues. If he's not willing, you can't force it. But if he won't discuss it, you need to decide whether you have a future with him.

Summary

Difficult and risky as it is to raise dissent with your employees and colleagues, you ratchet both up when you surface it with your boss. However, risky though it is, you may be paying an even bigger price by continuing to live in an environment that punishes you for thinking, creates a level of distrust of others, and forces you to act as if your survival were at stake. It is sometimes worth taking the risk to change that unhealthy state. The next chapter covers another way you can help the organization promote dissent and innovation.

Main Points

- In surfacing dissent with your boss, first decide whether he is worth helping.
- Surfacing dissent with your boss will depend on your skills, your relationship with your boss, your boss's past history, and the timing.

Kickstarting Your Innovation Culture

Although changing the culture is every manager's responsibility, creating one that supports innovation does need a boost, particularly at the initial stages. Appointing an Innovation Manager can do this.

Making Change

In the underground dissent quiz you took a while back, one of the sections assessed the health of your organizational culture. Some cultures are very dysfunctional. Not only is there not much innovation, the organizations are not even very efficient. And they're usually horrible places to work. They would be worth fixing no matter what. But your company's culture being troubled doesn't absolve you of the need to become more innovative. Your competitors won't stop working on the next breakthrough just so you can catch your breath. Much as it might be preferable to let the patient get well before you send him out to climb the mountain, you may not have the time. You may need to start out immediately. However, as with any other sickness, the illness will slow you down, will make it more difficult to climb rocks that other, healthier, organizations bound over easily. Almost everything you do will be resisted, usually covertly. You will have to spend an inordinate amount of time building your employees' trust. It will probably be a long time before you get a great, employee-generated idea and even longer before it is a consistent phenomenon. You will have a tougher time becoming an innovative culture than cultures that are healthier. But there you are. You have to play the hand you're dealt.

The basic components of moving toward an innovative culture don't differ, no matter how dysfunctional your starting point. There are three and I'll cover each component in a separate chapter. The foundation piece is the individual manager. If she does not migrate her behavior from one almost completely focused on efficiency to one that holds innovation and efficiency in balance, all will fail. We've already covered how individual managers can avoid suppressing naturally occurring dissent and surface it when it goes underground. But frankly, important though these are (and they are), all you've done with these is *not* kill the goose that can lay the golden eggs. Now managers have to learn how to create an environment in which the goose actually lays them. How to do this will be covered in Chapter 15, Encouraging Continued Dissent.

The second thing organizations need to do in pursuit of an innovation culture is to change some of their processes and mechanisms. Understandably, those currently in place are focused on maximizing efficiency and minimizing risk. But now that we understand we might have to sacrifice a little efficiency and tolerate a little more risk to get the innovation we need, the processes that support the old way must be examined. I'll do that in the next chapter.

The final (although it's actually the first) thing you need to do is build an infrastructure to support the transition from the old, non-innovative culture to the new innovative one. This is a critical piece most organizations miss.

In what I see as touchingly naïve, most executives seem to believe that if they stand before crowds of employees and exhort them to greater and better innovation, it will happen. They might even stress that employees' jobs depend on it. Well, if words were all that were needed, we could have said them long ago. Organizations are just blowing out so much hot air if they don't have a way of spreading this imperative throughout the organization.

In addition, an innovation culture actually requires different skills and attitudes than one focused exclusively on efficiency. A manager who never acquires the ability to keep dissent in the open will not encourage innovation no matter how much he might understand the need to. And again, if these were easy to acquire, we would already have them.

So not surprisingly, you need an infrastructure that will help the organization make this transition. When you try to move to a new culture, you will find the old culture enormously good at preventing any change. That's why hiring a few innovative individuals does nothing to create an innovative culture. They simply get co-opted or spit out by the forces of the old. Unless you have some way to protect this new initiative in its formative stages, the old culture will kill it off before it even gets going. It is incredibly easy to do. For example: Innovation is a strategic objective. Strategic usually means long-term, long-term means not today, not today means not urgent, and not urgent doesn't get done. Simply by paying attention to other things, innovation will die. And when it does, chalk up another failure.

To successfully introduce an innovation culture, you have to juggle a fundamental management paradox—the need to run the day-to-day operations focused on short-term success while changing the organization to ensure it in the long-term. Jack Welch of GE says, "The toughest part is designing a new organization while you operate the old one. You can't slam dunk the new way. You have to run the two systems in parallel."[1] You have to couple the structures and behavior necessary for normal efficient management with the informality and instability that characterizes moving to a new way of doing business. So the first key: the formation of an innovation unit, headed by an innovation manager, and separate from day-to-day operations. That's the subject of this chapter. The first part of the chapter is more relevant to executives who have the power to form the unit and the latter is for managers who want to head it up.

The Innovation Manager and Her Unit

An innovation manager's job is to help move the organization to be more consistently innovative. The focus is not solely or even primarily on new product or service development. Instead, her tasks are *to build capacity in the organization to foster dissent and innovation* and also *to strengthen or create processes that support innovation over the long term.* While a product development unit concentrates on generating new items to tempt customers, an innovation unit focuses on helping the organization develop the practices, attitudes, and skills that foster innovation in all aspects of work.

The innovation manager needs to report to a very senior executive, preferably the CEO, and not be buried in the bowels of HR. Since sustained innovation is *the* critical success factor for the future, the point man should an operational person.

Under the direction of the innovation manager, an innovation unit would do a wide range of things. It would be the focal point for implementing the process changes outlined in the next chapter. It would also encourage managers to support continuing dissent through various mechanisms such as training and changing the

---

[1] Gareth Morgan, *Riding the Waves of Change: Developing Managerial Competencies for a Turbulent World* (1988), p. 43

reward system. In addition, it would develop and gather data on metrics to quantify how innovative the organization is currently. It would recommend where the company should be (e.g., 3-M's measure that 30% of its revenue has to come from products that didn't exist four years ago). It might design a process that allows executives to identify innovations bubbling in the organization. It would train managers on how to be political handlers of innovators and coach them on coaching dissenters. It would conduct the underground dissent survey, identify the problems, and help managers develop appropriate solutions.

When I propose this unit, I'm not suggesting doubling your headcount or even creating a sizable organization. It should be very, very small, perhaps no more than two or three people. You don't want a structure that in any way suggests a power base outside the normal lines. Or worse, that "innovation" is taken care of in that unit and the rest of the organization can get on with real business.

The unit employees, including its head, should understand this is a temporary assignment. Their objective is work themselves out of a job. Once the organization has hit the innovation targets based on the metrics discussed above, the unit would be disbanded. The expectation that the innovation unit is a permanent part of the landscape will lower the chances that the rest of the organization will assume fostering innovation is part of their job.

Finally, if your organization is very large, very diverse, or geographically dispersed, you may want to add a network of managers and/or employees to help roll out the innovation mandate.

Working with or through the Innovation Manager

A new position, particularly a senior one, always creates a little uncertainty. No one knows how to work with or through this new function. Here are some guidelines. The first set is for the innovation manager's boss. The second are for other managers who need to work with the innovation manager.

Guidelines for the Innovation Manager's Boss: Who Owns the Change?

I'm a little worried when I provide a list of functions for an innovation manager. I picture the CEO sending it to some minion with, "This is your new job description. Get back to me when you're done." If he's very progressive, he might even say, "And why don't you let me know how it's going occasionally? My door's always open."

It won't work like that. There must be no doubt in anyone's mind (particularly yours) that you own this change. The innovation manager will support you and do most of the work, but you are where the buck stops.

This makes eminent organizational sense. Fostering innovation is a disruptive process. Say you want to become more like 3-M whose innovative capacity is the envy of the world. They have a standard operating procedure that would make most managers' hair stand on end. If an innovator can't get his own manager to support his idea, he is free to shop it around to any other manager to get funding. Think how disruptive that would be in most organizations. If Bill gets funding from Advanced Technologies, do I lose his head count when he goes over there to work on it? Do I have to take him back if the idea bombs (as I know it will)? And if it's a huge success, shouldn't I get some credit since I hired him originally? And anyhow, if his innovation pans out, it will compete with the products in my division, which is exactly why I wouldn't agree to support it. How can I meet my targets if I have an enemy working against me from within?

And that's just one small change. Imagine the disruption as you implement all the structural and other changes needed. When the innovation manager gets into action, your direct reports will comply only if they know she's acting on your behalf. This is true even of managers who support the idea of an innovation unit. Nobody likes to have a peer telling them what to do, no matter how politely phrased. It's different coming from the boss. Otherwise, and quite properly, they'll tell their peer to take a hike or at very least, the request will go to the bottom of their pile. The only person who can legitimately drive this type of massive and disruptive change is the CEO.[2]

You may need to clarify your role even with the innovation manager. In her zeal to get things moving, she may inadvertently cross the line between helping and ordering. This is a critical issue. You own the change; the innovation manager helps you. You (in conjunction with whoever is appropriate) make the decisions, the innovation manager ensures they happen. Of course, if the relationship works, only the naive or clueless will miss that you listen to her. That is as it should be. But everyone should also believe that you're still your own person. The innovation manager is not the Power behind the Throne. If she is ever perceived that way, you, she, and the hopes of sustained innovation will be in trouble.

---

[2] I am using the term "CEO" to mean the person who has the power to decide to move the culture to a more innovative one.

Guidelines for Working with the Innovation Manager

If you are an operational manager, you also need to decide how to work with the innovation manager. First, you need to recognize you and she have fundamentally different roles. The innovation manager's job is to shake up the whole organization. She will challenge managers to think about when they are sacrificing the innovative capacity of their people for efficiency goals. But your role is to keep the ship stable and keep making money during all this turmoil. You two may not always see eye to eye on tactics and even timing. You shouldn't sacrifice your efficiency to the innovation altar, but neither should you blow off her suggestions to build in capacity for people to reflect, experiment, and mess around. Not everything she suggests is going to work in your environment but if you recognize that you both have important jobs with different objectives, it will be easier to give her some slack.

An innovation manager can also threaten staff people, particularly those in HR, since many things she undertakes will have a people focus. As a staff person, you might believe the VP of HR should have been appointed to the position. But the knowledge revolution has made people (and the knowledge and potential innovation they carry in their heads) the new competitive advantage. So it is quite appropriate for a senior operational person to be appointed to focus on this strategic objective.

In any case, this is all water under the bridge. There is an innovation manager and she's not an HR person. You need to suck it in and move on. Given this unpalatable reality, what should you do? She needs your help—not just tactically but strategically. Provide her with the expertise she needs. If the CEO has made the right choice for the innovation manager, you can build an alliance that will be good for you, her, and the organization.

Whether operational manager or staff person, you should avoid using the innovation manager as a conduit for news that otherwise would be difficult to get to the senior levels. An important task for the innovation manager is addressing the ways in which managers suppress dissent. You may have a boss who is particularly egregious and want to be sure he is on whatever hit list you think is being developed.

YOU	*Hi, Beth. Congratulations on the new job. Innovation Manager! Wow!*
Beth	*Thanks. It'll be a challenge.*
YOU	*So I guess you make sure ideas get to the right people.*
Beth	*Yeah...*

> **YOU**   *Great. I wanted you to know about Gerry. He wouldn't know a good idea if it knocked on his door. And command-and-control! He can be really vicious!*

Let's stop here. Nope, this is not how you can work most effectively with the innovation manager. Although she should be trying to minimize suppression of dissent, her job is not targeting individual managers, however unproductive their styles. If she did, the position would be nothing more than an officially sanctioned witch-hunt. The innovation manager's job is to build capacity in the whole organization to deal with these types of situations. Rather than whispering into the CEO's ear about Gerry, she might provide training to him (along with other managers) on how to encourage dissent. She would work with the HR department to design a reward and compensation system that nudges people away from suppression and toward encouragement. She might even coach you on confronting Gerry!

In the longer term, as these system changes take effect, it will either become obvious to Gerry's boss that Gerry doesn't fit where the organization is going or Gerry will leave because the pressure to change is more than he can tolerate. Either way, it's not going to be a quick fix. It will take more time than anyone (except Gerry) would like to see.

Applying for the Innovation Manager Job

Rather than just working with the innovation manager, you may feel you have the skills and interest to do the job. While this position has great potential to do good both for the organization and for you, it is not without its perils. It's uncharted territory both for you and the CEO. He should eventually be looking to you for advice and guidance. To get to this stage with him, you need to be on the same wavelength in three important areas—the sense of urgency, willingness to step up to hard decisions, and boldness.

Talk to him about each one. You might introduce the topic with: "I know we'll be tackling some really leading-edge stuff, so we won't always know what's coming up. But I thought it would be worth discussing your take on a couple of issues." Then you can launch into a discussion of the three points.

Degree of Urgency

You already agree innovation is important. But is it urgent? Or more precisely, how urgent? If he thinks the whole organization has to be more innovative in the next six months and you think it needs two years, you'll be making sure things are well integrated while he's chomping at the bit. Conversely, if he sees the position as preparation for the future and you see thunderclouds gathering, you'll constantly be advocating actions he thinks are premature and ill advised. The sense of urgency will drive some important decisions. If you agree things are very urgent, you may give people (particularly senior people) less time to get with the program before you get tough.

Let me distinguish between how long it will actually take and how long you two *think* it will take. Transforming an organization is a much more extended process than anyone imagines. You and the CEO will have to come to terms with that at some later point. That's not the issue here. What we're discussing is whether you agree on how long it *should* take— whether there's a fit in perception. If you agree, you're in business. If you differ but you can live with his assessment, it's also a go. If you disagree in a substantive way, you need to rethink whether things will work out.

To open the discussion on urgency, you might say, "What's your sense of this whole initiative? Is this positioning us for the longer term or more focused on today's market? When would you want to see substantial results?"

Willing to Take Hard steps If Required

The CEO will need to make some tough decisions. This transition will require questioning all sacred cows and revisiting problems that had been too messy, complex, or touchy to address in the past.

Let's say one decision is to restructure to allow a more flexible composition of work. Teams would be formed when a big contract was won and disbanded when the work was completed. This will allow bringing in exactly the type of person needed for each project. Many people will move from employee to contractor status. Max, the VP of Ops and most affected by the change, rigorously opposes it. After much debate, the executive group adopts it anyhow. You're responsible for the transition. It will be impossible without Max's at least grudging cooperation. He gives no indication he'll give it.

In conversation with the CEO, you need to raise whether he's willing to contemplate taking decisive action if you're right. This should be done very generally. Not "I don't think Max Pierpoint will get on board. What will you do if he doesn't?" But more like "Sometime, during a big change, some people can't make the transition. How do you see handling this if it comes up?" The CEO will know who you're talking about. However, phrasing it as a principle will make it easier to consider an uncomfortable situation.

Understandably, and particularly if Max has been a high performer, the CEO will be reluctant to talk about it. This is Max who pulled off that great Marinimax coup, who delivered the Korean buyer, who plays golf badly, and who brought that ridiculous present to Ginny's wedding. These are important ties that need to be respected.

But all you're looking for is an indication that he'll allow you to raise this difficult issue if necessary. It would be inappropriate and unwise to expect a commitment. You just want to open the door in case you need to step through later.

Boldness

Does the CEO get excited or scared by bold moves? Will he generally want to tinker with a business process that isn't working or chuck the whole thing out and start over? Generally speaking, you're looking for someone who will entertain big new ideas and radical solutions—not adopt necessarily but at least listen.

In fact, I'd be wary of anyone who jumps on the nearest bandwagon. We've all suffered from flavor-of-the-month bosses. Beware of a CEO who has a pattern of shifting enthusiasms *and* isn't able to adequately explain why he wants to change flavors. If you find that combination, I'd give the job a miss. But if the CEO is willing to toss around new ideas and think about how they might work while keeping his eye on the politically and financially feasible, that's ideal. You could introduce this by saying, "How do you see us creating an innovative culture? Is this breaking new ground or building on what we've already got?"

In all of these, you're not looking for the ultimate ("I'll do anything to make this organization innovative, I'll try anything, I'll be ruled by your sense of urgency."). In fact, if you get it, it may be a showstopper. It may mean the CEO's planning to hand the whole thing over to you and can promise anything since he's not going to have to deliver. What you want to hear is some middle ground ("It's a possibility of course, but I'd have to see what the circumstances were." "I'd consider it, but other factors might be more important.").

If you match the CEO in your sense of urgency, willingness to deal with difficult situations, and boldness, you are probably well on the way to working successfully with him. If you take the job, look seriously at literature on change management. It is beyond the scope of this book to go into details about how to manage an organizational change but believe me, you need to know. But if you and the CEO are singing from the same song sheet on these three issues, you will have upped your chances both to become a trusted advisor and be successful.

Are You Willing to Be Attacked?

Initially, the CEO's direct reports probably supported your appointment. But inevitably, if the change is radical (and it needs to be if we're talking innovation), it will cause real discomfort. Resources have to be shifted, favorite products abandoned, underground powers dethroned. When this happens, the VPs are in a quandary. They dislike losing power as we all do, but how can they trash the idea of being more innovative? Nor can they attack the CEO who signs their paychecks. Who's left? Right. You.

The attacks may or may not be direct. Direct would be something like "This innovation stuff is the cat's pajamas. Couldn't support it more. But the Director of Innovation is too aggressive, pushy, demanding, timid, unfocused, ineffective. We need to change her and everything will be all right." The indirect will be harder to detect but will center on trying to make you look bad or incompetent.

If the CEO agrees with them, the process of altering the status quo is halted while a new person is found and brought up to speed. The move to an innovative culture has been successfully derailed because influential resisters have convinced the CEO that the pain and discomfort of the change is the innovation manager's fault.

Unfortunately, it is possible you are indeed too aggressive, timid, or any of the other adjectives listed above. Unless you can discuss these charges frankly with the CEO, you create a different sacred cow: The Innovation-Manager-Can-Do-No-Wrong. So you must be open to considering how your actions are affecting the process.

Summary

Culture change is one of those amorphous, everywhere, nowhere kind of things. And it almost always seems to be somebody else's responsibility. While in the longer term, it will be critical that everyone in the organization migrates their behaviors to those that encourage rather than suppress innovation, in the shorter term, you need someone to be the point man in the innovation effort. However, the role of the innovation manager is to work herself out of a job so that the organization's culture consistently supports innovation.

Main Points

- An innovation manager is needed to build capacity in the organization to innovate and put structures and mechanisms in place to support it.
- If you want the job, you need to discuss the CEO's degree of urgency, willingness to take hard steps, and boldness.

CHAPTER 14

ಠಠ

Structures
and Mechanisms
for Dissent

*The most important way an organization can encourage
dissent and innovation is through its managers, but it can
also put some structural and procedural mechanisms in
place that will up the chances that dissent and
innovation will be both tolerated and heard.*

Making Innovation Happen

How do you make innovation happen? Well, unless you have been asleep at the switch for the entire book, you already know you can't. Having said that, however, encouraging dissent and innovation is harder if you're swimming upstream against organizational processes that discourage it. Structures and processes make a difference. They don't make innovation happen, but they prepare the ground so that any innovative ideas that want to happen will have a soft landing. This is where executives have a special responsibility. They are usually the only ones who can make the structural and other changes needed to make it easier for innovation to flourish. This chapter will suggest ways senior managers can change the organizations so that it will be easier to promote innovation. The innovation manager could implement the recommendations in this chapter.

These mechanisms are grouped around ways to concretely encourage dissent, such as encouraging a greater capacity for risk, making tangible the belief that you're not always right, and avoiding punishing failure.

Encouraging a Greater Capacity for Risk

While we know people need to take risks to be innovative, organizations have some pretty sophisticated ways to discourage it. They can be as subtle as a supervisor's frown or as overt as having to ask permission to use the color copier.

Sometimes, there are good reasons for caution. When my life is on the line, I don't want my doctor thinking, "It hasn't worked yet, but hey! let's give it a go!" Even in the less critical business world, rules about who can spend what and who can go where aren't necessarily bad. But rule-makers aim to minimize the likelihood of downsides for the company. And as *Fortune* writer Gary Hamel points out, "In attempting to guarantee that there's never a downside, [you] place a ceiling on the upside."[1] We need to find ways to loosen our very efficient but not very innovative approach to risk-taking. Here are some.

Train

Training is the first thing managers think of when faced with a new problem. And very successful organizations do this. New 3-Mers take a course with their supervisors and are told they must be willing to defy them. However, as an old (make that former) trainer, I know that training is a necessary but not sufficient condition for change. You need it to start the risk-taking ball rolling but it alone will not sustain the momentum.

The strength of training is its ability to teach new skills. Taking risks is new for many people so it makes good sense to provide a venue to practice without fear of reprisal. But the rubber hits the road back on the job. Even if the employee is top of his class in knowing how to take a risk, he won't do it if he gets stomped on when he tries. (Unless of course he is a natural dissenter. But then he didn't need the course in the first place, did he?) So training is important but think of it like Spanish lessons—a necessary first step but useless unless you're in an environment that allows you to use the skill.

Reward and Recognition

The second thing that comes to mind to solve any HR problem— reward (or incent—is this a word?) employees to take risks. I don't think money will encourage dissent (see the sidebar for more on this) but you may be able to reward the outcome of dissent—innovation.

---

[1] Gary Hamel, "Reinvent Your Company," *Fortune* (June 12, 2000), p. 110. Truthfully, I'm doing a little bit of violence to Hamel's words as he was referring only to the capital budgeting process in organizations but I think he would agree with me that it applies elsewhere too.

Right now, most compensation plans are set up to reward stewards—people who use money, time, and other company resources in a responsible way. Excellent idea. But innovators and stewards don't have much in common. Using resources in what seem like irresponsible ways may even be a hallmark of innovators. You need a different system to reward them. But rather than have compensation specialists huddle in a room to come up with a great new plan, consider *Fortune* columnist Michael Schrage's suggestion that you "let people decide what portion salary will take up of their total benefits, let them trade vacation days, let innovators create incentive packages for innovating."[2] This way, you provide the incentive in a way that appeals to innovators because it allows maximum autonomy.

Rewards shouldn't be just money. As mentioned before, Hewlett-Packard has an "award of defiance" for those who have gone the extra dissent mile. The president of another company (who asked to remain anonymous to protect the identity of the employee) used the simple power of her attention to recognize achievement. She asked an employee who had developed an exceptionally innovative technology to give a formal presentation of it to her and her staff while the employee was in the midst of suing the organization on an unrelated matter. Thus she signaled her willingness to tolerate some level of "troublemaking" if it is coupled with innovativeness. Also mentioned earlier was Nortel's designation of Dr. Rudolph Kriegler as a Nortel Fellow even though he disobeyed direct orders of his superiors to stop work on a major project.

One of the biggest rewards for dissenters and innovators is participation in their community of practice—a group of knowledge workers who keep in touch with others in their field. It can be membership in a professional association but may also be more informal. Research is beginning to show that communities of practice are *the* way knowledge comes into organizations and new knowledge is created. They are important for companies interested in innovation but also for a dissenter or innovator whose first allegiance is to the work and who looks for respect from his peers. Giving him time to work on association activities, publish his work, or present at conferences can be powerful ways to motivate him. You may also want to institute peer reviews of work since innovators and dissenters find the opinions of their peers compelling.

Although this group doesn't necessarily respond well to the incentives they're supposed to (such as promotions, praise from the boss, and money), they still want recognition. It's just the form and source that are different.

---

[2] Michael Schrage, "Cafeteria Benefits? Ha! You Deserve a Richer Banquet," *Fortune* (April 3, 2000), p. 274.

Paying Dissenters to Cooperate

How do you get the dissenter to cooperate enough so you can move forward? Can we "incent" them to cooperate? Of course, we're not talking about rewarding them to lay down and play dead. That won't help innovation. But would it work to motivate them with money to be more temperate in their objections? I don't think so. Dissenters didn't become dissenters because it paid well so it's unlikely they'll desist for the same reason. Beyond that, financial incentives get people to do more of what they're already doing. Not better or different, just more. And while that's terrifically useful for efficiency, they're are an "incredibly weak tool" for innovation, according to *Fortune* magazine. Finally, past a certain point, money simply doesn't motivate. Studies looking at the importance of money find it ranks 11th for knowledge workers behind things such as recognition and responsibility.

Autonomy

Innovators have a very great need to be autonomous. They want to innovate but on their own terms and in their own way. To the extent possible, you need to let them have their head. But how can you do that and still deliver? It is possible. Rosabeth Moss Kanter makes a useful suggestion in a *Harvard Business Review* article.[3] If you want autonomy that can be managed, give people a methodology for decision-making rather than making the decisions for them. Ones I have used in the past[4] include teaching people why the decision is important, setting parameters, agreeing when you will intervene, and providing a methodology to assess the risk of their actions. If people follow decision-making guidelines, they can be independent while still following the strategic direction. One caveat: If they follow your guidelines, you have to live with the outcome even if you wouldn't have made the same decision. But that's the definition of autonomy, isn't it?

Mobility

If it's easy to leave a hidebound boss or move toward an exciting new project, you have a more risk-friendly environment. Enron, one of the most admired companies in *Fortune*'s survey, has an internal labor

---

[3] Rosabeth Moss Kanter, "Discipline!" *Harvard Business Review* (January/February 1992), p. 7.
[4] See Frances Horibe, *Managing Knowledge Workers: New Skills and Attitudes to Unlock the Intellectual Capital in Your Organization* (Toronto: John Wiley and Sons, 1999) for more on this.

market. People choose projects that appeal to them. In fact, their trading site, EnronOnline, was built by the project manager recruiting individuals working for other managers. It had 350 staff before senior executives even knew about it. EnronOnline did $100 billion in trades in its first year of operation.

Enron lets people keep their titles, no matter where they move. Once a VP, always a VP. Same for compensation. Thus, people are more willing to move to a new or risky venture because it's not a demotion and they don't suffer monetarily. Also, Enron's performance evaluations are done by committees of 24 people. That way, says Jeffrey Skilling, Enron COO, "your performance rating comes from the organization, not your boss, so you have very little risk to mobility."[5]

Access for Dissenters

Encouraging risk-taking without a way to signal it's being blocked just creates frustrated employees. An organization I worked in had a well-developed and well-accepted way to express dissent. The company was very large with numerous regional operations, many of which had larger budgets and staffs than headquarters. Strategic direction came from HQ but there were often conflicts about whether a regional employee had to do what some HQ minion said.

The process used to handle this will sound cumbersome but was in fact both efficient and effective. Say I'm a mid-level HQ manager. I want my regional counterpart to do something he doesn't want to. We both report to different bosses in different organizational structures. The only person with responsibility over both of us is the CEO. If Joe and I can't agree, I ask my boss to speak to Joe's. If the issue can't be resolved at that level, it moves up to the next pair of managers in the regional and HQ structure, until eventually, it reaches the CEO.

This sounds bureaucratic but it didn't work out that way. Because it was a well-accepted practice, nobody felt blindsided. In fact, an important component was me telling Joe my plans to go higher so he could fill in his boss. In addition, human nature kicked in. The higher the disagreement went, the more pressure there was to compromise. Senior managers knew it would reflect badly on them if *their* bosses were bothered with stuff that should have been settled at a lower level. Usually only the biggest policy and strategic issues reached the top. Thus employees had a way to express disagreement in an organizationally sanctioned way.

You can skip the hierarchy completely to provide access as Motorola does. Any employee can file a "minority report" above their supervisor's

[5] Hamel, op. cit.

head to lodge a different point of view. But this system works only if these reports don't bring retribution on employees. If they do, you're going to get precious few. If you are not sure whether you have that culture (and most organizations don't), you might want to try the admittedly less streamlined process described above.

Model Risk-taking

Employees know that what matters is not what managers say but what they do. You can exhort employees to take risks, train them, and even reward them, but if you aren't modeling it yourself, it ain't gonna happen.

H. Lee Scott Jr., the current CEO of Wal-Mart, credits Sam Walton, Wal-Mart's founder, with his learning on this point. Scott was a hard-driving manager who didn't realize his staff were suffering under his constant ultimatums. They used Sam Walton's open-door policy to complain. Through the discussion, Scott realized he was penalizing the 95% who were doing a good job for the 5% who need bearing down on. Equally important, at the end of the meeting, Walton asked Scott to shake hands with everyone to congratulate them on having the courage to use his policy to fix the problem. This is a great story about rewarding risk. But it is also a model because Scott tells the story himself. He models his willingness to hear bad news, even about himself.

Schwab modeled another kind of risk-taking. The company created e.Schwab for online trading, not realizing doing so would force customers to choose between it and the traditional business. This caused huge internal problems with brokers fighting over the same clients. In a "painful, expensive process, the company integrated e.Schwab. It had to reprice its core products, retrain all of its employees and renovate all of its systems."[6] The result: Schwab is the best-positioned retail brokerage firm. It demonstrated it could take risks and recoup when they didn't work out.

Demonstrating That You're Not Always Right

Encouraging a greater capacity for risk is an important step. But in addition, innovative organizations need to step beyond their internal processes such as strategic planning and other directives. Although they're important efficiency tools, they all make the implicit assumption that somebody Up There knows the Right Answer. But right answers can come from anywhere, and limiting who gets to decide

---

[6] Stewart Alsop, "Eat or Be Eaten," *Fortune* (November 8, 1999), pp. 85–7.

makes an efficient but not necessarily innovative organization. There are some things you can do to demonstrate you know that.

3-M's 15% Rule

Did you know that 50% of biomedical products were discovered when scientists were researching something else? 3-M has a sense of that and that's why they have their famous 15% rule. Dave Gagnon, a technical manager of Research and Development with 3-M, calls it "formalized bootlegging," which is "the freedom we give employees to spend 15% of their time working on projects not sanctioned by the job they're in." Using his 15%, Dr. Kent Neilson developed a "mating disruption spray"—an environmentally benign spray using microencapsulation technology to stop certain harmful insects from reproducing. It has been a huge success.

Allowing employees to develop their own projects on company time is a powerful signal that you know you're not the only one with ideas. But you need to protect that time from the natural encroachments of organizational life. Geoff Nicholson, international VP of Research and Development has told employees that if anyone gives them a hassle about using their 15%, they should tell them, "Leave me alone," and call him if they continue to run into interference. Another way to protect innovators and dissenters.

Pilot Projects and Flying Leaps

Ideas need time to be developed but sooner or later, they usually also need money—to hire particular skills or more people or do a prototype. Organizations good at innovating provide seed money. GE Capital has "popcorn stands" to experiment on a small scale and assess the potential of an idea. Nortel Networks, the fiber optics giant, allocates pools of money at different organizational levels. They can be used to fund any idea the manager thinks has potential but he is not accountable for a result. It is an innovation slush fund.

Corel, maker of WordPerfect and CorelDRAW, has an interesting program that balances efficiency and innovation. Corel's CEO Derek Burney says, "My main competition is not Microsoft...it's the two-or-three-person start-ups that siphon away the most talented people. They provide an excitement and an involvement that's hard to match in a large corporation." So to try to recreate this, he has instituted the "I" program—for innovation, ingenuity, inquiry, invention. Even the name of the program is kept purposely loose. When an employee has a bright idea, she can apply for a two-week pass to be allowed to work on it. One or two other people are assigned to her project to provide different expertise or perspective. For the next two weeks, they are in a "virtual garage" focused exclusively on developing the idea. At the end of the two weeks, the team can apply for another two-week pass and so on as long as the idea continues to look like it has potential. The program has been such a success that a New Ventures unit has been set up to exploit these ideas. And here is where efficiency and innovation merge. As Steve Quesnelle, Human Resources VP for Corel, points out, "We have great people and no shortage of ideas. The trick is to keep encouraging the new ideas while still keeping an eye on the bottom line." The New Ventures unit is not allowed to develop more than five new products at any one time. They need to keep the "virtual garages" producing new ideas, but they also maintain the focus on those ideas that have the greatest revenue potential.

Internal Venture Capitalists

Useful as the seed money examples are, they have a disadvantage. They assume one person—not the innovator—will decide whether the idea is worth pursuing. An even more interesting way to demonstrate that you know you're not always right is to re-create what venture capitalists do.

Silicon Valley has grown in large part because of venture capitalists (VC)—people with money and a taste for risk. They take on ventures that don't have a proven track record. Their advantage lies not only in their money and risk proclivities but also in their number. If one of them can't see the brilliance of your idea, you can try someone else. There isn't one all-knowing seer who doles out the money. Organizations can use the same approach. At 3-M, if an innovator can't get support from her own boss, she is free to shop the idea around to see if anyone else will buy it. Teradyne, a manufacturer of testing equipment for semiconductor chips, telephone networks, and software, uses another VC idea. For a new product, it funds an ersatz start-up. The start-up reports not to a boss but to a board of directors; it has venture capital, not a budget. This is another way to provide more freedom and autonomy to the innovator than might otherwise be possible in the normal management structure.

Peer Funding

Some organizations have gone beyond management-supported seed money, either through one person or multiple sources, by turning a pot of money over to employees who decide which ideas should be funded. 3-M is probably the grandfather of this movement with its Genesis

Grant. If innovators can't get funding from the sources already mentioned, they can turn to this fund for help. Their peers decide whether management has missed the boat on something worth pursuing.

Similarly, Shell has appointed an innovation panel of freethinking employees to allocate $20 million to game-changing ideas submitted by peers. When considering whether to fund the idea, they assess what Shell would lose if they pass and the opportunity turns out to be all its sponsors claim. Of Shell's five largest growth initiatives in 1999, four had their beginnings in the GameChanger initiative.

Funding Innovation Positions

Another important way to protect your innovative capacity is at budget time. Geoff Smith, VP of Business Development at Mitel, has put 10% of the R&D budget aside to fund head count in a "strategic technologies" unit—i.e., a unit of people whose job it is to look far out into the future and experiment with the next big breakthrough that doesn't contribute to the bottom line today but is essential to it in future years.

Changes in Hierarchy

Finally, there's a radical way to demonstrate you know you're not always right. Nokia, a 135-year-old corporation in Finland, surpassed Motorola in 1998 to become the world's leader in mobile phones. Nokia CEO Jorma Ollila wants the company to be "a place where you are allowed to have a bit of fun, to think unlike the norm, where you are allowed to make a mistake."[7] Each Nokia group can be as creative as it likes. Outside some shared systems, there are almost no rules. In fact, *Fortune* found it to be "one of the least hierarchical big companies on earth, a place where it is often profoundly unclear who's in charge." Sounds a bit radical, doesn't it? A place where nobody knows who's in charge? How can that work? And yet it has for Nokia.

That one may be too rich for your blood, but all the suggestions in this section challenge a common assumption. In *Images of Organization*,[8] Gareth Morgan points out that organizations are often seen as machines. Everyone has a role. With this view of the world, it is useful and important to distinguish between what you do and what I do so that we don't step on each other's toes. Duplication of effort is bad and inefficient. The aim is an orderly relationship between clearly defined parts. However, other ways of looking at organizations prompt very

---

[7] Justin Fox, "Nokia's Secret Code," *Fortune* (May 1, 2000), pp. 161–74.
[8] Gareth Morgan, *Images of Organization: The Executive Edition* (San Francisco: Berrett-Koehler Publishers, Inc., 1998), Chapter 2.

different thinking. What if an organization was not a machine but more like a brain? A brain has centers that perform the same or similar tasks. If one part is injured, another can sometimes take over. In this model, redundancy is good and eliminating it is destructive rather than positive.

The farther we get into the information age, the more I think organizations will need to act like brains and less like machines. As Corel, Nortel, 3-M, Nokia, and Shell have demonstrated, innovation seems to thrive when things are messier and less cut and dried than a machine view of the world will allow.

Not Punishing Failure

Risk-taking is not only about rewarding successful outcomes but also about avoiding punishing failure. But many of our systems are set up to do that, even at the societal level. In Italy, for example, if you declare bankruptcy, you can't ever get a personal or business loan. Failure will haunt you the rest of your life. We do the same thing in organizations. A failure often makes people look at us a little funny. "Sure," we can almost hear them saying, "he says it was risky, but maybe he just wasn't up to it." We're never going to get rid of backroom gossip, but we can do some things to avoid punishing failure.

Change Risk Assumptions

In business as in life, we'd really prefer options with no risk, no downsides, and a huge, assured payoff. But wishes aren't reality. No risk, no downside, no payoff. But still our planning focuses on minimizing risk and maximizing outcomes. Very rational, very efficient. But not very innovative. We need to change our assumptions about risk and even what constitutes success.

Venture capitalists assume 5 out of 10 of their investments will be total writeoffs—they will make not a penny back. Four will be modest successes and one will return 50 to 100 times the investment. The last pays for all the others. Naturally, if they could, VCs would go only for the big win. But they understand a principle that has yet to catch on in most organizations: You've gotta kiss a lot of frogs to get a prince. And you can't know which is which until after you've kissed them. Expending a lot of energy deciding who looks most prince-like among the available frogs, planning the kissing strategy, and projecting the minimum number of frogs to be kissed to ensure a prince—nice to do but ultimately useless. You just need to go out and start kissing. It's not that you invest in anything but you must encourage alternative and even competing solutions. One may be the breakthrough innovation you need even if the other nine turn out to be kind of useless.

How VCs fund is another thing organizations should look at. They base their decision not so much on the risk but on the upside potential. They take for granted anything with the possibility of a big payoff will have enormous risk and high likelihood of failure. But that's not a reason to avoid it. Can you imagine how different your organization would be if it was assumed that high risk was not a bar to action?

By the by, a small change your company can make is to stop using the same rules to justify small investments as large. I have seen organizations require complete business plans, with communication objectives, environmental impact, and customer support promises, to release a couple of thousand for a worthwhile but not earth-shattering improvement. Lighten up.

Fail Fast

Dave Gagnon, a manager of Research and Development with 3-M, knows it's difficult to determine the business value of projects employees are working on so they should be left alone to fully explore whatever they are attempting. But since only about 10% of ideas pan out, "the trick is to fail fast."[9] John Roth, CEO of Nortel Networks, agrees: "If something's going to fail, it's better we cancel it early than cancel it late."[10]

How do you do this? Negotiate with employees the criteria by which you decide whether this project is going to fly. You should do this before the employee starts on the great new idea. Be specific about the outcomes you need but also recognize that new innovations often don't look all that promising. They can be clunky or limited or hard to use. They may not look like a significant advantage over the mature technology they are designed to replace. A case in point: During the Vietnam war, the U.S. armed forces used computers but "beans, bullets and blankets" were tracked with a manual paper system because food, ammunition, and accommodation were too vital to the war effort to be entrusted to this unreliable technology.

Noble Failures

If you have done the kind of risk assessment we discussed above, you will be in a better position to make a distinction between someone who fails on a project with a 20% chance of success and one who blew a 99%

---

[9] David Brown, "Cut Employees Some Slack," *Canadian HR Reporter* (October 23, 2000), p. 3.
[10] Larry MacDonald, *Nortel Networks: How Innovation and Vision Created a Network Giant* (Toronto: John Wiley and Sons, 2000), p. 164.

"sure thing." But let's face it, we don't often do that. The innovator who expends every ounce of her ingenuity but fails to bring home an iffy starter is equated with the incompetent who needed only to avoid annoying the client to close the deal. They are both considered poor risks for bigger and better things. But they should be treated as opposites. The one who blows the sure thing either needs to increase his skills or be moved out. The innovator should be given another high-risk, low-probability-of-success project to use what she learned on the last one. She needs to be rewarded for the good work, not the outcome.

In addition, our vocabulary needs to change. Let's be more like Schwab where they talk about "noble failures"—projects that were worth pursuing but didn't work out. A noble failure is a good thing—a, well, noble thing. It's something we all want to have on our resumés.

Summary

Organizations want to support innovation but their structures, processes, and procedures often take them in exactly the opposite direction. They need to change them, along with the underlying assumptions, to open up the organizations to more risk, more innovation, and more dissent. These are, however, additions to and not substitutes for individual managers encouraging dissent and innovation in their own units. This will be dealt with in the next chapter.

Main Points

- Some structures and processes in organizations discourage dissent and innovation.
- To encourage a greater capacity for risk, managers need to train; reward risk-takers; provide autonomy, mobility, and access for dissenters; and model risk-taking themselves.
- Seed money should be available either from innovation slush funds controlled by managers or awarded by peers to peers.
- Not punishing failure means changing our risk assumptions, learning to fail fast, and viewing failure as noble.

References for This Chapter

Brown, David, "Cut Employees Some Slack," *Canadian HR Reporter* (October 23, 2000), p. 3.

Colvin, Geoffrey, "What Money Makes You Do," *Fortune* (August 17, 1998), p. 213.

Dess, Gregory G., "Leadership in the 21st Century," *Organizational Dynamics* (Winter 2000), p. 30.

Hamel, Gary, "Reinvent Your Company," *Fortune* (June 12, 2000), pp. 99–118.

Hamel, Gary, "Driving Grassroots Growth," *Fortune* (September 4, 2000), pp. 173–87.

Horibe, Frances, *Managing Knowledge Workers: New Skills and Attitudes to Unlock the Intellectual Capital in Your Organization* (Toronto: John Wiley and Sons, 1999).

Loomis, Carol J., "Sam Would be Proud," *Fortune* (April 17, 2000) p. 131–44.

Nemeth, Charlan Jeanne, "Managing Innovation: When More is Less," *California Management Review* (Vol. 40, No. 1, Fall 1997).

Stewart, Thomas A, "3-M Fights Back," *Fortune* (February 5, 1996), p. 97.

Stewart, Thomas A., "How Teradyne Solved the Innovator's Dilemma," *Fortune* (January 10, 2000) p. 188–90.

Stewart, Thomas A., "Taking Risk to the Marketplace," *Fortune* (March 6, 2000), p. 424.

Thurow, Lester, "Knowledge as the New Organizational and Societal Wealth in the 21st Century," Address to Canadian Centre for Management Development (November 7, 2000).

Encouraging Continued Dissent

*Getting employees to dissent once or on one item does not
promote an innovative culture. It must be an ongoing
process in which employees become increasingly comfortable
challenging what is happening. The manager needs to
understand how he can help to promote this culture.*

Introduction

As we have seen, transforming a culture into one that is more innovative requires three things. The first is an infrastructure that helps the
transition from the old culture to the new. The second are changes to
the current processes and mechanisms that currently support an effi-
ciency-only culture. The final and most important piece is the ability
of all managers at all levels to actively promote dissent. This is where
the rubber hits the road, where cultural change either happens or dies.
Not through some magic bullet fired from the top of the organization,
but by every one at every level making an honest attempt to foster
innovation in their little patch of the world.

The actions described below can and should be used by all levels of
management, from the most junior to the most senior. Executives as
well as supervisors need to be able to encourage dissent and innovation
in their direct reports. If executives encourage dissent among their
managers, they sanction it for the rest of the organization. Those direct
report managers are more likely to encourage the behavior among their
own staff.

This chapter will cover five things you can do with your group to promote continued dissent: speak last in group meetings, seek out dissenting views, protect dissenters, help would-be dissenters speak out, and challenge your group's status quo. We will also discuss the not-all-that-hidden fear that promoting dissent will result in an out-of-control operation.

Speak Last

Ronald Heifetz is one of the world's leading authorities on leadership and director of the Leadership Education Project at Harvard. He knows that your position as manager can inadvertently discourage innovation: "If you're the boss, the people around you invariably sit back and wait for you to speak. They will create a vacuum of silence, and you will feel a compelling need to fill it. You need to have a special discipline not to fill that vacuum."[1] As a subordinate, if your manager wants to go left, it's always been a wise career move for you to head off in that direction. As a boss, making clear what you want off the top is excellent for efficiency. But it's bad for innovation. Because as soon as the boss speaks, all other options become less possible. And once there is only one acceptable solution, innovation quietly drops off.

To avoid this, you can do a pretty simple thing: speak last. Easy and obvious—let everyone have their say before you express an opinion. However, obvious as it may sound, most managers find it difficult to do. Managers have been promoted because they are go-ahead guys. They see a problem, tackle it head on, knock it off, and move onto the next. If they know the solution, it's frustrating not to immediately jump in and provide it. But you need to encourage dissent by listening to everyone before you put your two cents in. You should do it even if asked directly "What do you think, Carmen?" You can say, "You know, I'd like to hear the rest of the discussion before I make up my mind."

There are two exceptions. Speak up if the group is using incorrect data. Something like: "No, I just saw the competitive intelligence report and it's possible CommQual is working on a similar enhancement." But not "Since CommQual always has problems launching, we have a shot at being first to market." See the difference? The first provides information, the second starts to direct the thinking.

The other exception should be used sparingly. The solution is completely obvious. You are aching to get it out and save everyone a lot of time. You could say something like "I'm not sure this would work but has anyone thought about...." To emphasize it's just an opinion, you might add, "Of course, the ops people will have our heads, so it may not be viable." Don't push—just let the idea lie there. If it's the right

---

[1] William C. Taylor, "The Leader of the Future," *Fast Company* (June 1999), p. 134.

time for the group to hear the solution, someone will pick it up. If not, they will drift off to other things and you need to just let it happen, annoying though it is.

Nothing about speaking last suggests you don't have the final say. If you're worried people won't realize this, start the meeting with "I'd like a full airing of the options before I decide." As long as everyone knows, the conversation can stray quite far afield into options you don't support and you can still keep quiet. Or, if you must, say something like "An interesting possibility. To make that work, how would you handle (the killer objection)...?"

You can and should participate in discussions, but you need to watch what you say and when you intervene to promote a climate of dissent.

Seek Out Dissenting Views

A lot of management today occurs in groups, aimed either at developing something new or settling a difficult problem. To do either successfully requires some level of innovation. Thus groups are an ideal setting to encourage dissent.

In previous chapters, I outlined how dissent is suppressed, from trying to argue the person out of her views, to making fun of her, to ignoring. Managers do this but so do groups. Groups automatically try to get people to conform to their norms. Otherwise, they wouldn't be groups. This pressure can be especially powerful in cohesive ones that share a common vision. Often, that's very positive. Peer pressure to go the extra mile or increase quality is much more effective than a supervisor's exhortations. But the very cohesion that makes the group efficient can also discourage "unacceptable" views that may be the precursor to innovation.

The ways they do this are varied. They practice safe behaviors—kind of like practicing safe sex, only it can be done in boardrooms. For example, they tend to avoid conflict. However, whether it's coming up with new ideas or solving a thorny problem, most group decisions have conflict built in. If the solution were self-evident, easy, or didn't cause heartburn somewhere, it's unlikely a group would be needed to address it. Without a way to surface conflict and deal with it directly and openly, the group tends to avoid proposing anything that might embarrass or disadvantage a team member. If a threatening recommendation is proposed, it is quietly ignored, on the understanding that if I don't attack you, you won't attack me. Risky proposals are usually discounted. Equally dangerous for innovation is the tendency to prefer proposals from those who are personally popular or particularly credible. Thus, what gets attention may be determined more by who you are than the quality of the thinking.

By valuing solidarity and smooth relationships over dealing openly with dissent, groups can succumb to their own pressure and act in opposition to their stated purpose. In one very large organization, a radical review of all functions was delegated to a multifunctional group. Their instructions were to outsource to the max and streamline to the fullest to free up resources for e-commerce. As a way to demonstrate its worth and ensure its existence, the organization's internal management consulting unit snapped up coordination of the process.

As the discussions proceeded, it became obvious that this internal group's tasks could easily be outsourced, even though they were providing a valuable transition function at the moment. Don, the rep from the group, was visibly shaken at this conclusion. He burst into an emotional plea for the jobs of his fellow unit members, pointing out that they had become so specialized that other employment would be difficult to find. The group was stunned into silence and embarrassed as they faced a concrete example of the disruption they were causing with their recommendations. Even though the internal management consulting unit met all the criteria for outsourcing, all but one member of the group voted to keep it.

We can sympathize with Don's distress and understand why the group chose to alleviate it. But because the consulting group had an eloquent spokesman who (however inadvertently) played on the emotions of the group, it escaped the fate of other areas. By protecting one of their own, the group produced a fundamentally flawed outcome. The fairness of the whole process is called into question. While it's very human to want to avoid pain, the group acted in a way that had more to do with group dynamics than the company's best interests.

There are many ways internal dynamics can prevent a group from being innovative and much of that stems from an almost built-in inclination to suppress outsider views. The Founding Fathers of the United States had a similar dilemma. While majority rule is preferable to autocracy, they knew it was not without pitfalls, one of them being that legitimate issues can be submerged in a wave of popular opinion. Despite their belief in democracy, they were very concerned about the "tyranny of the majority."

What can you do as a leader? When we make a decision, we typically take a head count of the "ayes" and if they total more than 50%, we shrug our shoulders at the nay-sayers and move on to the next item. And for small ticket items, you should continue this practice because it is efficient. However, when the issue is contentious or it is critical that all options be explored, the tyranny of the majority may take you down a doubtful path. You can help alleviate this tendency by actively seeking out dissent. It can be as easy as "Carol, I noticed you didn't say much during the discussion." Let's roll out an example based on this idea.

Your company produces a series of health publications. In addition, you sell a line of alternative health products and have an active consultation business. The latter two businesses provide much higher profit margins than the publishing. Market studies show most customers for these two lines are in the upper income brackets. If the publications were moved to your Internet site, the company could cut out printing and distribution costs. You could continue to charge for them but at a reduced price. They would be a marketing tool for the other services. Most of the group thinks this is a good plan. Carol hasn't said much in the discussion prior to the decision. I've assumed that Carol and the group are not underground in their dissent but are sensitive to group expectations.

YOU	*Carol, I noticed you didn't say much during the discussion.*
Carol	*Well, there's no point, is there?*
YOU	*Really? Why?*
Carol	*You've made up your minds.*
YOU	*Well, possibly but I'd like to hear your views.*
Carol	*Do you know how many low-income families and older people use our materials? How are they going to get them now? Do you think they have access to a computer?*
YOU	*So you don't buy retargeting our market?*
Carol	*But what are these people supposed to do? Do we just say, sorry, we can't make enough off you so you can rot?*
YOU	*So you think we should be doing something for them?*
Carol	*Well, yeah. When all we had was* Healthy Eating and Living, *they bought it as well as the rich ones. They still need the advice. We can't just dump them because we want to up our profit margins.*
YOU	*Can you think of a way to do what you're suggesting?*
Carol	*I don't know, but there must be some way.*
YOU	*I see your point. They're loyal customers and we don't want to leave them high and dry. But I'm looking for a way to satisfy them and still leverage the whole e-commerce thing.*
Carol	*I dunno...couldn't we at least make the publications available to libraries or other places that low-income people and seniors go?*
YOU	*You mean, give them permission to download for their clientele?*
Carol	*Something like that.*
YOU	*Hmm...might work. Could you do some research about costs and logistics?*
Carol	*Sure.*

I bet your first reaction is—great, the decision gets delayed. You're right. In this fast-paced world, this conclusion seems to be going in exactly the wrong direction. But you only need do this with big or contentious issues. And you need to because grudging acceptance or covert resistance will make the project difficult if not impossible to bring home.

You notice you didn't jump in immediately with "No, you've got it all wrong..." Instead, you kept paraphrasing "So you don't buy retargeting our market?" to make sure you understand the argument. It's an important way to signal you are listening.

In addition, you were able to avoid rising to the bait of implied slurs such as "We can't make enough off you so you can rot." People don't always choose their words as carefully as they should. While that's annoying, reacting negatively to the phrasing makes it less likely the idea will come through. Your objective is to see beyond the anger and even impracticality of the suggestion to that nugget of wisdom that may be there.

If Carol had been active in the debate, you know her views have not been incorporated into the final decision. That isn't always necessary but when consensus is important, you might say, *"What would it take to have you be okay with the decision?"* Whenever I've done that, it has prolonged the discussion, yes, but the group has also come up with a better decision. Once Carol makes her proposal, others can raise issues of price and whether that might eventually mean giving away the magazine—important and useful aspects of the debate that were hitherto omitted. You don't have to change the decision in Carol's favor. But the debate forces the group to come up with a better solution when people like Carol can challenge the prevailing views. It is an example of helping the dissenter to be heard.

Positive Deviance

The previous section encourages you to seek out dissent rather than just let it happen. You can take it a step further. Jerry Sternin of Save the Children worked with the Vietnamese government in the 1990s to combat malnutrition in villages.[2] In every community he found some children healthier than others even though the mothers had exactly the same resources. When he studied the mothers of healthier children, he found that these "positive deviants" acted differently. For one thing, they used what others considered low-class or unacceptable food—such as the tiny shrimps and crabs that thrived in the rice paddies—to provide their children with a source of protein.

---

[2] David Dorsey, "Positive Deviant," *Fast Company* (December 2000), pp. 284–92.

We see this in organizations—dissenters who are more tolerated than others. You might observe dissenters who have been around for a while in your company to figure out what makes them, if not palatable at least less unpalatable, to your culture. You might identify behaviors your dissenter could consider trying. Using this approach reduces the possibility that you would urge on him behavior changes that inadvertently destroy the innovative capacity you are trying to encourage.

Out-of-control Discussion

Managers often fear letting dissent out of the box because they will lose control. And that is nowhere more evident than in a group meeting. A free-for-all, where no one is listening except to the personal attacks, where carefully nurtured relationships are destroyed, where nothing gets accomplished—this is everyone's nightmare. It's not surprising managers fear dissent if this were the result. But it doesn't have to be.

Three things tend to happen in out-of-control discussions: people don't stay on topic; a dissenter/troublemaker keeps pushing an idea well past its sell-by date; or the conversation turns into personal attack. These problems can be dealt with in a straightforward way if you are chairing the meeting—and even if you are just a participant.

If people don't stay on topic, you can say something like one of the following:

We seem to have taken a bit of a detour. We were discussing item three.

I know this is important but I'm not sure we can resolve it here. Could Bill and Andrew take it offside to discuss?

The meeting is supposed to end at five but we have two more big items. Do we want to extend to, say, six or seven or should we move on?

I know technical issues are important, but let's decide whether to add it to our product line before we tackle the how. If it isn't valuable, we don't need the technical discussion.

If a dissenter continues to push his point, you can respond with something like one of the following:

You've made that point before, Ed. Is there something you haven't mentioned that expands the idea beyond what you've already presented?

Do you feel people don't understand your point? If so, please add any-thing new to clarify.

I feel I have a pretty good handle on what you are saying. Can I just run it back to make sure I've got it? [after the paraphrase] *Is that right? Okay, then I think we understand your point.*

I get the impression people understand your view but don't agree. I'm not sure it's helpful to repeat what they've already heard.

If the conversation turns into personal attack, you can say some-thing like one of the following:

Can we confine our comments to what people are saying? Let's be hard on the issues but soft on the people.

I can see this is pretty uncomfortable. Why don't we break for 15 min-utes? Bill and Andrew—why don't we caucus to see if we can't get this back on track?

I don't think calling names is getting us anywhere. Why don't we restate our main positions instead?

I think we're all getting pretty excited. Maybe we should slow down a bit. Bill, can you tell me Andrew's main objection? And Andrew, I'll ask you the same.

Even if the dissenter lacks the interpersonal skills to know when his idea has not been bought, it doesn't automatically mean you have a non-productive meeting. You can rein him in once he has had his say and you're sure he isn't being opposed just because he's raised an uncomfortable issue.

Naturally, groups take on a personality of their own. Yours may have lots of yelling and name-calling but is very good natured. If this is shutting no one down, it may be perfectly okay. However, even if the rambunctiousness works well for you, think about cultural diversity issues. Ensure everyone is participating. If they are not, you may want to address whether things can be toned down enough to encourage all.

Cultivate a Loyal Opposition

In the British parliamentary system, the party not in power is officially called the Queen's Loyal Opposition. I like this because it reflects a truth about democracies—that you can be both loyal and oppose: We agree on the fundamental tenets of freedom but we have different views on how to get there.

Organizations would do well to think about how to apply this principle to their operations. Is it possible to cultivate a "loyal opposition"—a group of people who show their loyalty, not by always agreeing, but by opposing? If we could create culture where loyal opposition was valued, our capacity for dissent and innovation would blossom.

Protect Dissenters

I know there are times when it feels like you should be protected from dissenters rather than you protecting them. They can be difficult, especially if they challenge when silence would be more appropriate or argue well past the point that things are settled.

These qualities are as much of a problem for their colleagues as they are for you. This is particularly true if the dissenter poses uncomfortable questions about how the group is acting. Group members will use ignoring, silence, and ostracizing to force the dissenter to toe the line. Your role may be in fact to protect the dissenter from attack so she can continue to say the things nobody else is willing to. Let's use the outsourcing and e-commerce example from earlier. You are chairing the meetings and the vote has been taken to keep Don's management consulting group. Alice was the lone dissenter. Let's see how things might play out (note: Unlike other conversations, there will be other people involved beside you and Alice).

YOU	*Okay, so the majority want to keep Don's group in the company.*
Alice	*Wait a minute—that doesn't make sense. Don's group fits all the criteria for outsourcing. How can we apply it to others but not his?*
Brad	*Come on, Alice, Don's right. Their group has done a great job in the transition.*
Alice	*Absolutely. So, in gratitude, we ignore the rules we ourselves put in place?*
Bob	*It's not just that—I'm sure they'll be useful even afterward.*

Alice	*I agree—but isn't that true for all the groups we're outsourcing? Like IT and HR?*
Brad	*Well, maybe—but this is a special case.*
Alice	*In what way?*
Brad	*Because…because…*
Alice	*Because Don made it one.*
Bob	*Hey, Alice, I think you're getting a little personal.*
Alice	*Personal? But he did, didn't he?*
Brad	*So what? He made a good point.*
Alice	*Which was? That his group has done a great job so we should exempt them from the rules?*
Bob	*Boy, you're really coldhearted, aren't you? Don't you put any store by loyalty or integrity?*
YOU	*Wait a minute, Bob. What was it that Alice said that made you think that?*
Bob	*Don's right. His group has done a great job and I think it says something about us if we can't recognize it by keeping them in the company.*
Alice	*But why come up with criteria if we're going to dump them whenever we want?*
Bob	*Can't you see this is a special case?*
YOU	*You know, Bob, you said that before but I'm not sure I got how Don's group is a special case. Could you explain?*
Alice	*Yeah, Bob, give it a go.*
YOU	*Okay, Alice. Let's hear what Bob has to say.*
Bob	*Because he's done such a good job.*
Alice	*And the others haven't?*
Bob	*That's not the point!*
YOU	*So what is the point, Bob?*
Bob	*…I just think we're pretty coldhearted if we can't recognize and reward good work.*
Sue	*I see that, Bob, but you know, this whole project isn't really about rewarding good work. It's about changing the direction of the company. You could be doing the best work in the world, but if it doesn't fit, it's not a go.*
Bob	*I suppose so, but…*
YOU	*But?*
Bob	*I dunno—it seems pretty coldhearted, that's all.*
Alice	*Yes, and so are the other decisions we're taking. I think it's unfair to apply one set of rules to one group and another to the rest.*
Bob	*I see your point—I don't have to like it, but I see it.*
YOU	*Okay, other opinions?*

Let's leave the discussion at this point. Other people may come back with arguments to keep Don's group or may have been swayed by the discussion to change their minds. The important point is not, for our purposes, the outcome but making sure that dissent was not suppressed by the group itself. Managers can play an important role in protecting dissenters from their colleagues' tendencies to pressure them to go along.

You notice that you're not necessarily taking a stance (speak last, remember?), but rather challenging people to be clear in their thinking ("I'm not sure I got how Don's group is a special case. Could you explain?"). Don't allow the group to slough a good point (e.g., "Have you changed the rules?") by attacking Alice's "coldheartedness."

Protecting dissenters is not easy as dissenters can make themselves somewhat unpopular by how they phrase their objections (e.g., "Don is a special case only because he made himself one"). People's backs go up and they react not to the value of the thought but to how it is expressed. You can help innovative thinking by getting the group to see beyond the unfortunate phrasing to the underlying idea.

However, protecting dissenters doesn't mean you take over the fight. I'd let the discussion flow unless the group starts to attack ("Don't you put any store by loyalty or integrity?") or gang up on the dissenter. Similarly, however, when you are protecting her, you shouldn't allow her to take potshots at others ("Yeah, Bob, give it a go") behind your cover.

Your objective in protecting dissenters is to prevent the group from suppressing unacceptable sentiments. If you can help the group focus on Alice's real message, others will probably join in the debate and take it from there.

Help Would-be Dissenters Speak Up

Some people have a natural proclivity to speak up. Others need more encouragement. They may not speak much anyhow or may come from cultures where challenging authority is unthinkable and questioning colleagues impolite. But quiet people don't have fewer good ideas than verbal ones. When appropriate, encourage speaking out and speaking up.

Juling is an excellent employee. She rarely speaks in meetings but works enthusiastically at testing new software. Until recently, she worked directly for you but as the group expanded, you brought in a manager to handle that part of the business. She reports to him. She comes to your office late in the day.

YOU	*Hi, Juling! How're things going?*
Juling	*Very well, thank you. You are busy?*
YOU	*No, come on in. How are things with Frank?*
Juling	*He is very energetic. He has many new ideas.*
YOU	*Well, that's great, isn't it?*
Juling	*Yes...*
YOU	*But?*
Juling	*No, nothing...*
YOU	*Nothing?*
Juling	*It's not right.*
YOU	*What's not right?*
Juling	*I should not have come...*
YOU	*Is there a problem?*
Juling	*You will not tell Frank?*
YOU	*Not unless we agree I should.*
Juling	*I'm testing the new version of MiroMax.*
YOU	*Yes...and...?*
Juling	*Well, Frank has cut my testing time in half.*
YOU	*Why?*
Juling	*He wants to ship quickly. He says we can fix bugs in the next version.*
YOU	*Well, there's lots of software like that.*
Juling	*But it's not what we do. Our new versions are to enhance the product, not fix mistakes.*
YOU	*True, that's what we've always done.*
Juling	*So, could you speak to Frank?*
YOU	*Have you brought it up with him?*
Juling	*Oh, no, I couldn't!*
YOU	*Why not?*
Juling	*He's my boss. It wouldn't be right.*
YOU	*Why not?*
Juling	*That's not how things should be done.*
YOU	*But you've come to me.*
Juling	*It is appropriate for a boss to correct an employee. It is right for you to tell Frank.*
YOU	*I understand this is uncomfortable, Juling, but it creates a difficult environment if we can't speak honestly to each other about problems.*
Juling	*But if you do it, it will become right.*
YOU	*But if I do it, it means you and Frank are not straight with each other.*
Juling	*It is not my place to...*

YOU	*I guess I don't agree. I think it's everyone's job to speak up. Are you afraid of him?*
Juling	*No, no. But it would be very impolite.*
YOU	*And yet, there is a problem.*
Juling	*But if you...*
YOU	*Juling, I'd be willing to coach you on what to say to Frank. Or mediate a discussion between you two. Or hire an outside coach.*
Juling	*Wouldn't it be simpler just for you to talk to Frank?*
YOU	*Yes, it would. But what happens next time something like this comes up?*
Juling	*I could come back to you.*
YOU	*And so we create the climate I was talking about—where we don't feel we can raise work issues.*
Juling	*I don't know, I don't know if I can.*
YOU	*I realize you're not used to this. But it's an important skill. Do you know how you want to proceed?*
Juling	*So you won't speak to Frank?*
YOU	*I wouldn't like to think of it as the first course of action. Let's consider some others first.*
Juling	*All right. I'll think about the others.*
YOU	*Why don't you drop by tomorrow and discuss it more?*
Juling	*All right. But you won't tell Frank?*
YOU	*Not unless we've agreed on what I'm going to say.*

Obviously, you didn't resolve the problem in the way most comfortable for Juling, even though it was probably an act of courage for her to come to you at all. But in the long term, it doesn't do people any favors to solve problems for them they need to learn to solve themselves. Like anything else, it's impossible to build expertise if you never get to practice.

In addition, an employee who won't speak up for fear of negative consequences prevents the possibility of a positive outcome. Because Juling won't raise the issue, Frank doesn't know she's unhappy and isn't given the option of either changing his mind or providing an explanation that sits well with her. She is like the old man who sprinkled gold dust around his cabin every night to keep tigers away. Night after night, he did it and sure enough, no tigers came. He was so convinced that the gold dust kept them away that he sold all his possessions to get it. He couldn't take the risk that, if he stopped, the tigers wouldn't come.

You should not completely rule out speaking with Frank yourself. It may be an acceptable interim step. And of course, if the issue had been critical or life-threatening, it would take precedence over helping Juling build her skills.

I think Juling will either avoid the follow-up meeting or re-introduce the solution most comfortable for her—you speak with Frank. You may need to replay the conversation you just had. That's okay. Changing ideas of what is proper is not an easy task and one that the employee—to the extent possible—should be allowed to accomplish at her own pace.

When different cultures meet, whether at the societal level or in the company, ideas about how things should be done often clash, as they did in this example. To resolve it, we typically make the assumption that others should change to be more like us. And we can enforce this view because we are in power—either as the boss in an organization or as the dominant culture in a country. But assuming that the dominant person or country has the right rules and the right way is, in itself, anathema to innovating. Self-satisfied people are not good innovators. So when you ask people to do something not consistent with their cultural background, ask yourself whether you should be rethinking your assumptions about what works best. For example, free-flowing talk is usually considered the hallmark of a good meeting. Everybody just jumps in whenever they have a thought. However, in some cultures, this is considered rude and pushy, so some people with excellent ideas may not speak up. One solution might be to strengthen their group skills but other methods are to occasionally ask everyone to express an opinion in turn, ask for ideas in writing, or table an idea on someone else's behalf. Using these techniques occasionally will tap these hidden resources.

I'm not suggesting you completely alter how you work or that you adopt these ideas holus-bolus. But varying how you solicit ideas to recognize differences in the group will increase the likelihood of a steady stream of them.

Challenge Your Group's Status Quo

One of the hardest and most valuable ways to encourage dissent is to challenge your group not simply to solve work problems creatively but to continually improve *how* they solve them.

Let's return to Alice—the lone dissenter in the group on outsourcing. You were able to protect her from being shut down. But for the group to manage dissent well, they need to acquire the skills you already have. What would happen if you asked the group to think about that issue? Again, more than two people will be speaking.

YOU	*Okay, any other agenda items? If not, I have one under Other Business.*
[pause]	*You remember last week, Alice brought up how we had inadvertently made one rule for Don's group and another for everyone else.*
Linda	*Yeah, but we got past that.*
YOU	*Yes, we did. But it made me wonder how we're working as a group.*
Linda	*What do you mean?*
YOU	*We were all pretty upset. It was embarrassing to have Don in the room.*
Don	*Hey—should I leave?*
Alice	*Yeah and me?*
YOU	*No, I think it's good for you both to be here. I'm not talking about that particular incident or trying to point fingers, but it got me thinking.*
Alice	*About?*
YOU	*Well, Alice, I think everybody was pretty uncomfortable when you spoke up.*
Alice	*You can say that again.*
YOU	*Why do you think that happened?*
Alice	*They didn't want to face the truth.*
Linda	*Alice, you're not being fair. I think we're doing a pretty good job, under the circumstances.*
Alice	*But it was a stupid decision.*
YOU	*Okay, hold it. I don't want to rehash the decision itself. I want to talk about how we got to where we did. Linda, you were saying the group was doing a pretty good job.*
Linda	*Well, yeah. Do you think it's easy knowing you're fooling around with people's lives?*
YOU	*No, of course not. But on reflection, did Alice have a point?*
Linda	*Well, yeah. I thought about it after the meeting. I guess we did go a bit overboard.*
YOU	*So, in some ways, we were lucky Alice was willing to speak up.*
Don	*I'm not sure I feel that way.*
YOU	*No, Don? How come?*
Don	*Well, my group is going to be outsourced. Otherwise, we might have been okay.*
YOU	*Was it the wrong decision?*
Don	*No, I guess not—not if we wanted to use the same rules for everyone.*

YOU	*So it sounds like Alice brought up a point we needed to discuss. But you know what I find interesting—and I think this could have happened to any of us—what I find interesting is that we made it pretty hard for her to make her point.*
Linda	*What do you mean?*
YOU	*Well, I remember her being called coldhearted.*
Don	*That was just the heat of the moment. I don't think anybody meant anything.*
YOU	*Yep, I can see that. But although we want to consider all points of view, it felt like this was an instance where we didn't.*
Linda	*Don't you think you're making too much of this? It was just a blip. It won't happen again.*
YOU	*As I say, I'm not interested in rehashing that particular incident so much as how come we got to that.*
Linda	*Just a blip, as I said.*
YOU	*I guess I'm not so sure.*
Don	*What do you think happened?*
YOU	*Maybe we have trouble hearing things that don't fit well with our feelings. We could all see Don's point and wanted to respond. So we didn't want to hear what Alice had to say.*
Linda	*You may have a point. I was feeling pretty ticked.*
YOU	*Sure, and yet, it was important. Is there a way we could act differently to make it easier for any of us, not just Alice, to bring up a point that's important but maybe sensitive?*
Linda	*Hmmm…we could be more aware when that's happening.*
YOU	*Yeah, great idea. But we were feeling pretty worked up when it came up. Is there a way we could be reminded to suck back and listen?*
Don	*Why don't you remind us?*
YOU	*I can do that if that's what everybody wants. Or Alice could.*
Alice	*No way—you're way better at this than me.*
YOU	*Okay, if that's what people want—but you have to promise not to jump on me when I do. A deal?*
Linda	*Okay.*

Because groups are unique, the conversation may be easier or harder than I have depicted. Expect some resistance as you bring up an issue most groups work very hard to keep off the radar screen. However difficult, the main point is the same. It is about asking people to go beneath the surface and inquire about the underlying issues influencing their behavior. This discussion helped the group realize that the understandable wish to avoid confrontation and hurt feelings resulted in a bad decision.

Early in the conversation, there was a question whether Alice or Don should be in the room. It is important to have them there. Talking about them in their absence is another way to avoid feeling negative feelings—theirs or our own—but we go for the comfortable at the expense of the useful. It adds to the problem to discuss an issue without the main people in the room.

Don't assume Alice will necessarily develop a sensitivity to the group's hot buttons either during or after this conversation. Alice is just going to be Alice—and she is valuable for that reason. If you think she is so over the top that she is making it hard on herself, you might want to coach her using the tips covered in the chapter on coaching dissenters.

You may be concerned that by using Alice's example, you look like you're favoring her—sort of going to bat for her. To avoid this perception, mention that anyone could have been in Alice's shoes. In addition, you will notice you used "we" a lot when speaking of the problem. Although this might be a small distortion of what actually happened, it is a good way to signal that you see yourself as part of the solution.

Finally, don't settle for a vague solution—like we'll all try to be better people. Although I am sure the intent is pure, unless there is a concrete action involved, people often forget their resolution. Having someone designated to be the official reminder can be a good thing.

What is important to maintain in yourself and encourage in others is a spirit of inquiry. Dissent is about raising issues, even uncomfortable ones, to the surface so that they can be examined. At first, people will suspect this as a thinly disguised way to blame them, but if you continue in the spirit of inquiry, people will start to believe that it really is about helping the group tolerate and even welcome dissent.

Needless to say, you don't want to dig down deep on every issue. If you did, you'd never get anything done. But a good rule of thumb: If an issue has come up more than once or twice, it's a mask. There is something underlying that is the real reason it keeps coming back to the table.

Summary

You encourage continuing dissent by protecting natural dissenters from peer pressure. You can also do it by helping people to speak up and by asking the group to inquire into why they act the way they do. All these things will help, but only if they are done in a true spirit of inquiry—a true wish to have issues tabled rather than underground, settled rather than floating around.

If you do it enough, you will find both that your group tolerates dissent more easily but also that they begin to respect those who do it and perhaps even thirst for it. When they begin to seek out dissent as a normal part of the innovation process, you know you have arrived. However, even if you do this, there are still cases and people who truly don't have the organization's best interests at heart and who will use this opening up to their personal advantage. Sometimes enough is enough, and the next chapter will help you deal with dissenters who cannot and should not be tolerated in an organization.

Main Points

- For an innovative culture, you have to actively promote dissent.
- You need to seek out dissent in your group.
- You need to protect dissenters from attack.
- You can help would-be dissenters speak out.
- You can challenge your group to improve *how* they solve problems.

CHAPTER 16

∞

Knowing When Enough is Enough

It is hard to know how much dissent to encourage but it is even harder to know when the dissenter has gone beyond the bounds of what is healthy. This chapter will help managers identify when dissent and dissenters have gone beyond what the organization should tolerate and how to handle it.

The Hard and Soft Side of Management

Some managers think that people are the "soft" side of management. Finances, operations, that's the "hard" stuff. A large part of your job is motivating and leading but calling this the soft side implies there isn't a "hard" side to people management. There is and should be. All your efforts are for naught if you can't be tough when needed. We've all worked for managers who were really nice guys but who also couldn't or wouldn't fix personnel problems. We suffered and so did the work because these managers had the soft but not the hard down pat.

The hard part of people management kicks in when the soft side is no longer sufficient—when you have done all the coaching, mentoring, requiring, and motivating that you can. When every positive avenue has been exhausted, you need to think about moving to the hard side. And the hardest is to let people go.

How Do You Know When to Let a Dissenter Go?

Let's say Mary has been a thorn in your side for a long time. How do you know when enough is enough? Obviously she's a troublemaker.

But as we've discussed, the trick is to distinguish between those people who are difficult, frustrating, and annoying but valuable and those who are destructive. Unfortunately, they look similar.

The first thing to ask yourself is "Does she have inventive thoughts?" You don't have to agree with them, you don't have to like them, you may even dislike them a great deal. But are they different from the mainstream? If the answer is yes, will you throw out the inventiveness baby with the troublesome bathwater? However, even when the answer is yes, you may still need to move toward termination. Here are some of the times it is probably warranted.

The underground dissenter. An underground dissenter is constantly sabotaging your efforts. The techniques suggested in Chapter 11 on surfacing dissent with your employees are effective but they don't work with everyone. There are some whose background and experience make them seemingly incapable of responding to open and honest treatment. They are so deeply suspicious of humanity that they believe they must trick and manipulate to survive. In a work setting, it's unlikely you can help this type of employee resolve enough of her problems to become as productive as you need her to be.

The abusive dissenter. I've asked you to tolerate some guff from dissenters in the pursuit of an innovation culture—impoliteness, aggressiveness, fits of temper, even somewhat childish behavior. However, it's not a carte blanche for unacceptable behavior. Naturally any physical menace is completely out of bounds as are the psychological equivalents. Out-of-control temper, intimidation, acts of revenge—all these create an unpleasant and unhealthy work environment. So while I am advocating a little more leeway for dissenters, it should not be at the expense of other employees. If the dissenter is creating a tense and unproductive environment, it is your responsibility to stop it.

The belittling dissenter. I once had an employee whose work was far superior to anyone else's. However, she also consistently belittled others. In meetings, the tone and language of her suggestions always implied that her colleague was stupid not to have thought of them first. People stopped speaking in meetings for fear of being attacked. Even after several discussions about this, she could not seem to stop. So, much as I valued her work, I let her go.

In general, you need to consider letting a dissenter go if the manner of her dissent depresses the productivity and/or creativity of those around her. A belittling dissenter is the most obvious way to do that but the tension or fear created by uncontrolled outbursts of an abusive dissenter or the environment of secrets and gossip fostered by an underground dissenter also qualify. If you don't move these types of dissenter out, you will end up with a unit unable to meet its goals, much less innovate.

You also need to take action when the dissenter cannot or will not change. While it is more frustrating to believe that the dissenter is capable of changing but chooses not to, the outcome is the same. He exhibits behaviors beyond what is tolerable for the good functioning of the group. The source of the block doesn't matter; you must take action.

One option short of termination is placing a supervisor between you and the troublesome employee. This keeps an innovative employee on staff and is less painful than outright dismissal. Sometimes it makes good sense. If the employee can't focus, more supervisory time might be helpful. You can also do this if the problem stems from a personality clash (which I think is rare, by the way). But by and large, I think it is a cop-out. Unless the manager to whom you are assigning the employee has extraordinarily better people management skills than you, he's unlikely to be any more successful. And if he isn't, all you've done is push the problem out of sight. So bite the bullet. If you don't think she is salvageable, go directly to termination; don't pussyfoot around with the interim measure of a different manager.

Involving Legal and HR

Presumably Mary has been a performance problem for a while. With HR's help, you've coached her, let her know your expectations, gotten her the appropriate training or counseling, tried to adjust her job duties, etc. None of this has worked or been successful enough. You have set performance expectations that she is able to work well with her colleagues and with you and she has been unable to fulfill those requirements. The next step is termination because she is unable to meet job expectations.

The size of your organization usually determines how many procedures and policies there are about letting an employee go. The bigger the company, the more likely Legal and HR have taken over the process. The smaller the company, the more likely you're on your own. Both have downsides. If you don't know what you're doing, it can be a difficult process with a potential for problems well after you let the person go. Wrongful dismissal charges are increasingly common. On the other hand, being able to control the process can be very positive.

The fear of legal action prompts Legal and HR departments to dump the employee into a rigorously controlled, antiseptic, legally correct process that is devoid of human feeling. Managers have told me that they have been instructed to read the reasons for the termination to the employee from a prepared text, refuse to answer any questions, and leave the room immediately. They are even discouraged from saying good-bye or thanking the person, so fearful are Legal and HR that these words could be used as the basis for litigation.

I know these staff people have the best interests of the company at heart but my observation has been that treating an angry, hurt, and disgruntled employee like she has Ebola fever is likely to make her more litigious rather than less. In my experience, even very angry people who are treated with respect can come around to, if not a pleasant parting, at least one that is not fraught with legal and other tensions.

That's not to say you don't need Legal and HR's help. You do. You need to know the dangers you run and how to handle them. But remember termination, like marriage, is not simply a legal relationship—it is also about working toward a common purpose, collegiality, and matters of the spirit. I understand this employee has been disappointing in one or more of these ways, but it doesn't negate the fact that when you terminate work, you terminate the others too. So while protecting the company's interests, you also need to pay attention to these issues.

Whistle-blowers—Potential and Actual

Sometimes there is a fear that a disgruntled employee will become a whistle-blower. The U.S. Government Accountability Project defines whistle-blowing as "disclosing information that an employee reasonably believes is evidence of illegality, gross waste, gross mismanagement, abuse of power, or substantial and specific danger to public health or safety."[1]

Movies have been made about whistle-blowers (e.g., like Karen Silkwood, Erin Brockovich) because we admire their guts and the good they tried to do. As citizens and consumers, we are all in favor of whistle-blowing when it points out a dangerous or abusive situation. But sometimes, what is dangerous and abusive in the eye of the whistle-blower is good management practice in others. In the recent past, the Canadian government was trying to decide whether to close down cod fishing off its Atlantic coast to conserve the stock. Canada's East Coast depends heavily on fishing for its livelihood and is one of the country's poorest

---

[1] Government Accountability Project, *Survival Tips for Whistle-blowers*, (September 1999) www.whistleblower.org.

regions. Closing fishing would create significant economic and social hardship. The Canadian government delayed announcement of the closure. The scientists who had done the research at the department of Fisheries and Oceans were furious. They went to the media with their complaint.

Without getting into the merits of the case, this is the kind of whistle-blowing all organizations fear—that based on a differing view of the right course. One part of the organization or one person feels strongly, even passionately, that their view is right. Other considerations—in this case, the effect on unemployment and the social fabric of the region—are not considered as important as the piece of data owned by the disgruntled employee. If it is ignored, the employee feels management is covering up.

If you have a whistle-blower who has already gone public with her allegations, immediately step out of the ring. This situation should be handled by the Legal department since over 90% of whistle-blowers report that their speaking out resulted in retaliation such as being harassed, socially ostracized, demoted, or even fired. Legal needs to guide your treatment of the whistle-blower while the case is being resolved.

But let's assume your dissenter has not blown the whistle, although it remains a possibility during the termination process. It is only prudent to take this into account. But I don't believe—and I know the lawyers will not agree with me—you need to shut her out of everything as a pre-emptive strike. Doing so may actually increase the chances she will retaliate publicly. Instead, consider using the approach I outline below.

Handling Termination Right

Those treated badly in a termination process often believe managers do it because they're callous or apathetic or even get pleasure from it. Although there may be a few who fit this description, I believe the process can be brutal because managers don't know how to do otherwise and are forced into a profoundly uncomfortable role.

Given the battles you've probably engaged in with the employee in the recent past, it's not surprising you'd want to distance yourself or, at very least, avoid more abuse. So managers use or allow others (like HR) to deliver the termination news, avoid the person before and after the news is broken, try to "jolly" her into faking pleasure at leaving ("People will be knocking down your door with job offers"), or spend enormous time planning the logistics of the departure but no time on the real issue—dealing with the feelings of loss and betrayal. They deal with their own discomfort by causing more pain to the terminated employee.

Look at it from Mary's point of view. Unless she is completely insensitive to all human contact, she knows she's disliked. Her co-workers have probably already marginalized her. Even though she may exhibit a fair amount of bravado ("I can take anything they dish out"), she is likely very hurt. And she can be hurt even if she brought it on herself. Also, remember Mary is probably firmly convinced her point of view is right and honestly bewildered by the hostility she meets. She feels persecuted.

Not surprisingly, when she is thrust into a rigid, antiseptic, and unfeeling termination process that seems more aimed at protecting the company from her (which it is) than treating her respectfully, it is bitterness piled on top of the unhappiness she is already experiencing. But it doesn't have to and shouldn't be that way. You can set up a process that, through your actions, communicates a fundamental value to Mary: You have a right to retain your dignity and to be provided as many degrees of freedom in the process as possible. You can do this by implementing the following.

- *Handling the termination interview yourself if possible.* Consult extensively with HR and Legal by all means. You may even want them in the room with you. But conduct the interview yourself. It's your decision, you're her supervisor, and she deserves to hear it from you.[2]

- *Making counseling available.* Alert the Employee Assistance Counselor or use an outplacement firm. If your company provides neither, encourage Mary to discuss these events with someone outside the situation like friends or family.

- *Thinking about the end of the interview.* Mary might be very upset or even crying. Does she have to walk past her colleagues to leave? Can the interview be held away from the work site or after work hours?

- *Allowing Mary to decide when to hear the details.* It's easier to give her all the severance details right in the interview, and some people want to know immediately. However, some need to deal with the shock before they're ready to listen. Give Mary the option of discussing the package right away or meeting later to do it.

- *Discussing the announcement of her leaving.* How will her colleagues be notified? Will you do it or will she? If a notice typically goes

---

[2] I realize there are some companies with such rigid termination procedures that not only is what I say heresy but also a firing offense for a manager to implement it. Obviously, I'm not asking you to put your career on the line. But you shouldn't assume HR and Legal know what is best for the employee. Their interest, and it is legitimate, is protecting the company.

out, she should see it before it's final. The announcement needs to be respectful but honest. If everyone knows she's being turfed and you say, "Honest, she's dying to go out on her own, been looking for the golden handshake for years," nobody will believe you and you damage your credibility and that of the process. I'm not saying don't ever do it (the employee may want it that way), but think about it first.

- *Giving her an adjustment period.* Some companies frog-march the person out the door the moment the termination interview ends. I don't think this is a good idea. If you remember the social and emotional aspects of work, you know these need to be rounded off as much as the packing up of personal mementos. Giving a person a period of adjustment before she has to leave allows her to do that. "But what if she destroys files or bad-mouths the company?" you may ask. I don't think most employees would but Mary has been difficult so it's a possibility. But you can raise that issue with her. Work out what files need to be transferred to whom and what she will say to customers ("We agreed it was the right time to move on. After all, no one spends her whole career in one company. This is the right time for me."). Make it clear that if she can't or won't do what you've agreed to, you will end her adjustment period immediately. And by the by, during this adjustment period, don't act like Mary has died. Keep talking to her.

- *Handling the return of company property.* Turning in the ID card or giving up the cell phone may be small things but they are symbols of the severing. And, like all symbols, they need to be treated with more care than the item itself might warrant. Again, talk to Mary about how this will happen. Agree on when and where this will happen. Will it be easier for her to give this stuff to HR rather than come back to the office? Will it all come in on the last day or does she want to do it over the course of the adjustment period?

Reactions of Other Employees

You may think, "Well, yes, all very nice, but realistically, what does it matter? Once she's out the door, she's no longer my concern." I think we should treat the departing employee well simply as a right. That reason alone is sufficient. In addition, however, the employees who remain watch how one in trouble is treated and draw their conclusions accordingly. If she is treated poorly, they assume they will be similarly treated. How you deal with or speak about Mary during the period before you decide to terminate, at the time of termination, and after she has left, will establish with your staff that you are acting responsibly and not simply taking revenge on a difficult employee.

During the Troubles

Usually, some time prior to termination, your difficulties with Mary will become known. She will probably spread the word herself, complaining to her co-workers about you. Naturally, she'll spin what's happening to her advantage.

Given the kind of people we are discussing, the other employees may dislike her and actually be relieved you're reining her in. However, as they continue to hear only her side of the story, they will begin to wonder if there isn't fire where all the smoke is coming from. In addition, they want to know you're taking action against her because of problems like abuse and belittling. If they know that for sure, they'll be more likely to believe you're not giving her a hard time just because she's outspoken.

Unfortunately, much as they need to know that, and much you would like to reassure them, you can't. The problems between you and Mary must remain confidential. It would be a abdication of your management responsibilities to discuss them. You must resist the temptation to give your side of the story even if other employees actively encourage you to do so.

YOU	*So are we done?*
Duncan	*Yeah, think so. I'll get back to you about the Maxwell thing. (pause) So how are things going for you?*
YOU	*Hectic as ever.*
Duncan	*Looks like Mary's giving you a merry chase.*
YOU	*Well, there are lots of things keeping me busy.*
Duncan	*I just want you to know that the rest of us are really glad you're finally cracking down on her.*
YOU	*Duncan, I know this is well meant but I feel uncomfortable talking about what's happening. You know I believe praise is public but problems are private.*
Duncan	*Yeah, but I thought you should know what she's saying about you…*
YOU	*Duncan, I know you want to be helpful and I really appreciate it. But I don't think we should discuss it.*
Duncan	*But she's really bad-mouthing you.*
YOU	*I'm sorry that's the case and certainly I wish I could set the record straight, but I need to respect her confidence.*
Duncan	*You're sure…*
YOU	*Yeah, I am. But thanks for the thought.*

I know you're dying to know what Mary is saying about you and about the situation. But don't ask. It's probably going to be a distortion anyhow, at least from your point of view. And trying to correct the misperception would violate the confidentiality Mary has a right to expect. In this instance, it really is better not to know.

Duncan tried more than once to engage you in discussing Mary. This is another time when being a broken record works. Keep repeating variations on two thoughts: You know he means well and you would be betraying confidences if you spoke about the situation. If you can, even avoid explicitly admitting you and Mary are having problems. If is implied of course, in statements like "I wish I could set the record straight," but nothing you say to a third party should add fuel to an already blazing fire.

Much as Duncan is dying to talk, either because he is loyal or because he wants more grist for the gossip mill, he is probably relieved you refused. Even if employees want to know the dirt, their trust in your reliability is shaken if you betray a confidence to do so. If you're willing to talk about Mary, you'll talk about them in the same unguarded manner.

You can do some things to suggest you are dealing honestly and appropriately with Mary behind closed doors. Keep talking to her—deal with her civilly on work issues, continue the pleasantries like "good morning" and "good night," invite her to join in the impromptu gab fests, ask her opinion in meetings. They sound minor but in the highly charged atmosphere that probably exists, these are the tea leaves everyone is reading.

What they will likely observe is you continuing to treat Mary as you would any other employee and she reacting ungraciously. She may well stop the pleasantries, refuse to join in social activities that you are a part of or stay mute at meetings. That's fine—she is hurting and she is expressing it. But you can indicate that you are treating her fairly in your private discussions by continuing to do so in public. Your employees are not stupid. They will draw their own conclusions about what is going on, despite Mary's spin doctoring.

At Termination

Even if it is expected, and even if desired, the termination of an employee for cause still sends shock waves through a unit. Layoffs are one thing, but terminations clearly target one person.

However much the dissenter was disliked, there is still a sense of unease. Employees still wonder, "What does this mean? Sure, Mary was over the top in some ways, but is management punishing people who speak their minds?" If the conclusion is yes to that last question, you are on the verge of underground dissent and the death of innovation.

You need to show you acted correctly and appropriately. While you cannot discuss the details, talk about what happened in general terms once Mary has left. Not to do so encourages an environment in which some things are undiscussable. Again, not conducive to innovation. In a staff meeting, say something like, "As you know, Mary has left. It wouldn't be fair to her to go into the particulars but I think you know it was a difficult transition. However, I want to assure you that the reason we needed to part company was *not* that she spoke out when she thought things were wrong. Quite the opposite. I thought it was a very positive characteristic." Someone will probably ask you why she left but you don't have to answer. "Sorry, Duncan, I'd be straying into confidential things if I answered that. But I wanted to make the point that I want to continue the kind of debates we've always had."

In the Aftermath

Even after Mary leaves, employees will be looking for signs that you are as good as your word. This will be true even if you do what I suggest, even if they believed you when you did it, and even if they generally like and respect you. They still need assurance you haven't suddenly turned into a control-freak and that Mary wasn't just the first in a string of casualties to come.

In the weeks after Mary's departure, pay special attention to how and how frequently you encourage dissent. Make a point of reflecting out loud on whether you are taking the right decision about whatever work issue is on the table. Encourage others to voice objections. In fact, ask people explicitly to do so. "Come on, there's got to be a flaw in this plan. Let's hear it." Or "Okay, I want to spend a couple of minutes brainstorming all the reasons why this won't work."

Once employees know you're still your old self, they will relax and conclude you were telling the truth about wanting an open environment. They won't tell you that, but you will know it by how quickly the atmosphere gets back to the freewheeling one that existed prior to the problems with Mary.

Summary

Taking tough decisions in a humane and respectful way is the hallmark of a truly great leader. One of the toughest decisions both to make and to do well is letting a dissenter go. But it is possible to move an employee out of your organization in a way that is maximally respectful to her, minimally damaging to the rest of your staff, and effective in its outcome.

Main Points

- Managers need to be tough on people issues when warranted.
- Dissenters who are underground, abusive, or belittling to others may need to be moved out.
- HR and Legal departments should be involved in a termination process but you need to take responsibility for and keep control of it.
- Handling a termination well involves communicating that the employee has the right to retain her dignity through the process.
- The reactions of the employees who remain need to be managed as well as the termination process.

CHAPTER 17

&

Conclusions

Some concluding comments.

The Paradox of Our Times

I was watching a program on Britain in the Second World War. As you probably know, Britain entered the war several years before the United States. Things were going badly. Hitler had conquered all of Europe. The British army had been pinned at Dunkirk and their heroic rescue from those beaches by hundreds of ordinary fishing boats couldn't hide the fact that it was a crushing military blow. The next obvious move was Germany's invasion of Britain. There were so few resources to defend the country that some British villages sharpened sticks to plant in the ground to stop German tanks. Britain was running out of equipment, fighting men, and food. The United States was holding secret talks with Canada (part of Britain's Commonwealth) to transfer the British Royal Navy to their side of the Atlantic *when* Britain was defeated. Winston Churchill was under intense pressure from his own Cabinet to give in to Hitler. But instead, he gave the world, "We shall fight them on the beaches...we shall fight them in the fields and in the streets....we shall never surrender."

Can you imagine where we would be today if Churchill had listened to those sincere and honest voices who told him what was as plain as the nose on his face—that it was time to surrender? How easy, sensible, and appropriate to sue for peace. How reckless, risky, and foolhardy to hold out. And yet he did.

Sometimes leaders do their countries great service by being unwilling to see any other point of view but their own—when they are fanatics, monomaniacal, holding to their beliefs in the face of all evidence to the contrary. This is as true in business as it is on the world stage. Research shows that managers tend to be deniers of reality and unrepentant optimists and, by being so, they have accomplished great things and have led one of the greatest economic booms in recent memory.

But while it may help to have blinders on to get a job done, almost the exact opposite is true for innovation.

Do you know that nobody realized color blindness even *existed* until John Dalton described it in 1794? It had always been there, but it took John Dalton's particular talent to see what nobody else had. While the discovery of color blindness isn't exactly an innovation, it nevertheless shares the same quality. There is something about innovation that requires people who don't just look around but actually see a world different from everyone else's. Who see patterns where there were none before, who link thoughts that have hitherto been on parallel tracks.

So leaders need to look only in one direction to accomplish great things as well as look where they've never looked before and in ways they've never looked before. They are in that crazy-making position of needing both blinders *and* 360-degree vision. Is it any wonder that organizations have trouble generating and sustaining innovation? Rather, it's surprising we can do it at all.

That's why we need dissenters—why Andy Grove, former chairman of Intel, believes you keep your strategy innovative by talking to people on the periphery and to the most challenging audiences and why 3-M founder Bill McKnight urged managers to "listen to anyone with an original idea, no matter how absurd it might sound at first."[1] Those of us intensely focused on one point on the horizon need those who are gazing off in all directions.

So here we have a paradox managers must adapt to—to be single-minded in the pursuit of a goal *and* to look where no one else is looking. But it is a paradox no more daunting than many others we manage every day—innovate but avoid mistakes, think in the long term but deliver results now, collaborate and compete, decentralize and retain control, specialize but be opportunistic. It's not easy but at least it has the virtue of being familiar. Well, cold comfort is better than no comfort at all, isn't it?

---

[1] Marshall Loeb, "How to Make the CEO Buy Your Idea," *Fortune* (December 11, 1995), p. 210.

So Where to from Here?

We understand dissent and innovation are two sides of one coin. You can't have one without the other. But the drive to and continued need for innovation will prompt other changes in the way we manage organizations. Here are some I think will be prominent in the coming years.

A New Role for Loyalty

The received wisdom is "there is no loyalty anymore. It's everyone for themselves." We may have almost convinced ourselves it's an industrial age concept. But you need loyalty more than ever. Why? Obviously, it increases the chances employees will stay with your company and that alone would be worthwhile. But there is also an innovation reason why loyalty is important.

In his interesting economic analysis called *Exit, Voice and Loyalty*,[2] Albert Hirschman found that when it's easy to leave an organization, people are less likely to speak up when something is wrong. Why fight city hall if you can just move elsewhere? He also found that those most likely to leave were also most likely to know what was wrong *and* most able to fix it. This is disaster for an organization. The firm loses the very people they most need to recover. You try to fix the problem that is driving out the most able with the help of those less able and less sensitive to it.

There is one exception to this dismal picture: if employees are loyal. That is, if they stay past the point when it would be in their best interests to jump ship. It's how baseball teams and political parties can come back—they have a base of loyal supporters that allows them the time and provides the expertise to recoup. So baseball teams, political parties, and organizations need loyalty. Now more than ever, your brightest also need to be your most loyal. This is the new challenge for organizations.

Managers' Search for Dissenting Voices

To this point, even though not explicitly in the job description, every manager worth his salt knew he should suppress dissent. Because it was efficient. But as it becomes clear that dissent is a necessary component to and precursor of innovation, it is now the manager's job to seek it out. Rather than being the guardian of the one right way, managers need to lead the way to more open inquiry and challenge of the status quo.

---

[2] Albert O. Hirschman, *Exit, Voice and Loyalty: Responses to Decline in Firms, Organizations and States* (Cambridge Mass.: Harvard Business Press, 1970).

But if the manager undertakes this role of devil's advocate and gadfly, she needs to be prepared for resistance and even counterattack as employees try to fend off uncomfortable feelings. People like stable states. I like stable states. I like to know that I have an income, that I'm good at what I do, that I can plan my life. All require some stability and predictability in the world. Actively encouraging instability will not win popularity contests. And yet, I feel convinced the most successful leaders in the future will be those who can keep just enough unpredictability and even chaos in place to open the door to innovation and that the also-rans will have the kind of tied-down, in-control shop that only a few years ago would have got them Manager of the Year Awards.

Consent of the Governed

The farther we move into the information age, the more apparent it is that our ability to be successful rests on how we treat people. Although there has always been some bowing to this idea in the past, it wasn't the serious issue it is now. The old economy mostly needed hands and not heads and there were plenty more where you came from. But now value is created primarily by using knowledge innovatively, and this occurs in the heads of knowledge workers. In this new economy of innovation, it is more important than ever to get the commitment of people to where you are going and how you are getting there.

But how do you create this environment that both accomplishes its goals and innovates? Vision, values, mission—all these have worked to some extent but as discussed earlier, they are usually unidirectional—that is, their main objective is to get commitment to a goal established by senior management. And while they are effective vehicles and necessary for productivity, they are inherently about compliance—enthusiastic compliance, creative compliance even, but compliance. They are not about questioning whether the goal is correct or whether what is valued has changed. But an innovative climate requires exactly that quality—a culture where even fundamental issues can be questioned. If we want innovation, we have to move beyond compliance, however enthusiastic.

There are institutions that are trying to do that, although the source may surprise you. The *government* is trying to adapt itself to the information age in ways that can provide us with some insights. The essence of democratic governance is the understanding that people have free will, cannot be coerced but must be persuaded. So democratic governments have always sought the *consent of the governed*. Usually, this took the form of elections. However, as the public has become more sophisticated and the issues more complex, this "Let's assume I'm right and then you can tell me if you agree four years from now" is no longer viable.

Governments got a wake-up call at the World Trade Conference in Seattle in 1999, where citizens used the Internet to exchange information about their objections. Through their protests, they affected both how the conference was conducted and its success. Recognizing the old way no longer suits the times or the sophistication of the citizenry, government is struggling to find new ones. They are increasing citizen involvement in policy development and trying (sometimes not too successfully) to make their deliberations more open. They don't have all the answers but they understand that consent is critical to how they govern.

Most organizations have not got that far. They have made some bows to democratic trappings, like consulting people on their preferences or allowing them to choose between two equally acceptable options. But they mostly have a top-down, I'll-tell-you-what-to-do approach. Vision and values may be a kinder, gentler top-down but it is top-down nevertheless. But when what is going on in employees' heads is now the engine of success in the new economy, this may not be enough. Employees, like citizens, must also be persuaded rather than coerced.

But before we go any farther, I feel an objection looming. We need to address whether likening organizations to democracies is appropriate. Because after all...

Organizations Are Not Democracies

You're right. Organizations are not set up nor intended to be democracies. People don't vote for their leaders, they decide only what management allows them to, they get paid for their participation—all different from a democracy. And I'm not suggesting that organizations should become democracies to encourage innovation.

But there are some conundrums about organizational life in a democratic society that must give us pause. Whether we wish it to be or not, organizations are systems of governance and therefore intrinsically political. Leaders have to find a way to create order and direction among diverse and conflicting views. So there may be some value in learning from the government arena where trying to suppress dissent has not been all that successful (Roswell fanatics aside).

In addition, for the most part, employees are denied rights they have as citizens such as holding opinions different from those in power and being treated as equals. There is a disconnect between the freedom people take as a matter of course in society at large and the freedom they have inside their workplace.

So while it is true organizations are not democracies and are not intended to be, can these conundrums continue to exist without some pressure to change? What will happen as knowledge workers approach the clout of citizens in their power to determine the success or failure of their leaders?

But still, organizations cannot and will not use exactly the same methods as governments to acquire the consent of the governed. However, there are organizational models that bridge the gap between democracy and organizational realities. Charities and other not-for-profits have some of the characteristics of democracies. Volunteers usually elect their leaders (the Board of Directors), get involved in strategic issues, and don't get paid. They have the right to be heard. In fact, Sol Kasimer, executive director of the YMCA, notes that volunteers who do not feel appreciated and heard "vote with their feet and volunteer organizations who don't pay attention to how they govern soon don't exist." The Y ensures that the voice of the governed is part of their structure, from the Board of Directors elected by members to advisory committees chaired by volunteers to program implementation, often delivered by volunteers. Because voluntary organizations have multiple constituencies—multiple types of customers—they're very good at getting the consent of groups who may not agree with each other. This is a skill the private sector would do well to learn as they begin to realize they must widen the scope of their stakeholders from simply customers and stockholders to customers, stockholders, employees, suppliers, and the community. So there are organizations that have taken on some of the characteristics of a democracy and still operate as organizations. I think they reflect more of the future than anyone imagines.

As workers begin to understand they have choices and should have a voice, I think they will increasingly insist they be treated more like citizens and less like employees. I believe we are moving into a era in which consent of the governed will be the hallmark not just of government but of organizations as well. Whether you like it or not, you are in the business of managing with their consent.

The Light Use of Position Power

A corollary of getting the consent of the governed is the light use of power. I know you've been exhorted to do this for a long time. The good news is you already know how to evolve from planner and controller to guide and mentor. The bad news is that you can't rest on your laurels. A world where innovation is paramount will respond only to the lightest touch on the reins. We will find employees need new freedoms, ones that we were sure were ours by managerial birthright.

In particular, we will need to pay attention to systems we put into place. A teacher friend was discussing school reform. The old system had allowed a lot of crazy things to go on—crazy bad things and crazy good things. Teachers out of control who didn't prepare students for life and teachers out of control who were inspired. The school authorities tried to rectify the situation by standardizing the curriculum and putting tighter controls on hiring. Their aim had been to get rid of the bad, but in the end all they did was get rid of the crazy. The crazy bad, yes, but the crazy good also.

So we must guard against those systems that, while worthwhile in their objectives of efficiency, teamwork, and responsible behavior, also suppress the magic from which all creativity and innovation flow. Because it's where we all want to go—to that place where the crazy good can flourish.

Main Points

- Leaders have accomplished a lot by refusing to see anything but what they want.
- But innovation requires a capacity to see the world in a different way.
- Dissenters can provide this capacity.
- In the future, there will be a new role for loyalty, the manager will seek out dissent and consent of the governed and will have to use his power lightly.

Index